GOOD WIVES

ALSO BY
LAUREL THATCHER ULRICH

A Midwife's Tale

The Age of Homespun

Well-Behaved Women Seldom Make History

A House Full of Females

All God's Critters Got a Place in the Choir
(with Emma Lou Thayne)

Tangible Things: Making History through Objects
(with Ivan Gaskell, Sara J. Schechner, Sarah Anne Carter)

GOOD WIVES

*Image and Reality in the Lives of Women
in Northern New England
1650–1750*

Laurel Thatcher Ulrich

*Vintage Books
A Division of Penguin Random House LLC
New York*

FIRST VINTAGE BOOKS EDITION, JUNE 1991

Copyright © 1980, 1982 by Laurel Thatcher Ulrich

All rights reserved. Published in the United States by Vintage Books, a division of Penguin Random House LLC, New York, and distributed in Canada by Penguin Random House Canada Limited, Toronto. Originally published in the hardcover by Alfred A. Knopf, a division of Penguin Random House LLC, New York, in 1982.

A portion of this book was first published in *Feminist Studies*.

Vintage and colophon are registered trademarks of
Penguin Random House LLC.

The Library of Congress Cataloging-in-Publication Data
Ulrich, Laurel.
Good wives : image and reality in the lives of women in northern New England, 1650–1750 / Laurel Thatcher Ulrich.—1st Vintage Books ed.
p.   cm.
Reprint. Originally published: New York : Knopf, 1980.
Includes bibliographical references and index.
1. Women—New England—History. 2. Women—New England—
Social conditions. I. Title.
[HQ1438.N35U47   1991]
305.42'0974—dc20   90-55673
CIP

Vintage Books Trade Paperback ISBN: 978-0-679-73257-0
eBook ISBN: 978-0-307-77297-8

Book design by Virginia Tan

www.vintagebooks.com

Printed in the United States of America

FOR

Alice Siddoway Thatcher

Here lyes
A Worthy Matron of unspotted life,
A loving Mother and obedient wife,
A friendly Neighbor, pitiful to poor,
Whom oft she fed, and clothed with her store;
To Servants wisely aweful, but yet kind,
And as they did, so they reward did find:
A true Instructer of her Family,
The which she ordered with dexterity.
The publick meetings ever did frequent,
And in her Closet constant hours she spent;
Religious in all her words and wayes,
Preparing still for death, till end of dayes:
Of all her Children, Children liv'd to see,
Then dying, left a blessed memory.

Anne Bradstreet, 1643

Contents

	Preface	*xiii*
	Introduction	3
Part One	BATHSHEBA	11
1	The Ways of Her Household	13
2	Deputy Husbands	35
3	A Friendly Neighbor	51
4	Pretty Gentlewomen	68
Part Two	EVE	87
5	The Serpent Beguiled Me	89
6	Consort	106
7	Travail	126
8	Mother of All Living	146
Part Three	JAEL	165
9	Blessed Above Women	167
10	Viragoes	184
11	Captives	202
12	Daughters of Zion	215
	Afterword	237
	Abbreviations	243
	Notes	245
	Bibliographic Essay	277
	Index	283

Historical maps will be found
on pages xvii and 56

Illustrations

following page 108

A goodwife at her flax wheel
A gentlewoman and her spouse

Title page of Anne Bradstreet's *The Tenth Muse*
Sampler, by Mary Hollingsworth
Pie crust vents
Pocket

Needlework chair seat
Wattle-and-daub wall fill
Wooden scoop and samp bowl
Flatiron
Seventeenth-century hoe

Needlework panel, by Mary Dodge Burnham
Adam and Eve panel, by Mary Sarah Titcomb
Crewelwork bedhangings, attributed to Mary Bulman

Ashley Bowen's courtship
Portrait of Catherine Moffatt, by John Greenwood
Portrait of John Moffatt, by John Greenwood
Portrait of Elizabeth Oliver, by John Smibert
Portrait of Daniel Oliver, by John Smibert
Portrait of Mary Pepperrell, attributed to John Smibert

ILLUSTRATIONS

Eighteenth-century curling iron

Mantelpiece in Wentworth-Coolidge Mansion

Detail of mantelpiece

Portrait of Abigail Gerrish and Abigail Gerrish, granddaughter and grandmother, by John Greenwood

Go-cart

Title page of Mary Rowlandson's captivity narrative

Fragments of clay tobacco pipes

Plan of Montreal, 1760

Portrait of Esther Wheelwright

"Siamese twins"

Mary Cutler's gravestone

Alice Hart's gravestone

Lydia White's gravestone

Key from Otis Garrison

"Marks" of Hannah Duston and her daughters

Preface

IN SEVENTEENTH-CENTURY NEW ENGLAND, women of ordinary status were called Goodwife, usually shortened to Goody, as in Goody Prince or Goody Quilter or Goody Lee. The title of this book deliberately puns on that term. To write about good wives is to write about ideals; to write about goodwives is to write about ordinary women living in a particular place and time. I have tried to mediate between the two concerns, to explore values and at the same time to describe and to celebrate lives. The title consciously echoes Alice Morse Earle's *Colonial Dames and Good Wives* (Boston, 1895), honoring an early generation of women's historians who skillfully practiced what later scholars dismissed as "pots-and-pans history."

My emphasis on *good* wives betrays a propensity to search for normative elements in a history which from the time of Hawthorne has been dominated by outcasts and witches. Readers will find little about Anne Hutchinson or the Devil in this book. They will find much about housekeeping, childbearing, and ordinary churchgoing, about small conflicts experienced by forgotten women, and about little triumphs that history has not recorded.

Good Wives is a study in role definition, an extended description constructed from a series of vignettes. In organization and intent it is a little like those elongated samplers worked by young women in seventeenth-century England and America. Unlike eighteenth- and nineteenth-century samplers, which were made to be framed and hung on a wall, these first samplers were true patterns, one band of embroidery added to another, each incomplete in itself but capable of transfer and elaboration on a larger ground. In the best of samplers, and I hope in this book, the appeal of the whole lies in the aggregate texture of the associated parts.

I have written about northern New England because that is where I live and the tedious sifting of sources necessary for such a project was therefore possible, but I make no special claim for the region's uniqueness or cohesiveness. I suspect that much of what I have discovered can be found elsewhere. *Good Wives* describes a diverse and changing world, but its major objective is neither to elaborate nor to explain change but to delineate certain broad patterns within which change occurred. I offer it as a collection of "ensamples," a parade of exemplary lives, which, if not constructed in quite the medieval sense, have something of the same intent—to entertain and to instruct the reader.

I owe a special debt to Charles E. Clark, whose seminar on the historical writing of early America, which I took when a graduate student in English, reinforced my growing interest in history, and who first suggested what seemed at the time an awesome change in direction. I am pleased in having had him as my mentor. I am also fortunate in having had the guidance of Darrett Rutman, also of the University of New Hampshire. He has been a rigorous critic and an equally generous friend. For moral support and good ideas I am indebted to other colleagues at U.N.H., Karen Andrésen, Robert Mennel, Judith Silver, Steve Cox, Ray Wilbur, Ron Lettieri, Chuck Wetherell, and Stuart Wallace, all of whom have read and commented on portions of the manuscript. Mary Ryan offered helpful criticism of an article from which several chapters grew; Mary Maples Dunn generously read and responded to a late version of the manuscript; Claudia Bushman has continuously shared her appreciation of the ordinary. I thank all of these friends and critics without blaming any.

I would like to thank the directors of the Essex Institute in Salem and the Massachusetts Historical Society in Boston for permission to quote from unpublished manuscripts in their collections. I am also grateful to Irene Norton of the Essex Institute; Elizabeth Newton and Mary Conley of the Ipswich Historical Society; Elizabeth Barker and Margaret Kimball of the Warner House in Portsmouth, New Hampshire; Susan DeVito of the Lady Pepperrell House at Kittery Point, Maine; Mrs. Everett Billings of Kittery Point; and the Reverend Mr. James Christensen of South Berwick, Maine, for special assistance in locating materials.

The Woodrow Wilson National Fellowship Foundation and the

Frost Fund, University of New Hampshire, provided more than kind words, for which I am grateful. My children offered equally tangible support. Karl cooked, Melinda cleaned, Nathan typed, Thatcher washed dishes, and Amy kept quiet when it really mattered. My husband Gail did all of the above, and then bolstered my self-confidence by staying awake when he read the final revision.

Neither of my parents has read the manuscript, though both have contributed to it in specific ways. Dad was probably startled when I called him long distance one afternoon to chat about cows. Hearing him talk about the relationship between butterfat and pasture and describe how his mother helped with the milking made the agricultural past seem less remote. It is a great sorrow to know he will not see the finished book. Mother's contribution is only partly acknowledged in the dedication. Certainly I resisted her early lessons in housekeeping, but I have never forgotten the history lessons she didn't know she was giving—the stories that came with the pickles and the currant jelly, the rides up to Teton past the sugar factory, and especially the visit to "Grandma" Harrison and the other elderly women in our town. "The salt of the earth," she called them, and I have not forgotten it.

Laurel Thatcher Ulrich

Durham, N.H., and Idaho Falls, Idaho
April 1981

GOOD WIVES

Introduction

O N TUESDAY MORNING she had risen in good health. But before dinner, seized with what felt like a gas pain in her chest, she had gone to bed. By noon of the next day, when the doctor arrived, she was in agony. Though his cordials eased the pain, she continued to languish. Seven days later, on December 27, 1643, at six o'clock in the morning, Dorothy Dudley died.[1]

She had been a good wife, obedient to her husband, loving to her children, kind to her neighbors, dutiful to her servants, and, as her daughter Anne Bradstreet expressed it, "religious in all her words and wayes."[2] When Thomas Dudley sat down to write the news of her death to another daughter, Mercy Woodbridge, he confessed himself "melted with sorrow." Yet he was composed enough to reiterate this same list of qualities in a long passage of advice, reminding Mercy that she could honor her mother best by imitating her virtues.[3] Fifty years later Mercy's own children could comfort themselves at her death by repeating the familiar litany. Acknowledging their mother's goodness, they promised to "tread in her steps."[4]

Twentieth-century readers are likely to approach such pieties with impatience if not with cynicism. When we read on a gravestone that a woman was "Eminent for Holiness, Prayerfulness, Watchfulness, Zeal, Prudence, Sincerity, Humility, Meekness, Patience, Weanedness From ye World, Self-denial, Publick-Spiritedness, Diligence, Faithfulness & Charity," we smile, wondering what she was *really* like.[5] It is difficult for us to approach a world in which neither innovation nor individuality was celebrated, in which the rich particulars of daily life were willfully reduced to formulaic abstraction. Yet the purpose of an epitaph was not to commemorate, but to transcend, personality. A good wife earned the dignity of anonymity.

"Womans the centre & lines are men," young Seaborn Cotton wrote in his commonplace book early in the 1650s. The sexual connotations of the metaphor are obvious, yet its meaning has a larger resonance. Because female life has been centered on private duties, women have emerged from their idealized epitaphs less frequently than men. As wives and mothers, they have represented the fixed circle of human history, a presumed counterweight to the moving line which traces the founding of commonwealths or the development of ideas. Cotton's little book can be seen as an extended commentary on this theme. "Circles draw many lines unto the Centre/but love gives leave to onely one to enter," he wrote just before his marriage to Dorothy Dudley's granddaughter Dorothy Bradstreet. In the cramped pages of his book, college ballads abruptly give way to genealogical entries in a record continued for three generations. From Seaborn and Dorothy Cotton's first child, born November 21, 1655, to the last child of their granddaughter Dorothy Gookin, born August 10, 1734, there are more than two dozen terse entries. Only subtle changes in handwriting mark the transition from one cycle of reproduction—from one woman—to another.[6]

Yet change permeated the exterior life of northern New England in those years. Between 1650 and 1750 the settlements north of Boston experienced political upheaval, religious conflict, and four devastating wars. The coastal towns grew from frontier outposts to prospering links in an imperial trade network, and by 1750 in the remote "eastern parts" tiny agricultural settlements had begun to sprinkle the interior.

Historians have written of these changes. They have described the struggle between France and England which created havoc for three generations in the settlements in the north; they have discussed conflicting proprietary claims within the English colonies, the boundary disputes between Massachusetts and New Hampshire, and the political and economic conquest of the eastern parts by the Bay Colony; they have begun in recent years to examine in detail the internal conflicts of towns and parishes, to explore commonplace but little-understood aspects of material culture, to quantify the demographic explosion which in part fueled the dynamic changes of the eighteenth century. But as yet they have given little attention to the women who stood at the "centre" of life in these years.

This is understandable, for the chore facing the historian who would write of female experience in colonial America is no less than to reverse the process by which flesh-and-blood women became "good wives"—that is, to somehow rediscover the variegated humanity submerged in the ideal. What specifically did it mean to be a "loving mother," an "obedient wife," and a "friendly neighbor"? Women cooked. They spun wool. But what else did they do with their days? What were the concrete realities of their lives in northern New England? How did these differ for men?

On the surface it is obvious that some activities in colonial society carried gender labels and some did not. Men were elected to representative assemblies. Women nursed babies. Both men and women experienced religious conversion and Indian captivity. Few members of either sex wrote poetry. Yet within the larger outlines the patterns are far from clear. The first objective of this study, therefore, has been to recover lost detail, a formidable task since the archives contain no female diaries written in New England before 1750 and few female letters. Among published works there are only the brief "Valedictory and Monitory Writing" of Sarah Goodhue, the captivity narratives of Mary Rowlandson and Elizabeth Hanson, and the poetry of Anne Bradstreet. Yet significant evidence of female life lay buried in sermons, account books, probate inventories, genealogies, church records, court records, paintings, embroideries, gravestones, and the private papers of husbands and sons.

In interpreting this material, the major analytical tool has been "role analysis." In the sociologist's jargon, a role is "the sum total of the culture patterns associated with a particular status. It thus includes the attitudes, values and behavior ascribed by the society to any and all persons occupying this status." Role analysis has both normative and behavioral dimensions. A social scientist studying the role of housewife in twentieth-century America might ask a group of women what tasks they felt wives should perform as well as what jobs they actually did daily, weekly, or monthly. Such a study would focus not just on cultural expectations, the abstract "role," but also on "role performance," on how people behaved.[7]

Role analysis cannot be applied with scientific precision, but as a general concept it is useful in approaching the history of women in the traditional world. It recognizes that informal structures and unwritten codes can be as effective in determining behavior as legal and economic systems. It allows for diversity, and even for contradiction, in acknowledging that a complex role like that of a wife is really composed of many roles. But it is especially congenial in a study of colonial women because it approaches so closely the traditional manner of commemorating personality. Anne Bradstreet did not describe Dorothy Dudley as a unique individual but as the successful occupant of a series of discrete positions. She was a "worthy matron," an "obedient wife," "a loving mother," a "kind" mistress, and "a friendly neighbor." For seventeenth-century readers these stock phrases were cues that unlocked a whole store of specific images. They had no need for a complete role description. For twentieth-century readers the detail is essential because we have lost so many of the assumptions which governed the traditional world.

IN SOME ENGLISH DIALECTS the words *wife* and *woman* are synonyms. In northern New England in the century between 1650 and 1750 they were virtually so. Almost all females who reached the age of maturity married. This was in contrast to Europe, where during the same period an estimated ten percent of the population remained single. American women were probably younger at first marriage than English women, but not so young as folklore has imagined.[8] Mercy Dudley was eighteen when she married John Woodbridge, who at twenty-six was still unsettled in his profession, but on the average, women married somewhere between the ages of twenty and twenty-two. Husbands were four or five years older.[9]

Perhaps the wider the age gap the easier it was for a woman to "reverence, fear, and obey" as society and the scriptures taught. "Know that that God that hath gracyously placed thy good husband here will be here with thee and comfort thee if thou submytt and trust to him," Thomas Dudley told Mercy.[10] The blurring of the pronoun reference was perhaps unintentional, but it is no less instructive. Submission to God and submission to one's husband were part of the same religious duty. As God told Eve, "Thy desire shall be to thy husband and he shall rule over thee."

Obedience was not only a religious duty but a legal requirement. The classic statement of the legal subordination of wives is in William Blackstone's *Commentaries on the Laws of England:*

> By marriage, the husband and wife are one person in law; that is, the very being or legal existence of the woman is suspended during the marriage, or at least is incorporated and consolidated into that of the husband; under whose wing, protection, and cover, she performs everything.[11]

Although Blackstone's commentaries were not published until 1765, the principles which he described had been long imbedded in tradition and in language. The most obvious emblem of a woman's coverture was her loss of a name, a custom made more vivid by the seventeenth-century practice of referring to a married woman not as "Mary Brown" or as "Mrs. John Brown" but as "John Brown his wife." Unless her husband were willing to sign a special contract prior to marriage, a wife could neither own nor acquire property, nor could she enter into a contract or write a will.

Upon her husband's death, a wife became a *relict*. This now archaic synonym for *widow* evokes that state well: in etymology and in usage the term was identical to the modern *relic*. The death of a mother did not mean the dissolution of a family; the death of a father did. As one patriarchy dissolved and others formed, there was a shuffling both of people and of things. Household inventories taken by trusted neighbors soon after death are an important source of information for twentieth-century historians, but they are also a reminder that death in early America meant a redistribution of roles as well as resources. By law, a widow usually inherited at least a third of the household goods, and she was entitled to use or to receive income from a third of the real estate until she died or remarried. If she had minor children, she might retain practical control of the entire estate until her sons came of age, but the final disposition of family property would not be determined by her but by court order or her husband's will. A widow was ensured maintenance at whatever level the estate allowed, but only rarely did she retain full control of her house and yard or even the assembly of pots, beds, and cows which had once been her domain.[12]

If this were all there were to say, then the history of colonial women would indeed be the recital of disadvantage and subjection which some historians have made it. But the notion of male supremacy must not be wrenched from the larger concept of an organic social order in which rights and responsibilities were reciprocal and in which terms like *individuality* or *self-reliance* had little place. It was difficult for men and women of the premodern world to conceive of equality. In the hierarchical structure which sustained the social order, one human being was of necessity almost always subject to another—child to parent, servant to master, subject to ruler. Yet within this larger system of dependencies the relation of wife to husband was different. "Of all the Orders which are unequals," wrote Samuel Willard, "these do come nearest to an Equality, and in several respects they stand upon even ground. These do make a pair, which infers so far a Parity."[13]

William Secker employed a whole series of metaphors to express this notion. A husband and wife, he wrote, were like two instruments making music, two streams in one current, a pair of oars rowing a boat to Heaven (with children and servants as passengers), two "milch kine" coupled to the Ark of God, two cherubim, two tables of stone on which the law was written.[14]

As both ministers understood, the position of a wife was complementary and at the same time secondary to that of her husband. This was a function not just of ideology, but of the most pervasive realities of ordinary existence. Contradictory possibilities were built into a system which meshed law with sentiment, property with procreation, and gender specialization with communal obligation.

Some of the disabilities of colonial women can be attributed to sexism, others simply to sex. The colonial world, like our own, struggled to reconcile the ways in which women and men are different with the ways in which they are the same. Yet one thing which surely separated the premodern past from the nineteenth century was a tolerance for contradiction. Female life was defined in a series of discrete duties rather than by a self-consistent and all-embracing "sphere." For this reason, unitary definitions of status are especially misleading in any description of the lives of colonial women. Much better to follow the lead of Anne Bradstreet, searching for that forgotten web of social relations which gave form to the life of a "worthy matron." A married woman in early New England was simultaneously a housewife, a deputy husband, a consort, a mother, a mistress, a neighbor, and a Christian. On the war-torn frontier she might also become a heroine.

A *housewife* polished female specialties. Her role was defined by a space (a house and its surrounding yards), a set of tasks (cooking, washing, sewing, milking, spinning, cleaning, gardening), and a limited area of authority (the internal economy of a family).

A *deputy husband* shouldered male duties. These might be of the most menial sort—for a weaver's wife, winding quills for the loom; for a farmer's wife, planting corn—but they could also expand to include some responsibility for the external affairs of the family. A deputy was not just a helper but at least potentially a surrogate.

A *consort* tuned her life to her mate's. For the blessed, marriage harmonized spirituality and sexuality, two concepts frequently at odds in the western world. For the unblessed, it brought clacking and clanging and sometimes an appearance in the county court.

A *mother* spent herself to perpetuate the race. As a biological rule, motherhood bound women to alternating cycles of pregnancy and lactation. As a social rule, it elevated selflessness and love, finding in women a capacity for affection which counterbalanced the presumably more authoritarian government of fathers.

A *mistress* served those who served her. She trained, supervised, and often fed and clothed a succession of neighbors' daughters who rewarded her efforts by leaving her to marry, becoming mistresses themselves.

A *neighbor* sustained the community of women, gossiping, trading, assisting in childbirth, sharing tools and lore, watching and warding in cases of abuse. Relations between neighbors could be vertical or horizontal, embracing the obligations of charity and deference as well as ordinary helpfulness and sociability.

A *Christian* seized spiritual equality and remained silent in church. Among the congregationalist majority in New England, women could sign the covenant, enlarge the scriptures, write and even publish, but only among the Quakers could they hold office or preach in mixed assemblies. Sharing a common bench in church, female Christians nudged the edges of a contradictory religious identity.

A *heroine* burst the bonds of female anonymity, projecting private virtues into the public sphere. Visibility, more than anything else, separated her from an ordinary wife. Indian captivity amplified the trials of motherhood and tested Christian faith; garrison life magnified neighborliness; while the continuous threat of attack called forth the "manly resolution" already expected of deputy husbands.

None of these roles existed in isolation. Each must be studied not only in relation to the others but within the detailed context of ordinary life in a particular place and time. *Good Wives* is a study in role definition. It is also a description of neglected aspects of daily life in the province of New Hampshire and in the two Massachusetts counties which bordered it, Essex County to the south and York County (now Maine) to the north and east. The text is organized around three role clusters, each epitomized by a Biblical prototype frequently employed in New England. "Bathsheba" focuses upon economic life, "Eve" upon sex and reproduction, "Jael" upon the intersection of religion and aggression.

WHEN THOMAS DUDLEY WROTE to his daughter Mercy Woodbridge, telling her of her mother's death, he not only praised his wife's godliness, but, recognizing the void left in Mercy's life, he attempted to take up some of the specific duties Dorothy laid down that Tuesday morning when she was seized with a pain in her breast. He offered to pay for a midwife to attend Mercy on her coming confinement. He promised to send her through her Uncle Parker a "souce in a bagge." Finally, he begged her to "lett mee have now thy letters as thy mother had and I will answeare them."[15] As a loving parent, he understood the value of fine abstractions. But he also knew the worth of sausage. To enter the world of Dorothy Dudley and her contemporaries requires an appreciation for both.

Part One

BATHSHEBA

*Who can find a virtuous woman? for her price is far above
  rubies.*
*The heart of her husband doth safely trust in her, so that he
  shall have no need of spoil.*
She will do him good and not evil all the days of her life.
*She seeketh wool, and flax, and worketh willingly with her
  hands.*
*She is like the merchants' ships; she bringeth her food from
  afar.*
*She riseth also while it is yet night, and giveth meat to her
  household, and a portion to her maidens.*
*She considereth a field, and buyeth it: with the fruit of her
  hands she planteth a vineyard.*
*She girdeth her loins with strength, and strengtheneth her
  arms.*
*She perceiveth that her merchandise is good: her candle goeth
  not out by night.*
*She layeth her hands to the spindle, and her hands hold the
  distaff.*
*She stretcheth out her hand to the poor; yea, she reacheth forth
  her hands to the needy.*
*She is not afraid of the snow for her household: for all her
  household are clothed with scarlet.*

She maketh herself coverings of tapestry; her clothing is silk and purple.

Her husband is known in the gates, when he sitteth among the elders of the land.

She maketh fine linen, and selleth it; and delivereth girdles unto the merchant.

Strength and honour are her clothing; and she shall rejoice in time to come.

She openeth her mouth with wisdom; and in her tongue is the law of kindness.

She looketh well to the ways of her household, and eateth not the bread of idleness.

Her children arise up, and call her blessed; her husband also, and he praiseth her.

Many daughters have done virtuously, but thou excellest them all.

Favour is deceitful, and beauty is vain: but a woman that feareth the Lord, she shall be praised.

Give her of the fruit of her hands; and let her own works praise her in the gates.

PROVERBS 31: 10–31

Chapter One

THE WAYS OF HER HOUSEHOLD

By ENGLISH TRADITION, a woman's environment was the family dwelling and the yard or yards surrounding it. Though the exact composition of her setting obviously depended upon the occupation and economic status of her husband, its general outlines were surprisingly similar regardless of where it was located. The difference between an urban "houselot" and a rural "homelot" was not as dramatic as one might suppose.

If we were to draw a line around the housewife's domain, it would extend from the kitchen and its appendages, the cellars, pantries, brewhouses, milkhouses, washhouses, and butteries which appear in various combinations in household inventories, to the exterior of the house, where, even in the city, a mélange of animal and vegetable life flourished among the straw, husks, clutter, and muck. Encircling the pigpen, such a line would surround the garden, the milkyard, the well, the henhouse, and perhaps the orchard itself—though husbands pruned and planted trees and eventually supervised the making of cider, good housewives strung their wash between the trees and in season harvested fruit for pies and conserves.

The line demarking the housewife's realm would not cross the fences which defined outlying fields of Indian corn or barley, nor would it stretch to fishing stages, mills, or wharves, but in berry or mushroom season it would extend into nearby woods or marsh and in spells of dearth or leisure reach to the shore. Of necessity, the boundaries of each woman's world would also extend into the houses of neighbors and into the cartways of a village or town.

Housewives commanded a limited domain. But they were neither isolated nor self-sufficient. Even in farming settlements, families found it essential to bargain for needed goods and services. For prosperous and socially prominent women, interdependence took on another meaning as well. Prosperity meant charity, and in early New England charity meant personal responsibility for nearby neighbors.

None of this was unique to New England. In fact, each aspect of female life described here can be found in idealized form in the Bible in the description of the "virtuous woman" of Proverbs, chapter 31. The Puritans called this paragon "Bathsheba," assuming rather logically that Solomon could only have learned such an appreciation for huswifery from his mother. Forgotten in their encomia to female virtue was the rooftop bather whose beauty brought King David to grief. In English and American sermons Bathsheba was remembered as a virtuous housewife, a godly woman whose industrious labors gave mythical significance to the ordinary tasks assigned to her sex.[1]

As described in Proverbs, Bathsheba is a willing servant to her family: "She riseth also while it is yet night, and giveth meat to her household."

She is a skilled manufacturer: "She seeketh wool, and flax, and worketh willingly with her hands."

She is a hard-working agriculturist: "With the fruit of her hands she planteth a vineyard."

She is a resourceful trader: "She is like the merchants' ships; she bringeth her food from afar."

Because her realm includes servants as well as young children, her ability to direct, to inspire, and to nurture others is as important to her success as hard work. "She openeth her mouth with wisdom; and in her tongue is the law of kindness." Her industry and her charity give legitimacy to her wealth. Though dressed in silk and purple, "strength and honour are her clothing" and "she stretcheth out her hand to the poor." Her goal is not public distinction but private competence. Although her husband is "known in the gates," her greatest reward is in looking well to "the ways of her household." In doing so, she earns the devotion of her children, the praise of her husband, and the commendation of God.

To describe this virtuous Bathsheba is to outline the major components of the housekeeping role in early America. Some of these activities have received greater attention in the literature than others. For most historians, as for almost all antiquarians, the quintessential early American woman has been a churner of cream and a spinner of wool. Because home manufacturing has all but disappeared from modern housekeeping, many scholars have assumed that the key change in female economic life has been a shift from "production" to "consumption," a shift precipitated by the industrial revolution.[2] This is far too simple, obscuring the variety which existed even in the pre-industrial world.

Setting aside for the moment the social skills involved in housekeeping—the nurturing, managing, and charitable responsibilities described in the myth of Bathsheba—we can see how relatively subtle shifts in emphasis among the economic skills— service, manufacturing, agriculture, and trade—might create pronounced differences in patterns of daily work. Evidence derived from 401 household inventories from Essex and York counties (Table 1) sketches the major economic variations in the region.

Predictably, home manufacturing, as measured by ownership of dairying and textile-processing equipment, was more widespread in the farming settlements of Essex County in 1670 than in the more remote fishing and sawmill villages of frontier Maine. With few fences and little hay, frontier planters let their scraggly cows browse in the woods, killing them for meat in winter but expecting little milk in any season. In such a setting, few families bothered with sheep, which were easy prey for wolves. By 1700, however, the dairying statistics for the two counties had almost reversed themselves. Flax appeared almost as often in York County as in Essex, and sheep even more frequently. The hinterland was becoming agricultural. The proportionate decline in cows and churns in Essex County is explained by the increasing diversity of the Massachusetts economy as commercial centers like Salem began to diverge from their agricultural surroundings.

Extracting urban Salem inventories from the larger 1700 sample makes this shift obvious (see Table 2). Although the wives of Salem shopkeepers, craftsmen, and mariners still kept a pig or two "at the door," agriculture had become a less pronounced theme in their daily work. Many farm wives in Essex County con-

Table 1. *Some Indicators of Agriculture and Home Manufacturing in Household Inventories, Essex and York Counties, 1670, 1700, 1730*

TOTAL INVENTORIES	1670[1]	1700[2]	1730[3]
Essex County	97	95	92
York County	39	41	37
DAIRYING			
Cows			
Essex County	77%	64%	57%
York County	73%	79%	84%
Processing Equipment			
Essex County	30%	14%	10%
York County	18%	25%	10%
TEXTILES			
Sheep			
Essex County	43%	45%	39%
York County	18%	64%	46%
Spinning Wheels			
Essex County	38%	46%	38%
York County	21%	46%	40%
Looms			
Essex County	4%	6%	13%
York County	0%	2%	3%
Flax			
Essex County	8%	12%	18%
York County	0%	10%	13%
PROVISIONS (any type of food, any quantity)			
Essex County	56%	26%	32%
York County	37%	53%	30%

1. Taken from *The Probate Records of Essex County* (Salem, Mass., 1916–1920), II, 237–432, and *Maine Province and Court Records* (Portland, Me., 1931), II.
2. Book 307, manuscript probate records, Essex County Court House, Salem, Mass. Books I, II, manuscript probate records, York County Court House, Alfred, Me.
3. Book 321, manuscript probate records, Essex County. Book IV, manuscript probate records, York County.

tinued to milk cows, but most women in the region's largest town did not. At the same time, luxury items like looking glasses, framed pictures, or quilts, which were still rare in the country, had become quite visible. Thus, rather straightforward contrasts between frontier, farming, and commercial communities explain many of the variations in the inventory data.

*Table 2. Comparison of Selected Items
Urban Salem and Overall Essex County Inventories, 1700*[1]

	Salem (N = 12)	Essex (N = 83)
Cows	33%	71%
Dairy Tools	0%	17%
Sheep	16%	51%
Spinning Wheels	50%	47%
Swine	41%	51%
Looking Glasses	75%	31%
Pictures	25%	0%
Quilts	15%	2%

1. The overall Essex County sample was taken from Book 307, manuscript probate records, Essex County Court House, Salem, Mass. The twelve urban inventories drawn from that same source can all be placed on James Duncan Phillips' reconstructed map of the center of Salem, 1700 (*Salem in the Seventeenth Century*, Boston, 1937). In 1700 the town of Salem was still very large geographically and included rural as well as urban neighborhoods. The twelve decedents in this subsample obviously belonged to the commercial world of mercantile Salem. They included three mariners, one innkeeper, a tailor, a cooper, a joiner, and two cordwainers. Sidney Perley, *History of Salem* (Salem, 1924) I, 306, 435, 441; II, 38, 82, 178, 268, 386, 387; III, 29, 51, 52.

To more fully understand the diverse ways in which the Bathsheba model was reflected in daily life, we must turn from the general to the particular. Beatrice Plummer, Hannah Grafton, and Magdalen Wear lived and died in New England in the years before 1750. One of them lived on the frontier, another on a farm, and a third in town. Because they were real women, however, and not hypothetical examples, the ways of their households were shaped by personal as well as geographic factors. A careful examination of the contents of their kitchens and chambers suggests the varied complexity as well as the underlying unity in the lives of early American women.

LET US BEGIN with Beatrice Plummer of Newbury, Massachusetts.[3] Forgetting that death brought her neighbors into the house on January 24, 1672, we can use the probate inventory which they prepared to reconstruct the normal pattern of her work.

With a clear estate of £343, Francis Plummer had belonged to the "middling sort" who were the church members and freeholders of the Puritan settlement of Newbury. As an immigrant of 1653, he had listed himself as a "linnen weaver," but he soon became a farmer as well.[4] At his death, his loom and tackling stood in the "shop" with his pitchforks, his hoes, and his tools for smithing and carpentry. Plummer had integrated four smaller plots to form one continuous sixteen-acre farm. An additional twenty acres of salt marsh and meadow provided hay and forage for his small herd of cows and sheep. His farm provided a comfortable living for his family, which at this stage of his life included only his second wife, Beatrice, and her grandchild by a previous marriage. Had not death prevented him, he might have filled this January day in a number of productive ways, moving the loom into the sparsely furnished hall, for example, or taking his yoke of oxen to the wood lot "near the little river" to cut wood for the large fireplace that was the center of Beatrice's working world.

The house over which Beatrice presided must have looked much like surviving dwellings from seventeenth-century New England, with its "Hall" and "Parlor" on the ground floor and two "chambers" above. A space designated in the inventory only as "another Roome" held the family's collection of pots, kettles, dripping pans, trays, buckets, and earthenware. Perhaps this kitchen had been added to the original house as a lean-to, as was frequently the case in New England.[5] The upstairs chambers were not bedrooms but storage rooms for foodstuffs and out-of-season equipment. The best bed with its bolster, pillows, blanket, and coverlet stood in the parlor; a second bed occupied one corner of the kitchen, while a cupboard, a "great chest," a table, and a backless bench called a "form" furnished the hall. More food was found in the "cellar" and in the "dairy house," a room which may have stood at the coolest end of the kitchen lean-to.[6]

The Plummer house was devoid of ornament, but its contents bespeak such comforts as conscientious yeomanry and good huswifery afforded. On this winter morning the dairy house held four and a half "flitches" or sides of bacon, a quarter of a barrel of salt pork, twenty-eight pounds of cheese, and four pounds of butter. Upstairs in a chamber were more than twenty-five bushels of "English" grain—barley, oats, wheat, and rye. (The Plummers apparently reserved their Indian corn, stored in another location, for their animals.) When made into malt by a village specialist, barley would become the basis for beer. Two bushels of malt were already stored in the house. The oats might appear in a variety of dishes, from plain breakfast porridge to "flummery," a gelatinous dish flavored with spices and dried fruit.[7] But the wheat and rye were almost certainly reserved for bread and pies. The fine hair sieves stored with the grain in the hall chamber suggest that Beatrice Plummer was particular about her baking, preferring a finer flour than came directly from the miller. A "bushell of pease & beans" found near the grain and a full barrel of cider in the cellar are the only vegetables and fruits listed in the inventory, though small quantities of pickles, preserves, or dried herbs might have escaped notice. Perhaps the Plummers added variety to their diet by trading some of their abundant supply of grain for cabbages, turnips, sugar, molasses, and spices.

Even without additions they had the basic components of the yeoman diet described in English agricultural literature of the seventeenth century. Although the eighteenth century would add a little chocolate or tea as well as increasing quantities of tiny "petators" to the New England farmer's diet, the bread, cider, and boiled meat which fed Francis and Beatrice Plummer also fed their counterparts a century later.[8]

Since wives were involved with early-morning milking, breakfast of necessity featured prepared foods or leftovers—toasted bread, cheese, and perhaps meat and turnips kept from the day before, any of this washed down with cider or beer in winter, with milk in summer. Only on special occasions would there be pie or doughnuts. Dinner was the main meal of the day. Here a housewife with culinary aspirations and an ample larder could display her specialties. After harvest Beatrice Plummer might have served roast pork or goose with apples, in spring an eel pie flavored with parsley and winter savory, and in summer a leek soup or gooseberry cream; but for ordinary days the most common menu was boiled meat with whatever "sauce" the season provided—dried peas or beans, parsnips, turnips, onions, cabbage, or garden greens. A heavy pudding stuffed into a cloth bag could steam atop the vegetables and meat. The broth from this boiled dinner might reappear at supper as "pottage" with the addition of minced herbs and some oatmeal or barley for thickening. Supper, like breakfast, was a simple meal. Bread, cheese, and beer were as welcome at the end of a winter day as at the beginning. In summer, egg dishes and fruit tarts provided more varied nutrition.

Preparing the simplest of these meals required both judgment and skill. As Gervase Markham, an English writer of the seventeenth century, quipped, a woman who was "utterly ignorant" of cookery could "then but perform half her vow; for she may love and obey, but she cannot cherish, serve, and keep him with that true duty which is ever expected."[9] The most basic of the housewife's skills was building and regulating fires—a task so fundamental that it must have appeared more as habit than craft. Summer and winter, day and night, she kept a few brands smoldering, ready to stir into flame as needed. The cavernous fireplaces of early New England were but a century removed from the open fires of medieval houses, and they retained some of the characteristics of the latter. Standing inside one of these huge openings today, a person can see the sky above. Seventeenth-century housewives *did* stand in their fireplaces, which were conceived less as enclosed spaces for a single blaze than as accessible working surfaces upon which a number of small fires might be built. Preparing several dishes simultaneously, a cook could move from one fire to another, turning a spit, checking the state of the embers under a skillet, adjusting the height of a pot hung from the lugpole by its adjustable trammel. The complexity of fire-tending, as much as anything else, encouraged the one-pot meal.[10]

The contents of her inventory suggest that Beatrice Plummer was adept not only at roasting, frying, and boiling but also at baking, the most difficult branch of cookery. Judging from the grain in the upstairs chamber, the bread which she baked was "maslin," a common type made from a mixture of wheat and other grains, usually rye. She began with the sieves stored nearby, carefully sifting out the coarser pieces of grain and bran. Soon after supper she could have mixed the "sponge," a thin dough made from warm water, yeast, and flour. Her yeast might have come from the foamy "barm" found on top of fermenting ale or beer, from a piece of dough saved from an earlier baking, or even from the crevices in an unwashed kneading trough.[11] Like fire-building, bread-making was based upon a self-perpetuating chain, an organic sequence which if once interrupted was difficult to begin again. Warmth from the banked fire would raise the sponge by morning, when Beatrice could work in more flour, knead the finished dough, and shape the loaves, leaving them to rise again.

Even in twentieth-century kitchens with standardized yeast and thermostatically controlled temperatures, bread dough is subject to wide variations in consistency and behavior. In a drafty house with an uncertain supply of yeast, bread-making was indeed "an art, craft, and mystery." Not the least of the problem was regulating the fire so that the oven was ready at the same time as the risen loaves. Small cakes or biscuits could be baked in a skillet or directly on the hearth under an upside-down pot covered with coals. But to produce bread in any quantity required an oven. Before 1650 these were frequently constructed in dooryards, but in the last decades of the century they were built into the rear of the kitchen fireplace, as Beatrice Plummer's must have been. Since her oven would have had no flue, she would have left the door open once she kindled a fire inside, allowing the smoke to escape through the fireplace chimney. Moving about her kitchen, she would have kept an eye on this fire, occasionally raking the coals to distribute the heat evenly, testing periodically with her hand to see if the oven had reached the right temperature. When she determined that it had, she would have scraped out the coals and inserted the bread—assuming that it had risen enough by this time or had not risen too much and collapsed waiting for the oven to heat.[12]

Cooking and baking were year-round tasks. Inserted into these day-by-day routines were seasonal specialties which allowed a housewife to bridge the dearth of one period with the bounty of another. In the preservation calendar, dairying came first, beginning with the first calves of early spring. In colonial New England cows were all-purpose creatures, raised for meat as well as for milk. Even in new settlements they could survive by browsing on rough land; their meat was a hedge against famine. But only in areas with abundant meadow (and even there only in certain months) would they produce milk with sufficient butterfat for serious dairying.[13] Newbury was such a place.

We can imagine Beatrice Plummer some morning in early summer processing the milk which would appear as cheese in a January breakfast. Slowly she heated several gallons with rennet dried and saved from the autumn's slaughtering. Within an hour or two the curd had formed. She broke it, drained off the whey, then worked in a little of her own fresh butter. Packing this rich mixture into a mold, she turned it in her wooden press for an hour or more, changing and washing the cheesecloth frequently as the whey dripped out. Repacking it in dry cloth, she left it in the press for another thirty to forty hours before washing it once more with whey, drying it, and placing it in the cellar or dairy house to age. As a young girl she would have learned from her mother or a mistress the importance of thorough pressing and the virtues of cleanliness. She may also have acquired some of the many English proverbs associated with dairying. Taking her finished mound to the powdering tub for a light dusting, she perhaps recalled that "much saltness in white meat is ill for the stone."[14]

The Plummer inventory gives little evidence of the second stage of preservation in the housewife's year, the season of gardening and gathering which followed quickly upon the dairy months. But there is ample evidence of the autumn slaughtering. Beatrice could well have killed the smaller pigs herself, holding their "hinder parts between her legs," as one observer described the process, "and taking the snout in her left hand" while she stuck the animal through the heart with a long knife. Once the bleeding stopped, she would have submerged the pig in boiling water for a few minutes, then rubbed it with rosin, stripped off the hair, and disemboweled it. Nothing was lost. She reserved the organ meats for immediate use, then cleaned the intestines for later service as sausage casings. Stuffed with meat scraps and herbs and smoked, these "links" were a treasured delicacy. The larger cuts could be roasted at once or preserved in several ways. With wine, ginger, mace, and nutmeg, pork could be rolled into a cloth and pickled as "souse." But this was an expensive—and risky—method. Beatrice relied on more common techniques. She submerged some of her pork in brine, trusting the high salt concentration and the low temperature in the dairy house to keep it untainted. She processed the rest as bacon. Each "flitch" stood in salt for two or three weeks before she hung it from the lugpole of her chimney for smoking.[15] In the Plummer house "hanging bacon" must have been a recurring ritual of early winter.

Fall was also the season for cider-making. The mildly alcoholic beverage produced by natural fermentation of apple juice was a staple of the New England diet and was practically the only method of preserving the fruit harvest. With the addition of sugar, the alcoholic content could be raised from five to about seven percent, as it usually was in taverns and for export. The cider in the Plummer house was probably the common farm variety. In early winter the amber juice of autumn sat hissing and bubbling in the cellar in the most active stage of fermentation, a process which came to be described poetically as the "singing of the cider."[16]

Prosaic beer was even more important to the Plummer diet. Although some housewives brewed a winter's supply of strong beer in October, storing it in the cellar, Beatrice seems to have been content with "small beer," a mild beverage usually brewed weekly or bi-weekly and used almost at once. Malting—the process of sprouting and drying barley to increase its sugar content—was wisely left to the village expert. Beatrice started with cracked malt or grist, processing her beer in three stages. "Mashing" required slow steeping at just below the boiling point, a sensitive and smelly process which largely determined the success of the beverage. Experienced brewers knew by taste whether the enzymes were working. If it was too hot, acetic acid developed which would sour the finished product. The next stage, "brewing," was relatively simple. Herbs and hops were boiled with the malted liquid. In the final step this liquor was cooled and mixed with yeast saved from last week's beer or bread. Within twenty-four hours—if all had gone well—the beer was bubbling actively.[17]

All that we know of Beatrice Plummer of Newbury reveals her as a woman who took pride in huswifery. A wife who knew how to manage the ticklish chemical processes which changed milk into cheese, meal into bread, malt into beer, and flesh into bacon was a valuable asset to a man, as Francis Plummer knew. But not long after his death Beatrice married a man who did not appreciate her skills. To put it bluntly, he seems to have preferred her property. Like Francis Plummer before him, Edmund Berry had signed a prenuptial contract allowing Beatrice to retain ownership of the estate she had inherited from her previous husband. Subsequently, however, Edmund regretted his decision and began to hound Beatrice to tear up the paper.

The strategy which Edmund used was wonderfully calculated. Not only did he refuse to provide Beatrice with provisions, he denied her the right to perform her housewifely magic upon them. "Forr such was & still is his absurd manner in eating his victualls, as takeing his meat out of ye pickle: & broyleing it upon ye coales, & this he would tell me I must eate or else I must fast," she told the Salem Quarterly Court in June of 1677. Beatrice had lived peacefully with two husbands, as one neighbor testified, but in old age she had wedded a man who preferred her estate to her cooking. He said she should have nothing of him because he had nothing of hers, and he told one neighbor he did not care if "there were a fire in the south field and she in the middle of it." Berry was fined for his "abusive carriages and speeches."

What is really interesting about this case is not the ill-temper of the husband but the humiliation of the wife, who obviously found herself in a situation for which she was unprepared, despite the experience of two previous marriages. Legally, Beatrice had every right to hold fast to her dower, as Edmund Berry knew. The real issue, however, was not law but custom. Berry simply refused to play by the rules as his wife understood them. She offered to help him "wind his quills" (like his predecessor, he was a weaver), and she brought him "a cup of my owne Sugar & beare" and drank to him, saying, "Come husband lett all former differences be buried & trod under Foote." But he only replied, "Thou old cheating Rogue."[18] Neither the services of a deputy husband nor the ministrations of a wife could salve his distemper. Beatrice's loss is history's gain. The tumult which thrust her into court gives life to the assemblage of objects found in her Newbury kitchen, and it helps to document the central position of huswifery in the self-definition of one northern New England woman.

BEATRICE PLUMMER REPRESENTS one type of early American housewife. Hannah Grafton represents another.[19] Chronology, geography, and personal biography created differences between the household inventories of the two women, but there are obvious similarities as well. Like Beatrice Plummer, Hannah Grafton lived in a house with two major rooms on the ground floor and two chambers above. At various locations near the ground-floor rooms were service areas—a washhouse with its own loft or chamber, a shop, a lean-to, and two cellars. The central rooms in the Grafton house were the "parlour," with the expected featherbed, and the "kitchen," which included much the same collection of utensils and iron pots which appeared in the Plummer house. Standing in the corner of the kitchen were a spade and a hoe, two implements useful only for chipping away ice and snow on the December day on which the inventory was taken, though apparently destined for another purpose come spring. With a garden, a cow, and three pigs, Hannah Grafton clearly had agricultural responsibilities, but these were performed in a strikingly different context than on the Plummer farm. The Grafton homelot was a single acre of land standing just a few feet from shoreline in the urban center of Salem.[20]

Joshua Grafton was a mariner like his father before him. His estste of £236 was modest, but he was still a young man and he had firm connections with the seafaring elite who were transforming the economy of Salem. When he died late in 1699, Hannah had three living children—Hannah, eight; Joshua, six; and Priscilla, who was just ten months.[21] This young family used their space quite differently than had the Plummers. The upstairs chambers which served as storage areas in the Newbury farmhouse were sleeping quarters here. In addition to the bed in the parlor and the cradle in the kitchen, there were two beds in each of the upstairs rooms. One of these, designated as "smaller," may have been used by young Joshua. It would be interesting to know whether the mother carried the two chamber pots kept in the parlor upstairs to the bedrooms at night or whether the children found their way in the dark to their parents' sides as necessity demanded. But adults were probably never far away. Because there are more bedsteads in the Grafton house than members of the immediate family, they may have shared their living quarters with unmarried relatives or servants.

Ten chairs and two stools furnished the kitchen, while no fewer than fifteen chairs, in two separate sets, crowded the parlor with its curtained bed. The presence of a punch bowl on a square table in the parlor reinforces the notion that sociability was an important value in this Salem household. Thirteen ounces of plate, a pair of gold buttons, and a silver-headed cane suggest a measure of luxury as well—all of this in stark contrast to the Plummers, who had only two chairs and a backless bench and no discernible ornamentation at all. Yet the Grafton house was only slightly more specialized than the Newbury farmhouse. It had no servants' quarters, no sharp segregation of public and private spaces, no real separation of sleeping, eating, and work. A cradle in the kitchen and a go-cart kept with the spinning wheels in the upstairs chamber show that little Priscilla was very much a part of this workaday world.

How then might the pattern of Hannah Grafton's work have differed from that of Beatrice Plummer? Certainly cooking remained central. Hannah's menus probably varied only slightly from those prepared in the Plummer kitchen, and her cooking techniques must have been identical. But one dramatic difference is apparent in the two inventories. The Grafton house contained no provisions worth listing on that December day when Isaac Foot and Samuel Willard appeared to take inventory. Hannah had brewing vessels, but no malt; sieves and a meal trough, but no grain; and a cow, but no cheese. What little milk her cow gave in winter probably went directly into the children's mugs. Perhaps she would continue to breast-feed Priscilla until spring brought a more secure supply. In summer she might make a little cottage cheese or at harvest curdle some rich milk with wine or ale for a "posset," but she would have no surplus to process as butter or cheese. Her orchard would produce fresh apples for pie or puffs for autumn supper, but little extra for the cellar. Her three pigs might eventually appear, salted, in the empty barrels stored in the house, but as yet they represented only the hope of bacon. Trade, rather than manufacturing or agriculture, was the dominant motif in her meal preparations.

In colonial New England most food went directly from processer or producer to consumer. Joshua may have purchased grain or flour from the mill near the shipbuilding center called Knocker's Hole, about a mile away from their house. Or Hannah may have eschewed bread-making altogether, walking or sending a servant the half-mile to Elizabeth Haskett's bakery near the North River. Fresh meat for the spits in her washhouse may have come from John Cromwell's slaughterhouse on Main Street near the congregational meetinghouse, and soap for her washtubs from the soap-boiler farther up the street near the Quaker meetinghouse.[22] Salem, like other colonial towns, was laid out helter-skelter, with the residences of the wealthy interspersed with the small houses of carpenters or fishermen. Because there was no center of retail trade, assembling the ingredients of a dinner involved many transactions. Sugar, wine, and spices came by sea; fresh lamb, veal, eggs, butter, gooseberries, and parsnips came by land. Merchants retailed their goods in shops or warehouses near their wharves and houses. Farmers or their wives often hawked their produce door to door.[23] Salem had a charter for a fair, remarked one English traveler, "but it begins like Ingerstone Market, half an Hour after eleven a Clock, and Ends half an Hour before Twelve."[24]

In such a setting, trading for food might require as much energy and skill as manufacturing or growing it. One key to success was simply knowing where to go. Keeping abreast of the arrival of ships in the harbor or establishing personal contact with just the right farmwife from nearby Salem village required time and attention. Equally important was the ability to evaluate the variety of unstandardized goods offered. An apparently sound cheese might teem with maggots when cut.[25] Since cash was scarce, a third necessity was the establishment of credit, a problem which ultimately devolved upon husbands. But petty haggling over direct exchanges was also a feature of this barter economy.

Hannah Grafton was involved in trade on more than one level. The "shop" attached to her house was not the all-purpose storage shed and workroom it seems to have been for Francis Plummer. It was a retail store, offering door locks, nails, hammers, gimlets, and other hardware as well as English cloth, pins, needles, and thread. As a mariner, Joshua Grafton may well have sailed the ship which brought these goods to Salem. In his absence, Hannah was not only a mother and a housewife but, like many other Salem women, a shopkeeper as well.

There is another highly visible activity in the Grafton inventory which was not immediately apparent in the Plummers'—care of clothing. Presumably, Beatrice Plummer washed occasionally, but she did not have a "washhouse." Hannah did. The arrangement of this unusual room is far from clear. On December 2, 1699, it contained two spits, two "bouldishes," a gridiron, and "other things." Whether those other things included washtubs, soap, or a beating staff is impossible to determine. In a seaport town a building with a fire for heating rinse water, boiling laundry, and drying clothes could have been the base for a thriving home industry. But there is no evidence of this in the Grafton inventory. Like the "butteries" and "dairies" which appear in other New England houses, this room may have retained a specialized English name while actually functioning as a multipurpose storage and service room.[26] With its spits and gridiron Hannah Grafton's "washhouse" may have served as an extra cooking space, perhaps on occasions when all fifteen chairs in the parlor were filled.

But on any morning in December it could also have been hung with the family wash. Dark woolen jackets and petticoats went from year to year without seeing a kettle of suds, but linen shifts, aprons, shirts, and handkerchiefs required washing. Laundering might not have been a weekly affair in most colonial households, but it was a well-defined if infrequent necessity even for transient seamen and laborers. One can only speculate on its frequency in a house with a child under a year. When her baby was only a few months old, Hannah may have learned to hold little Priscilla over the chamber pot at frequent intervals, but in early infancy, tightly wrapped in her cradle, the baby could easily have used five dozen "clouts" and almost as many "belly bands" from one washing to another. Even with the use of a "pilch," a thick square of flannel securely bound over the diaper, blankets and coverlets occasionally needed sudsing as well.[27]

Joshua's shirts and Hannah's own aprons and shifts would require careful ironing. Hannah's "smoothing irons" fitted into their own heaters, which she filled with coals from the fire. As the embers waned and the irons cooled, she would have made frequent trips from her table to the hearth to the fire and back to the table again. At least two of these heavy instruments were essential. A dampened apron could dry and wrinkle while a single flatiron replenished its heat.[28]

As frequent a task as washing was sewing. Joshua's coats and breeches went to a tailor, but his shirts were probably made at home. Certainly Hannah stitched and unstitched the tucks which altered Priscilla's simple gowns and petticoats as she grew. The little dresses which the baby trailed in her go-cart had once clothed her brother. Gender identity in childhood was less important in this society than economy of effort. It was not that boys were seen as identical to girls, only that all-purpose garments could be handed from one child to another regardless of sex, and dresses were more easily altered than breeches and more adaptable to diapering and toileting. At eight years of age little Hannah had probably begun to imitate her mother's even stitches, helping with the continual mending, altering, and knitting which kept this growing family clothed.[29]

In some ways the most interesting items in the Grafton inventory are the two spinning wheels kept in the upstairs chamber. Beatrice Plummer's wheel and reel had been key components in an intricate production chain. The Plummers had twenty-five sheep in the fold and a loom in the shed. The Graftons had neither. Children—not sheep—put wheels in Hannah's house. The mechanical nature of spinning made it a perfect occupation for women whose attention was engrossed by young children.[30] This is one reason why the ownership of wheels in both York and Essex counties had a constancy over time unrelated to the ownership of sheep or looms. In the dozen inventories taken in urban Salem about the time of Joshua Grafton's death, the six non-spinners averaged one minor child each, the six spinners had almost four. Instruction at the wheel was part of the almost ritualistic preparation mothers offered their daughters.[31] Spinning was a useful craft, easily picked up, easily put down, and even small quantities of yarn could be knitted into caps, stockings, dishcloths, and mittens.

Unfortunately, there is no documented event in Hannah Grafton's life corresponding to Beatrice Plummer's colorful appearance in court. But a cluster of objects in the chamber over her kitchen suggests a fanciful but by no means improbable vignette. Imagine her gathered with her two daughters in this upstairs room on a New England winter's day. Little Priscilla navigates around the end of the bedstead in her go-cart while her mother sits at one spinning wheel and her sister at the other. Young Hannah is spinning "oakum," the coarsest and least expensive part of the flax. As her mother leans over to help her wind the uneven thread on the bobbin, she catches a troublesome scent from downstairs. Have the turnips caught on the bottom of the pot? Has the maid scorched Joshua's best shirt? Or has a family servant returned from the wharf and spread his wet clothes by the fire? Hastening down the narrow stairs to the kitchen, Hannah hears the shop bell ring. Just then little Priscilla, left upstairs with her sister, begins to cry. In such pivotal but unrecorded moments much of the history of women lies hidden.

THE THIRD INVENTORY can be more quickly described.[32] Elias Wear of York, Maine, left an estate totaling £92, of which less than £7 was in household goods—including some old pewter, a pot, two bedsteads, bedding, one chest, and a box. Wear also owned a saddle, three guns, and a river craft called a gundalow. But his wealth, such as it was, consisted of land (£40) and livestock (£36). It is not just relative poverty which distinguished Elias Wear's inventory from that of Joshua Grafton or Francis Plummer. Every settlement in northern New England had men who owned only a pot, a bed, and a chest. Their children crowded in with them or slept on straw. These men and their sons provided some of the labor which harvested barley for farmers like Francis Plummer or stepped masts for mariners like Joshua Grafton. Their wives and their daughters carded wool or kneaded bread in other women's kitchens. No, Elias Wear was distinguished by a special sort of frontier poverty.

His father had come to northern New England in the 1640s, exploring and trading for furs as far inland in New Hampshire as Lake Winnipesaukee. By 1650 he had settled in York, a then hopeful site for establishing a patrimony. Forty years later he died in the York Massacre, an assault by French and Indians which virtually destroyed the town, bringing death or captivity to fully half of the inhabitants.[33] Almost continuous warfare between 1689 and 1713 created prosperity for the merchant community of Portsmouth and Kittery, but it kept most of the inhabitants of outlying settlements in a state of impecunious insecurity.[34]

In 1696, established on a small homestead in the same neighborhood in which his father had been killed, Elias Wear married a young widow with the fitting name of Magdalen. When their first child was born "too soon," the couple found themselves in York County Court owning a presentment for fornication. Although New England courts were still sentencing couples in similar circumstances to "nine stripes a piece upon the Naked back," most of the defendants, like the Wears, managed to pay the not inconsequential fine. The fifty-nine shillings which Elias and Magdalen pledged the court amounted to almost half of the total value of two steers. A presentment for fornication was expensive as well as inconvenient, but it did not carry a permanent onus. Within seven years of their conviction Elias was himself serving on the "Jury of Tryalls" for the county, while Magdalen had proved herself a dutiful and productive wife.[35]

Every other winter she gave birth, producing four sons—Elias, Jeremiah, John, and Joseph—in addition to the untimely Ruth. A sixth child, Mary, was just five months old when her father met his own death by Indians in August of 1707 while traveling between their Cape Neddick home and the more densely settled York village.[36] Without the benefits of a cradle, a go-cart, a spinning wheel, or even a secure supply of grain, Magdalen raised these six children. Unfortunately, there is little in her inventory and nothing in any other record to document the specific strategies which she used, though the general circumstances of her life can be imagined.

Chopping and hauling for a local timber merchant, Elias could have filled Magdalen's porridge pot with grain shipped from the port of Salem or Boston. During the spring corn famine, an almost yearly occurrence on the Maine frontier, she might have gone herself with other wives of her settlement to dig on the clam flats, hedging against the day when relief would come by sea.[37] Like Beatrice Plummer and Hannah Grafton, she would have spent some hours cooking, washing, hoeing cabbages, bargaining with neighbors, and, in season, herding and milking a cow. But poverty, short summers, and rough land also made gathering an essential part of her work. We may imagine her cutting pine splinters for light and "cattails" and "silkgrass" for beds. Long before her small garden began to produce, she would have searched out a wild "sallet" in the nearby woods, in summer turning to streams and barrens for other delicacies congenial to English taste—eels, salmon, berries, and plums. She would have embarked on such excursions with caution, however, remembering the wives of nearby Exeter who took their children into the woods for strawberries "without any Guard" and narrowly avoided capture.[38]

Frontier danger drew scattered families together, sometimes compressing an entire neighborhood into a designated "garrison" for days at a time. Near sawmills, these structures were in some cases true garrisons—fortified houses constructed of machine-smoothed timbers laid edge to edge; just as often they were simply the largest or most substantial dwellings in each settlement.[39] Women like Magdalen Wear went to the doors of these same houses in times of peace, asking to borrow malt or offering to spin for a day.

Only the most prosperous families of Maine and New Hampshire built according to the parlor-hall houseplan which was becoming typical of Essex County by the end of the seventeenth century. The Wears probably lived in a single-story cottage which may or may not have been subdivided into more than one room. A loft above provided extra space for storage or sleeping. With the addition of a lean-to, this house could have sheltered animals as well as humans, especially in harsh weather or in periods of Indian alarm. Housing a pig or a calf in the next room would have simplified Magdalen's chores in the winter. If she managed to raise a few chickens, these too would have thrived better near the kitchen fire.[40]

Thus, penury erased the elaborate demarcation of "houses" and "yards" evident in yeoman inventories. It also blurred distinctions between the work of a husbandman and the work of his wife. At planting time and at harvest Magdalen Wear undoubtedly went into the fields to help Elias, taking her babies with her or leaving Ruth to watch them as best she could.[41] A century later an elderly Maine woman bragged that she "had dropped corn many a day with two governors: a judge in her arms and a general on her back."[42] None of the Wear children grew up to such prominence, but all six of them survived to adulthood and four married and founded families of their own. Six children did not prevent Magdalen Wear from remarrying within two years of her husband's death. Whatever her assets—a pleasant face, a strong back, or lifetime possession of £40 in land—she was soon wed to the unmarried son of a neighboring millowner.[43]

MAGDALEN WEAR, Hannah Grafton, and Beatrice Plummer were all "typical" New England housewives of the period 1650–1750. Magdalen's iron pot represents the housekeeping minimum which often characterized frontier life. Hannah's punch bowl and her hardware shop exemplify both the commerce and the self-conscious civilization of coastal towns. Beatrice's brewing tubs and churn epitomize home manufacturing and agrarian self-sufficiency as they existed in established villages. Each type of housekeeping could be found somewhere in northern New England in any decade of the century. Yet these three women should not be placed in rigidly separate categories. Wealth, geography, occupation, and age determined that some women in any decade would be more heavily involved in one aspect of housekeeping than another, yet all three women shared a common vocation. Each understood the rhythms of the seasons, the technology of firebuilding, the persistence of the daily demands of cooking, the complexity of home production, and the dexterity demanded from the often conflicting roles of housekeeper, mother, and wife.

The thing which distinguished these women from their counterparts in modern America was not, as some historians have suggested, that their work was essential to survival. "Survival," after all, is a minimal concept. Individual men and women have never needed each other for mere survival but for far more complex reasons, and women were *essential* in the seventeenth century for the very same reasons they are essential today—for the perpetuation of the race. As the Indians and Edmund Berry knew, English husbands could live without cheese and beer. Nor was it the monotony of these women's lives or the narrowness of their choices which really set them apart. Women in industrial cities have lived monotonous and confining lives, and they may have worked even harder than early American women. The really striking differences are social.

In this brief exploration of work we have merely hinted at the social setting in which work occurred. We have noted the intervention of Beatrice Plummer's neighbors in her conflicts with her husband, the importance of children in the household of Hannah Grafton, and the blurring of gender boundaries in the frontier environment of Magdalen Wear. In later chapters these patterns will be elaborated. Here we can simply assert that the lives of early American housewives were distinguished less by the tasks they performed than by forms of social organization which linked economic responsibilities to family responsibilities and which tied each woman's household to the larger world of her village or town.

For centuries the industrious Bathsheba has been pictured sitting at a spinning wheel—"She layeth her hands to the spindle, and her hands hold the distaff." Perhaps it is time to suggest a new icon for women's history. Certainly spinning was an important female craft in northern New England, linked not only to housework but to mothering, but it was one enterprise among many. Spinning wheels are such intriguing and picturesque objects, so resonant with antiquity, that they tend to obscure rather than clarify the nature of female economic life, making home production the essential element in early American huswifery and the era of industrialization the period of crucial change. Challenging the symbolism of the wheel not only undermines the popular stereotype, it questions a prevailing emphasis in women's history.

An alternate symbol might be the pocket. In early America a woman's pocket was not attached to her clothing, but tied around her waist with a string or tape. (When "Lucy Locket lost her pocket, Kitty Fisher found it.") Much better than a spinning wheel, this homely object symbolizes the obscurity, the versatility, and the personal nature of the housekeeping role. A woman sat at a wheel, but she carried her pocket with her from room to room, from house to yard, from yard to street. The items which it contained would shift from day to day and from year to year, but they would of necessity be small, easily lost, yet precious. A pocket could be a mended and patched pouch of plain homespun or a rich personal ornament boldly embroidered in crewel. It reflected the status as well as the skills of its owner. Whether it contained cellar keys or a paper of pins, a packet of seeds or a baby's bib, a hank of yarn or a Testament, it characterized the social complexity as well as the demanding diversity of women's work.

Chapter Two

DEPUTY HUSBANDS

MANY HISTORIANS HAVE ASSUMED, with Page Smith, that "it was not until the end of the colonial era that the idea of a 'suitable' or 'proper' sphere of feminine activities began to emerge." For fifty years historians have relied upon the work of Elizabeth A. Dexter, who claimed that there were more "women of affairs" proportionally in eighteenth-century America than in 1900. Colonial newspapers yield evidence of female blacksmiths, silversmiths, tinworkers, shoemakers, shipwrights, tanners, gunsmiths, barbers, printers, and butchers, as well as a great many teachers and shopkeepers. Partly on the basis of such evidence, Richard Morris concluded in his pioneering study of female legal rights that American women in the colonial period attained "a measure of individuality and independence in excess of that of their English sisters."[1]

Recently, however, a few historians have begun to question these assumptions. Mary Beth Norton has carefully studied the claims of 468 loyalist women who were refugees in Great Britain after the American Revolution. Only forty-three of these women mentioned earning money on their own or even assisting directly in their husbands' business. As a group, the loyalist women were unable to describe their family assets, other than household possessions, and they repeatedly described themselves as "helpless" to manage the business thrust upon them. She has concluded that these women were "almost wholly domestic, in the sense that that word would be used in the nineteenth-century United States."[2] In a study of widowhood in eighteenth-century Massachusetts,

Alexander Keyssar came to similar conclusions. Economic dependency, first upon husbands, then upon grown sons, characterized the lives of women in the agricultural village of Woburn.[3]

Both groups of historians are right. The premodern world did allow for greater fluidity of role behavior than in nineteenth-century America, but colonial women were by definition basically domestic. We can account for these apparently contradictory conclusions by focusing more closely upon the economic relationship of husband and wife. There is a revealing little anecdote in a deposition recorded in Essex County in 1672. Jacob Barney of Salem had gone to Phillip Cromwell's house to negotiate a marriage. Although both Cromwell and his wife were present, Barney had turned to the husband, expecting, as he said, "to have their minds from him." But because Cromwell had a severe cold which had impaired his hearing, he simply pointed to his wife and said that whatever she agreed upon, "he would make it good."[4] This incident dramatizes three assumptions basic to family government in the traditional world:

1. The husband was supreme in the external affairs of the family. As its titular head, he had both the right and the responsibility to represent it in its dealings with the outside world.

2. A husband's decisions would, however, incorporate his wife's opinions and interest. (Barney expected to hear *their* minds from *him*.)

3. Should fate or circumstance prevent the husband from fulfilling his role, the wife could appropriately stand in his place. As one seventeenth-century Englishman explained it, a woman "in her husband's absence, is wife and deputy-husband, which makes her double the files of her diligence. At his return he finds all things so well he wonders to see himself at home when he was abroad."[5]

To put it simply, Dexter's evidence points to what was permissible in colonial society, Norton's to what was probable. As deputy husbands a few women, like Mistress Cromwell, might emerge from anonymity; most women did not. Yet both sets of evidence must be analyzed apart from modern assumptions about the importance of access to jobs in expanding female opportunity. The significance of the role of deputy husband cannot be determined by counting the number of women who used it to achieve independence. To talk about the independence of colonial wives is not only an anachronism but a contradiction in logic. A woman became a wife by virtue of her dependence, her solemnly vowed commitment to her husband. No matter how colorful the exceptions, land and livelihood in this society were normally transmitted from father to son, as studies like Keyssar's have shown.

One can be dependent, however, without being either servile or helpless. To use an imperfect but nonetheless suggestive analogy, colonial wives were dependent upon patriarchal families in somewhat the same way seventeenth-century ministers were dependent upon their congregations or twentieth-century engineers are dependent upon their companies. That is, they owned neither their place of employment nor even the tools of their trade. No matter how diligently they worked, they did not expect to inherit the land upon which they lived any more than a minister expected to inherit his meetinghouse or an engineer his factory. Skilled service was their major contribution, secure support their primary compensation. Unlike professionals in either century, they could not resign their position, but then neither could they be fired. Upon the death of a husband they were entitled to maintenance for life—or until they transferred their allegiance (symbolized by their name) from one domestic establishment to another.

The skilled service of a wife included the specialized housekeeping skills described in the last chapter, but it also embraced the responsibilities of a deputy husband. Since most productive work was based within the family, there were many opportunities for a wife to "double the files of her diligence." A weaver's wife, like Beatrice Plummer, might wind quills. A merchant's wife, like Hannah Grafton, might keep shop. A farmer's wife, like Magdalen Wear, might plant corn.

Looking backward to the colonial period from the nineteenth century, when "true womanhood" precluded either business enterprise or hard physical labor, historians may miss the significance of such work, which tells us less about economic opportunity (which for most women was limited) than about female responsibility (which was often very broad). Most occupations were indeed gender-linked, yet colonial Englishmen were far less concerned with abstract notions like "femininity" than with concrete roles like "wife" or "neighbor." Almost any task was suitable for a woman as long as it furthered the good of her family and was acceptable to her husband. This approach was both fluid and fixed. It allowed for varied behavior without really challenging the patriarchal order of society. There was no proscription against female farming, for example, but there were strong prescriptions toward dutiful wifehood and motherhood. Context was everything.

In discussing the ability of colonial women to take on male duties, most historians have assumed a restrictive ideology in Anglo-American society, an essentially negative valuation of female capacity. Some historians have argued that this negative ideology was offset by the realities of colonial life; others have concluded it was not. This chapter reverses the base of the argument, suggesting that even in America ideology was more permissive than reality. Under the right conditions any wife not only *could* double as a husband, she had the responsibility to do so. In the probate courts, for example, widows who did not have grown sons were routinely granted administration of their husbands' estates.[6] Gender restrictions were structural rather than psychological. Although there was no female line of inheritance, wives were presumed capable of husbanding property which male heirs would eventually inherit.

To explain fully the contradictions in such a system, we must return to the day-to-day behavior of individual husbands and wives, first examining the factors which enhanced the role of deputy husband and then exploring conditions which muted its significance for colonial women.

HISTORIANS CAN READ WILLS, account books, and tax records, documents in which males clearly predominate, but they cannot so easily explore the complex decision-making behind these records. Scattered glimpses of daily interaction suggest that there was as much variation in seventeenth- and eighteenth-century families as there is today. Some wives were servile, some were shrews, others were respected companions who shared the authority of their spouses in the management of family affairs. Important conditions, however, separated the colonial world from our own. The most basic of these was spatial. Earlier we described an imaginary boundary stretching from house to yard, separating the domain of the housewife from the world of her husband. It is important to recognize that in reality no such barrier existed. Male and female space intersected and overlapped. Nor was there the sharp division between home and work that later generations experienced. Because servants and apprentices lived within the household, a family occasion—mealtime or nightly prayer—could become a business occasion as well.

In June of 1661 a young maid named Naomi Hull described a discussion which took place in the parlor of the Samuel Symonds' home in Ipswich, Massachusetts, early in that year. The case concerned the length of indenture of two Irish servants. According to the maid, all of the family had gathered for prayer when one of the Irishmen asked if a neighbor's son was coming the next day to plow. *Mistress* Symonds said she thought so. One of the men asked who would plow with him. *Mistress* Symonds said, "One of you." When the two men announced that their indenture was up and that they would work no longer, both the master and the mistress questioned the servants. At one point Mistress Symonds interrupted her husband. "Let them alone," she said. "Now they are speaking let them speak their own minds."[7] Because the involvement of Mistress Symonds was not at issue, this casual description of her participation is all the more impressive. Such an anecdote shows the way in which boundaries between male and female domains might blur in a common household setting.

Ambitious men in early America were often involved in many things at once—farming and running a gristmill, for example, or cutting timber and fishing. Because wives remained close to the house, they were often at the communications center of these diverse operations, given responsibility for conveying directions, pacifying creditors, and perhaps even making some decisions about the disposition of labor. On a day-to-day basis this might be a rather simple matter: remembering to send a servant to repair a breach in the dam after he finished in the field, for example, or knowing when to relinquish an ox to a neighbor.[8] But during a prolonged absence of her husband a woman might become involved in more weighty matters.

Sometime in the 1670s Moses Gilman of Exeter, New Hampshire, wrote to his wife from Boston:

> Loving wife Elisabeth Gillman these are to desire you to speake to John Gillman & James Perkins and so order the

matter thatt Mr. Tho. Woodbridge may have Twelve thousand fott of merchantable boards Rafted by thirsday night or sooner if poseble they Can for I have Absolutly sould them to him & if John Clough sen or any other doe deliver bords to make up the sum Give Receits of whatt you Receive of him or any other man and lett no bote bee prest or other ways disposed of untill I Returne being from Him who is yos till death

Moses Gilman[9]

If Gilman had doubted his wife's ability to "order the matter," he could have written a number of separate letters—to John Gilman, James Perkins, John Clough, and perhaps others. But securing a shipment of twelve thousand feet of merchantable boards entirely by letter would have been complicated and time-consuming. Instead, Gilman relied on the good sense of his wife, who would be respected as his surrogate, and who probably had acquired some expertise in making out receipts for forest products and in conveying instructions to lumbering and shipping crews. A "loving wife" who considered herself his "till Death" was more trustworthy than a hired servant or business associate. As a true consort, she would know that by furthering her husband's interest she furthered her own.

Thus, a wife with talent for business might become a kind of double for her husband, greatly extending his ability to handle affairs. This is beautifully illustrated in a document filed with the New Hampshire court papers. In February of 1674 Peter Lidget of Boston signed a paper giving Henry Dering of Piscataqua full power of attorney "to collect all debts due to him in that place and thereabout." On the reverse side of the document Dering wrote: "I Henry Dering have, and do hereby Constitute, ordaine, and appoint my loveing wife, Anne Dering my Lawful Attourney" to collect and sue for Peter Lidget's debts "by virtue of the Letter of Attourney on the other side."[10] (Anne Dering was the widow of Ralph Benning of Boston. She left her married name—and perhaps some of her business acumen—to her great-grandson, Governor Benning Wentworth of New Hampshire.[11])

Court cases involving fishermen give some glimpses of the kinds of responsibility assumed by their wives, who often appear in the foreground as well as the background of the documents. Depositions in an action of 1660 reveal Anne Devorix working alongside her husband, "taking account" as a servant culled fish from a spring voyage. She herself delivered a receipt from the master of the ship to the shop where the final "reckoning" was made. When her husband was at sea, she supervised spring planting on the family corn land as well as protecting the hogsheads, barrels, and flakes at the shore from the incursions of a quarrelsome neighbor.[12] Even more visible in the records is Edith Creford of Salem, who frequently acted as an attorney for her husband, at one point signing a promissory note for £33 in "merchantable cod fish at price current." Like the fishwives of Nantucket whom Crèvecoeur described a hundred years later, these women were "necessarily obliged to transact business, to settle accounts, and in short, to rule and provide for their families."[13]

At a different social level the wives of merchant sea captains played a similar role. Sometime in the year 1710 Elizabeth Holmes of Boston sat down with Patience Marston of Salem and settled accounts accumulated during a voyage to Newfoundland. Neither woman had been on the ship. They were simply acting as attorneys for their husbands, Captain Robert Holmes, who had commanded the brigantine, and Mr. Benjamin Marston, who owned it.[14] Family letters give a more detailed picture of Mistress Marston's involvement in her husband's business.

In the summer of 1719 Benjamin Marston took command of one of his own ships, taking his twenty-two-year-old son Benjamin with him. Young Benjamin wrote his mother complete details of the first stage of the journey, which ended at Casco Bay in Maine. He included the length of the journey, the state of the family enterprises in Maine, and the price of lumber and staves, adding that he was "Sorry you should sett so long in ye house for no Adv[ance] but perhaps to ye prejudice of your health." Patience was obviously "keeping shop." A week later Benjamin wrote again, assuring his mother that he was looking after the business in Maine. "My father w[oul]d have been imposed upon by m—c had I not interposed and stood stiffly to him," he explained. Was the son acting out some Oedipal fantasy here, or was he perhaps performing as his *mother's* surrogate, strengthening the resolve of the presumably more easygoing father? The next day he wrote still another letter, asking for chocolate, complaining boyishly that "ye Musketo's bitt me so prodigiously as I was writing that I can hardly tell what it was I wrote," and conveying what must by then have been a common request from the absent husband. Mrs. Marston was to get a witnessed statement regarding a piece of family business and send it by "the first Oppertunity."[15]

Because the business activities of wives were under the "wing, protection, and cover" of a husband (to repeat Blackstone's phrase), they are difficult to measure by standard methods. Patience Marston was a custodian of messages, guardian of errands, preserver of property, and keeper of accounts. Yet without the accidental survival of a few family papers there would be no way of knowing about her involvement in her husband's business. In Benjamin's will she received the standard "thirds." She may have become impatient with her chores or anxious about her husband's business acumen, but there is no indication of this in the only writings preserved in her hand. She served as "deputy husband" as circumstances demanded, and when her husband perished from smallpox soon after arriving in Ireland, she declared herself grateful for the dear son who returned "as one from the dead" to take over his father's business.[16]

The role of deputy husband deserves more careful and systematic study. But two cautions are in order. First, the biases of the twentieth century may tempt historians to give undue significance to what were really rather peripheral enterprises. Acting as attorney to one's husband is not equivalent to practicing law. To colonial women, it may even have been less desirable than keeping house. This leads to the second point. The value of any activity is determined by its meaning to the participant, not to the observer. In early America position was always more important than task. Colonial women might appear to be independent, even aggressive, by modern standards, yet still have derived their status primarily from their relationship to their husbands.

This is well illustrated in a New Hampshire court record of 1671. A carpenter named John Barsham testified about an argument he had heard between Henry Sherburne and his second wife, Sarah, who was the widow of Walter Abbott. Barsham had come to the house to get some nails he needed for repairing a dwelling he had rented from them. According to Barsham, Sarah became so angry at her husband's opposition that she "rose off from the seat where she was setting & came up to him with her arms akimbo saying we should have nayles & he had nothing to [do] in it." As if to add the final authority to her demand, she asked him "why he trode upon Walter Abbotts floor & bid him get out of doors, & said that he had nothing to do there."[17] Sarah Sherburne was an experienced and assertive woman. She had kept tavern "with two husbands and none." The house in which she and Sherburne lived had been part of her inheritance from her first husband.[18] But in the heat of the argument she did not say, "Get out of *my* house" or "Get out of the house *I* provided." She said, "Get out of Walter Abbott's house." Her identity was not as property owner, but as wife. To assert her authority over her husband, she invoked the memory of his predecessor.

FOR SOME WOMEN, the realities of daily life in coastal New England enhanced the role of deputy husband. For others, discrepancies in education as well as the on-again-off-again nature of the role made involvement in the family business just another chore. A woman who worked effectively as an assistant, especially with the authority of a living husband behind her, could still be insecure in handling complex business arrangements. Finally (and perhaps the most important point of all), most woman had other things to do. A closer examination of female economic life suggests not only separate education and separate duties but separate lines of trade.

Selectman's indentures from mid-eighteenth-century Newbury show the contrasting training offered boys and girls at the lowest end of the social spectrum in a commercial town. Between 1743 and 1760 the selectman indentured sixty children of the town poor. Forty-nine of these were boys, who were apprenticed to blacksmiths, shipwrights, cordwainers, coopers, weavers, tanners, tailors, joiners, blockmakers, riggers, mastmakers, and even a perriwig-maker in the town. The eleven girls, on the other hand, were promised instruction in the generalized skills of "housewifery" or "women's work," though occasionally spinning, carding, sewing, and knitting were also specified. Often the phrase "Art, Trade, or Mystery" on these printed forms was crossed out in the girls' indentures. All of the children were assured instruction in reading, but only the boys were to learn "to write a Ledgable hand & cypher as far as the Gouldin Rule" or "to write & Cypher as far as ye Rule of three or so far as to keep a Tradesmans Book."[19]

That more than four times as many boys as girls were apprenticed suggests that the support of poor girls was usually handled in some other way. Either they remained with their families or were placed as day workers or maids on a less formal basis among the housewives of the town. The crossed-out passages in the indentures highlight the anomalous position of these female apprentices. Clearly, the training of artisans and the training of their wives were two separate processes belonging to two separate systems. A female might learn the mysteries of blacksmithing or tanning—but only informally, by working as a helper to the men in her family. Predictably, in the region as a whole, women lagged far behind men in their ability to write, a discrepancy which actually increased over the eighteenth century.[20]

What this meant in the daily lives of ordinary women is suggested by extant account books from the period. Although many such books survive, in the entire century between 1650 and 1750 there is not a single one known to have been kept by a woman. Purchasing an account book was a significant step for a farmer or village craftsman. A Topsfield weaver recognized this when he wrote in the inside of his new book, "John Gould his Book of accounts I say my Book my owne book and I gave one shillin and four pence for it so much and no more."[21] Books like Gould's fall somewhere between the systematic, literate, merchant-oriented economy which came to dominate the external trade of New England and the local, personal, largely oral trade networks which were central to village life. As deputy husbands a few women might participate in the former, but for most wives economic life was centered in the latter.

Something of the range of bookkeeping methods employed in colonial America is preserved in an anonymous account book from Portsmouth, New Hampshire. One segment of this record was kept in the unformed scrawl typical of ordinary craftsmen and farmers; another was neatly posted in the hand of a professional clerk. But evidence of a third and quite different method is preserved in entries for a laborer named Richard Trip, who traded

Deputy Husbands

work in the "gundalow" (a Piscataqua sailing vessel) for "75 meals of victualls" and "75 nights of lodging brot from the acco[un]t kept in chaulk on the wall."[22] The wife of the unknown shopkeeper may have been responsible for the chalk account as well as for providing the "diet," "washing," and "mittins" recorded in Trip's debits. For this sort of bookkeeping she had no need for "cyphering."

Judging only from the account books, one might conclude that most married women were seldom involved in trade even on the village level. Yet account books represent but one strand of the village economy. Other sources point to an extensive, less systematic, and largely oral trade network in which women predominated. A court case of 1682 provides an interesting example. When a woman named Grace Stout appeared to answer several charges of theft, the witnesses against her included thirty-four persons, among them twenty-one housewives who were able to give precise accounts of the value of work performed or goods received. These were petty transactions—kneading bread for one woman, purchasing stockings knitted by another—not the sort of thing to turn up in a colonial trade balance but nevertheless an essential part of the fabric of economic life.[23]

The account books themselves give negative evidence of a separate female network. Although most ledgers include a few female names, the great majority of written accounts are with men, with credits reflecting the dominant commodities in each community. Ipswich farmers traded grain, farm labor, and animal products for shoes, weaving, rum, tobacco, skillets, and cotton wool. Householders from Marblehead paid for the same items in cash and fish, while those from Exeter usually offered pine, oak, and hemlock boards as well as labor.[24] Entries for the products of female craft are infrequent; most sustained accounts for butter, cheese, sewing, or spinning are listed under the names of widows. This pattern is especially striking in the few accounts which shift from the name of a husband to the name of his widow. Thomas Bartlett, a Newbury shoemaker, listed twenty-one entries under the name of Ephraim Blesdel from March 13, 1725, until October 16, 1730. Until the middle of July 1728 the credits included hides, cider, onions, codfish, veal, and cash. But on that date Bartlett reckoned with "the widow Debrath Blesdel." Nine of the twelve credits which follow are for spinning.[25] There is pathos in a second series recorded in Bartlett's book. From November 1729 until September 1733 he listed twenty-seven debits under John Wood's name, all for making and mending shoes. The credits already included some spinning as well as cash and skins when, on June 8, 1732, he noted in a taciturn entry: "husbands shoes sent back." From that point on, the account was with "Widow Anne Wood," who now attempted to pay for her shoes in dried sage from her garden and in additional spinning.[26]

Anne Wood was probably trading small amounts of sage long before her husband's death. The accumulation of minor transactions which composed female trade could become substantial without ever appearing in written accounts. Suggestive evidence of this appears in the account book of Thomas Chute, a tailor from Marblehead, Massachusetts, who became one of the first settlers of New Marblehead in frontier Maine. In May of 1737 Chute reckoned with Joseph Griffin of Marblehead, matching his own charges for tailoring against £8 debited in Griffin's book, finally balancing the whole with £4 pending, "By you [r] wives accoumpt with mine." A similar entry appears forty years later, in 1766, when he added to a £25 total accumulated by John Farrow of New Marblehead the sum of £3 "by yr wifes & mine acoumpts."[27] For the most part, the trade of Thomas Chute and the trade of his wife were harmoniously separate.

Informal, oral, local, petty—female enterprise appears as the merest flicker on the surface of male documents. That it existed seems clear enough. The problem is in determining its value to the participants.

Potentially at least, managing a female specialty might be even more attractive than simply helping in a husband's work. An Ipswich woman known in the records only as Mistress Hewlett became so successful in the poultry business that she was able to loan money to her husband. When a friend expressed surprise at this arrangement, arguing that the wife's income really belonged to him if he needed it, Ensign Hewlett replied, "I meddle not with the geese nor the turkeys for they are hers for she has been and is a good wife to me."[28] To the neighbor, loaning money to one's spouse was contradictory, an assertion of individual rather than communal values. But to Hewlett, no such threat was implied. His wife had "been a good wife." As long as independent female trade remained a minor theme within a larger communal ethic, it did not threaten either male supremacy or the economic unity of the family.

Yet consider the case of Mary Hunt of Portsmouth. Her encounter with Samuel Clark suggests both the opportunities and the limitations of female trade. When she found a cheese missing from her house after the fast day in October of 1675, she suspected Clark, who was a near neighbor. Storming into his house, she opened a drawer. There between two pieces of biscuit was the evidence she needed, an uneaten morsel notched, as she later testified, "with the very same marke which I put upon my best cheeses." Mary Hunt's accusation was brash, for Clark had once served on a jury which convicted her of stealing from the prominent Cutt family when she lived with them as a maidservant.[29] Her new status as a housewife and as a cheese dealer had obviously given her a sense of power as well as an opportunity for revenge.

The story does not end there, however. A marked cheese does not have the durability of a marked tankard or clock. Unfortunately, Mary Hunt's cheese did not make it to court in November, much less into the stream of physical artifacts from which we derive our understanding of a culture. Clark's servant apparently swallowed the evidence. Though Hunt won her case in the fall, Clark successfully appealed in June, standing on his dignity as a man never before suspected of "any crime much less so base a crime as theft and for so sorry a matter as cheese." Part of his long—and professionally inscribed—defense was a counter-accusation: it was well known in the neighborhood, he said, that Goody Hunt sold her products to "one and another" and was apt to do so without her husband's knowledge, crying theft if called to reckon.[30]

Clearly, the informal nature of female trade might work to the advantage of a woman who wanted a little extra income independent of her husband, yet ultimately the economic power of any woman was inseparable from her larger responsibility as wife. The role of housewife and the role of deputy husband were two sides of the same coin. Whether trading cheese or shipping barrel staves, a good wife sustained and supported the family economy and demonstrated her loyalty to her husband.

In the absence of a husband, the same skills might prove inadequate to independence. An anonymous document in the Essex Institute at Salem, Massachusetts, reveals the chasm which might develop between "female trade" and "male business." The unknown author of this little treatise had been accused of fraudulently securing a deed from an aged widow. In his defense he methodically itemized the charges against him, then answered each in turn. Two are of particular interest here—first, that the woman knew but little of the "common commerce of life," and, second, that she was unable to form a "just idea" of what belonged to her or its value. The man answered the first charge with a flat denial:

> I nor no other Person In this Neaborrhood I donte believe Ever heard of her not knowing how for to Trade.

But he at least partly acknowledged the second:

> How could she or any other Person forme any just Idia of what they are worth when it is Eveadent that Part of it was In Another Persons hands . . . and She Not Knowing how for to Right so as for to keep my Acc[ount] nor she could not Read Righting nor she could not Chipher so as for to Cast up my Acc[ount].[31]

These two statements summarize much of what we have said here. A talent for trade was one thing; the ability to handle complex business affairs was another. Although northern New England produced many Elizabeth Gilmans and Edith Crefords, women who successfully handled business in the absence of their husbands, it probably produced even more women like this anonymous widow of Salem. In her years as a housewife she had acquired considerable skill in the "common commerce of life" but little that would prepare her to deal with a sophisticated and aggressive assault on her property, especially when legal documents were involved. No longer able to rely upon a spouse or a son, she had truly become a "relict."

IN FEBRUARY OF 1757 Mary Russell of Concord, Massachusetts, wrote a letter to her brother-in-law Samuel Curwen of Salem in which she joked, "I should have answered Your letter long before this had I known when we were to come to Boston but you know I am a Femme Covert and cannot act for my self."[32] Her wit betrays a deeper feeling—if not yet a *feminist* sense of injustice, certainly a quite consciously *feminine* annoyance at the officious pedantry of the law, at least as it was discussed in her own parlor. Mary Russell knew that the restrictions of the common law had little relationship to the ordinary decisions of her daily life. Within her own domain she acted confidently and independently.

Yet the predicament which she described in jest became a reality for at least some women in the course of the eighteenth century as both business and law became increasingly sophisticated. The loyalist widows whom Mary Beth Norton described were in this position. Without their husbands or the familiar surroundings of home, they were forced to deal with the complexities of an English court. Little wonder that they declared themselves "helpless."

Norton's more recent work has shown, however, that the American Revolution affected many patriot women in a strikingly different way. At first reluctantly and then with increasing confidence and skill, these wives took up the management of farms and businesses while their husbands were away at war. Norton believes that the war had dissolved traditional boundaries, altering a "line between male and female behavior, once apparently so impenetrable."[33] Our evidence from early New England suggests a quite different conclusion. If there was an "impenetrable" gender barrier in mid-eighteenth-century America, it was a new one. The avowed helplessness of the loyalist women may be a measure of increasing specialization in economic life just before the revolution. The competence of the patriot women is even clearer evidence of the persistence of the old role of deputy husband. That patriot women failed to establish permanent changes in female roles is hardly surprising, since they acted within rather than against traditional gender definitions.

The economic roles of married women were based upon two potentially conflicting values—gender specialization and identity of interest. A wife was expected to become expert in the management of a household and the care of children, but she was also asked to assist in the economic affairs of her husband, becoming his representative and even his surrogate if circumstances demanded it. These two roles were compatible in the premodern world because the home was the communication center of family enterprise if not always the actual place of work. As long as business transactions remained personal and a woman had the support of a familiar environment, she could move rather easily from the role of housewife to the role of deputy husband, though few women were prepared either by education or by experience to become "independent women of affairs."

The role of deputy husband reinforced a certain elasticity in premodern notions of gender. No mystique of feminine behavior prevented a woman from driving a hard bargain or chasing a pig from the field, and under ideal conditions day-to-day experience in assisting with a husband's work might prepare her to function competently in a male world—should she lose her husband, should she find herself without a grown son, should she choose not to remarry or find it impossible to do so. But in the immediate world such activities could have a far different meaning. The chores assigned might be menial, even onerous, and, whatever their nature, they competed for attention with the specialized housekeeping responsibilities which every woman shared.

Chapter Three

A FRIENDLY NEIGHBOR

IN NORTHERN NEW ENGLAND a "neighbor" might be a woman living thirty feet away on a definable street in a well-developed group of dwellings clustered around a village meetinghouse. She might also be a housewife within shouting distance in the garrison house at the top of the next rise. Settlement patterns varied, but most folks had neighbors. It was dangerous to live alone. But beyond that, neighborliness was a cultural norm in all the New England colonies. When young Constance Oliver of Portsmouth, New Hampshire, opened the door one morning, she found her neighbor Mary Richards asking to borrow a kettle. Since her mother wasn't home, she asked Goody Richards to wait awhile, in the meantime going herself to another neighbor's house to fetch a coal of fire.[1]

Borrowing was part of the rhythm of life at all social levels. Families not only shared commodities. They shared the work which produced them. Not wanting to appear too interested in a friendly weaver, Faith Black of Topsfield sat down by his loom and began to shell peas. Only when she spent too much time at his house did her behavior become suspect.[2] Gadding was discouraged, but socializing was not. Johannah Green counseled her married daughter to become more involved with her neighbors, telling her "that she might better do her work an go to another bodys house than they that have a great family can go to hers."[3] Shared work in this form derived from the same needs and offered some of the same rewards as the more visible "huskings" and "quiltings" common to village life. Berrying, washing, spinning were female specialties which might bring neighbors together. Sharing work, women shared other responsibilities as well. When a little girl named Hannah Hutchinson was finishing her mother's wash at a neighbor's house, two other housewives were on hand to catch her in a lie.[4]

By twentieth-century standards, even the largest colonial towns were small. In 1754 Salem, Massachusetts, the most populous town north of Boston, had 3,462 people.[5] The average town population in 1750 has been estimated at 1,280 for Massachusetts (including Maine) and at 640 for New Hampshire.[6] Obviously, men and women who spent all their lives in a village of a few hundred persons knew their neighbors' names and probably their life histories and their personal idiosyncrasies as well. But it is a mistake to romanticize the concept of "neighborliness," to assume that material interdependence and physical proximity automatically ensured "meaningful personal relationships, a sense of participation, and a feeling of collective caring."[7]

Guides in historic houses in New England love to display the "latchstring" in seventeenth-century doors. When the string was out, so the story goes, visitors were welcome; when it was in, no company was sought. Such a subtle but commonly understood language may have been used. Surviving records show that at least some housewives employed even more colorful methods. An Ipswich woman snubbed her neighbor by hanging a dishclout out the door when she saw her approaching. A Hampton, New Hampshire, wife attempted to trap her neighbor, whom she suspected of being a witch, by draping the doorjamb with bay leaves.[8] As these women knew, a neighbor could provide commodities, household help, friendship—or aggravation.

Contention among neighbors has been a central theme in the recent social history of New England, yet most studies have concentrated on the political and institutional development of towns and have consequently had very little to say about women *per se*. This chapter will isolate themes of neighborliness of particular importance to women by examining the compact center of one town in one period—Ipswich, Massachusetts, circa 1670.

Settled in 1639 under the leadership of such pre-eminent Puritans as Thomas Dudley, Simon Bradstreet, Richard Saltonstall, and John Winthrop, Jr., the town gave intellectual, religious, and military leadership to New England in the seventeenth century.[9] But there are more important reasons for choosing it as a subject of study. Because Ipswich was the seat of one of the quarterly courts of Essex County, its citizens—including a number of housewives who might otherwise never have bothered to enter a suit—had easy access to formal justice. As a result, an unusual number of the petty squabbles and mundane struggles of housekeeping in this seventeenth-century community have been preserved to history. And because Ipswich was blessed at the turn of the twentieth century with an intelligent and energetic town historian, Thomas Franklin Waters, many of these events can be traced to a specific neighborhood.

LIFE IN IPSWICH was characterized by interdependence—and inequality. Although all of the original inhabitants of the town had land, some had a great deal more than others. One scholar has classified three-quarters of the population as "small landholders," whose allotments ranged from twenty poles to ninety acres. Among the remaining quarter, fifty-six men owned from 100 to 400 acres; eleven men owned more than 400 but fewer than 1,000; and five men owned 1,000 or more.[10] Three of these five largest landholders—Samuel Symonds, Daniel Denison, and Jonathan Wade—were still living in Ipswich in 1670. William Hubbard, one of the two ministers in the town, was a son of the fourth.

The town had been laid out as an open-field English village with most settlers living on small plots in the center and traveling to tillage land on the periphery. The "homelots" of Symonds, Denison, Hubbard, and Wade were distinguished less by their size than by their proximity to important public institutions. Denison and Symonds—when they were not attending General Court or visiting one of their large farms in the outlying countryside—lived near the meetinghouse green. Hubbard and Wade built their houses near the schoolhouse green on the opposite side of the river, as did John Rogers, the eminent first minister of the town. In each neighborhood the greater houses of the gentry stood near the lesser houses of craftsmen and small farmers and the cottages of the poor.[11]

The meetinghouse at the center of the village gave tangible

form to the social conservatism as well as to the utopian idealism of its builders. Rejecting popish ornament and ritual for the plain word of God, the saints nevertheless perpetuated the Anglican custom of "seating" the congregation in ranked order, according to sex, wealth, and age. Gender was the first distinction among God's children. The gospel of damnation and grace intoned from the pulpit was the same for all Christians, but men and women heard it from different sides of the room. Although women predominated among covenanted members of the church, men did the preaching, bore the titles of elder and deacon, and collected the tithes. Their wives sat on the opposite side of the room or in the gallery, and wrestled with small children—and sometimes with each other. Not until late in the seventeenth century were family pews constructed, and these were reserved for a few of the most prominent citizens of the town.[12] Women could not walk into the meetinghouse without being reminded of their separateness, of the primacy of their gender identity.

The meetinghouse green was the focal point of village life, but it was hardly the grassy oasis of nostalgic memory. Strewn with horse manure and rutted with cart tracks, it was set with such rude reminders of human and animal cussedness as the whipping post, the pound, the watchhouse, and the jail. Around the meetinghouse itself were the remnants of a stone fortification never used and always out of repair but not officially abandoned until 1702, when the town declared itself free of Indian danger by selling the rock and using the proceeds to buy a town clock.[13] Women—like men—were subject to the civil authority symbolized in the jail and the whipping post, but they did not participate in town meeting or serve in such offices as constable or keeper of the pound. Nor did they experience the military order of training day or the often drunken disorder at the tavern afterward when, for a few hours at least, social rank dissolved in a common maleness.[14]

There was hardly an aspect of life untouched by public authority in Puritan Ipswich. The same court which issued tavern licenses and enforced school law admonished Goodwife Brabrook for carrying a half-bushel of corn or peas with her when she went to meeting, and fined old Goodman Lee for swearing by his salvation. For women's history, the court's intrusiveness in daily life had important consequences.[15] Scraps of testimony collected in the parlors of Major-General Denison or Deputy-Governor Symonds, the two magistrates in town, tell us much about ordinary life in Ipswich. Beyond that, the depositions demonstrate that women, though excluded from formal authority, played a central role in the communication networks which bonded or sundered neighborhoods.

In the early 1670s, in a period of about eighteen months, almost two dozen actions originated in William Hubbard's neighborhood on the south side of the Ipswich River. Although only five of the twenty-six defendants in these cases were female, 85 of the 240 depositions were delivered by women.[16] In these actions it is almost impossible to distinguish private from public issues, sexual slander from economics, or the entanglements of women from the feuds of their spouses. The evidence presented in court merely hints at the complexity of interaction within the neighborhood itself. The chains of innuendo become almost ludicrous, as when Margaret and Elizabeth Boarman deposed that Laurence Clinton said that Goody Abbot told Goody Howard that . . . or when Goody Hunt testified that Thomas Knowlton came to her house and said that Joseph Lee had told him that he had heard that Knowlton had said that Goody Hunt had accused Betty Woodward of . . .[17]

A young man named Nathaniel Browne, who had set up a soap-boiling business in the neighborhood, learned at first hand the power of talk. He inadvertently returned the wrong pair of sheep shears and was accused of stealing. His wife, Judith, applied for admission to the church and found herself in a clamor of gossip (none of which was specifically reiterated in court). In his own testimony Browne blamed their troubles on the shoemaker Knowlton, another young man and relative newcomer to the neighborhood. Knowlton had "set neighbors together by the ears," Browne complained. He and Judith had tried to handle their grievance privately, but it had done no good. He had "asked Goody Leigh's advice, also Goodwife Rust," but when Goodwife Rust remained "as intimate as ever" with his enemy Knowlton, he was forced to petition the court.[18]

Goodwives Lee and Rust are barely visible in formal records from seventeenth-century Ipswich. They neither owned property nor held public office, yet in the world of Nathaniel Browne they

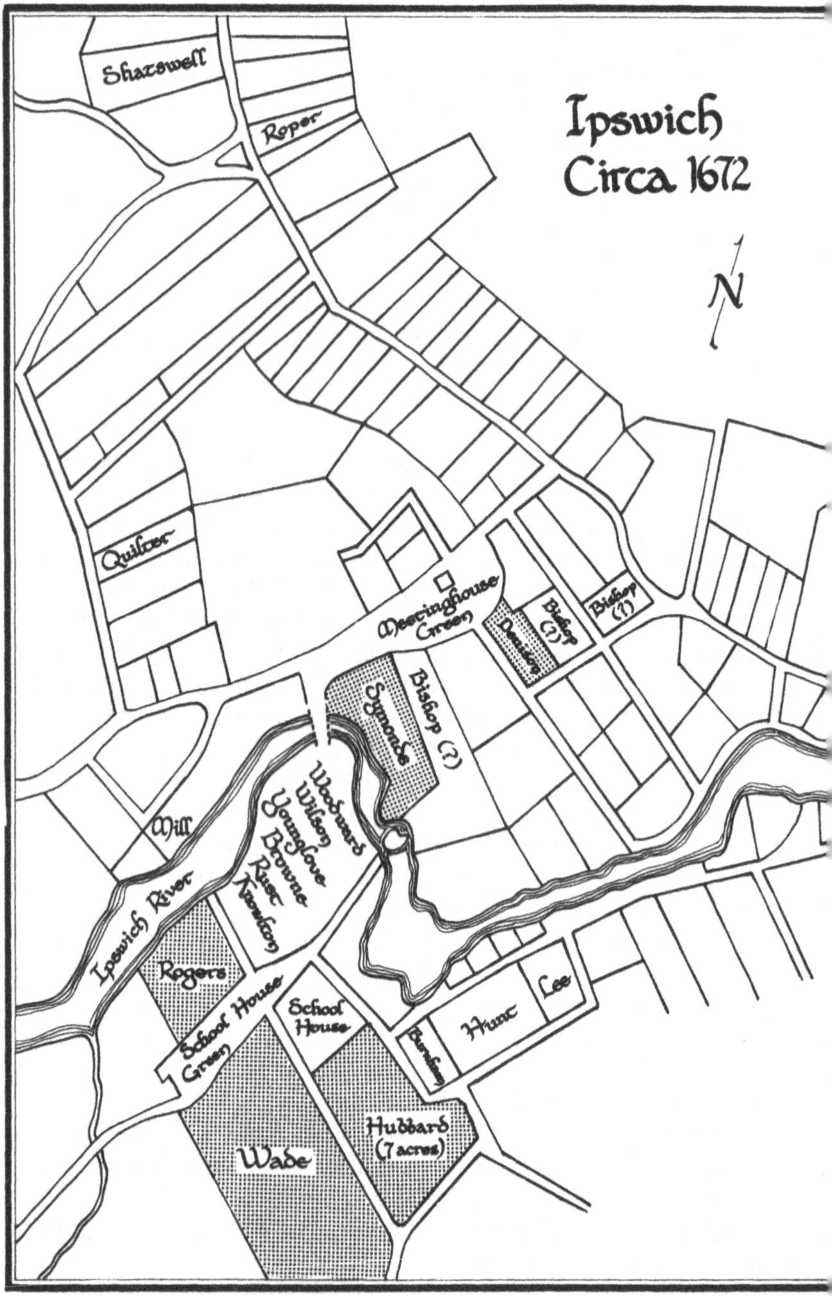
Ipswich
Circa 1672
N
Shatswell
Roper
Quilter
Meetinghouse Green
Bishop (?)
Bishop (?)
Denison
Bishop (?)
Symonds
Mill
Woodward
Wilson
Younglove
Browne
Rust
Knowlton
Ipswich River
Rogers
School House Green
School House
Burnham
Hunt
Lee
Hubbard (7 acres)
Wade

obviously occupied a position of eminence. The chains of hearsay which reverberated in Daniel Denison's parlor cannot be dismissed as idle gossip, certainly not as a mischievous outlet for otherwise powerless women. Gossip was an effective mechanism used by both sexes in the intimate arena of this Puritan town. When women talked, men as well as other women listened.

On one level, then, the Essex County court records demonstrate the intermeshing of male and female concerns. But on closer examination they also point toward a separate world of women, one which had rules and conflicts of its own. Housewives in colonial Ipswich can be divided into three social groups—the mistresses of the big houses (often the wives of magistrates or ministers); their near neighbors but social inferiors, the wives of small landowners and craftsmen; and an indeterminate but growing group who lived in rented houses or in semi-dependence upon employers or parents. The difference between the second and third groups was often determined by age as much as by wealth. Interacting with these housewives was a fourth group—the unmarried girls who worked as servants. Although there were a few indentured servants and slaves in New England in the seventeenth century, most household helpers were neighbors or neighbors' daughters. Families with more children than work to do exported maids; families with big houses or no children or very young children took them in. Interconnections among these four groups are apparent in the case of Sarah Row, a young woman accused of sexual misbehavior.

Sarah was one of eight daughters of the carpenter Ezekiel Woodward, but she had lived and worked for many years in William Hubbard's house, which stood just across the schoolhouse green from her parents' home. Before she was eighteen, Sarah married a fisherman named William Row, who spent much of his time at the Isles of Shoals in Maine, but who seems to have rented a house somewhere in Ipswich for at least one winter. Sarah's status after her marriage remained somewhat fluid. She maintained friendships with the servants in the Hubbard house and remained close to an unmarried girl named Sarah Buckley, who worked in the kitchen and cowyard of Nathaniel Rust, the glover. But she was also in and out of Judith Browne's house, and she was friendly with Hannah Knowlton, the twenty-five-year-old wife of the shoemaker.[19] Both groups of friends—the servants and the craftsmen's wives—had something to say when Sarah's case came to court.

In contrast, Sarah's former mistress, Margaret Hubbard, remained aloof from the squabbles which rocked her neighborhood. Although the Reverend Mr. Hubbard testified on Sarah's behalf, any opinions which his wife had were expressed in private. Mistress Hubbard was insulated less by the seven-acre homelot which surrounded her house than by her dignity as a minister's wife and a gentlewoman. The mistresses of the big houses moved in a social—and often familial—circle of their own. Margaret Hubbard's mother, the widow of the Reverend Nathaniel Rogers, lived beyond the schoolhouse on the other side of the green. So for a time did her brother John, soon to be president of Harvard College. John's wife, Elizabeth, was the daughter of Major-General Denison.

Eminence did not mean independence, however. The houses of the Hubbards, the Rogerses, and the Denisons were distinguished by books, pictures, gilt looking glasses, and rich textiles (Margaret Hubbard's father had even owned "a treble viol"), but their floors were swept and their beds were made by the young daughters of the small landowners of Ipswich. Just as Mistress Hubbard had employed the carpenter's daughter, Sarah Row, her mother, Mistress Rogers, had for years depended upon Mary Quilter, the daughter of a small farmer whose houselot was on the other side of the river. Patience Denison, the Major-General's wife, had engaged a number of servants over the years, including Sarah Roper, whose father, Walter, owned a house, barn, and homestead worth £80 on the High Street.[20]

Thus, relationships among female neighbors could form in a number of directions. They could be both vertical and horizontal, involving economic links between servants and mistresses as well as close friendships among women of comparable position. The rules which governed social intercourse cannot be fully reclaimed at this distance, but female testimony in a number of cases provides some vivid clues. The cases of Frances Quilter (an ordinary wife) and Patience Denison (a gentlewoman) clearly reveal what we might call the Rules of Industry and of Charity as they affected self-definition in this seventeenth-century village. A cluster of cases involving Elizabeth Hunt (the wife of an aspiring freeman) demonstrates the problems involved in maintaining the Rule of Modesty.

All three Rules are expressed in Proverbs 31. Bathsheba was involved in many discrete tasks, as we have seen, but behind all her effort was the Rule of Industry: "She looketh well to the ways of her household, and eateth not the bread of idleness." Because women's work was essentially supportive, tied not to products but to people, it was by nature often invisible. Women did not build houses or rig ships or preach sermons; they fed and clothed the men who did. As a consequence, "work" could never be isolated from the larger relationship of which it was a part. Nor could it often be directly measured. Because a day's effort was quickly swallowed, the measure of productivity was often in the worker herself—a good wife kept busy.

Like the virtuous woman of the Bible, she also "stretcheth out her hand to the poor; yea, she reacheth forth her hands to the needy." In the larger sense, this Rule of Charity meant neighborly concern, a general willingness to extend oneself to meet the needs of others. During the witchcraft uproar of 1692, for example, one suspected woman was saved by a petition of 116 residents of her town, who testified that she "was allways, readie & willing to doe for [her neighbors] w[ha]t laye in her power night & day, though w[i]th hazard to her health or other danger."[21] For wealthy women, however, it meant hand-to-hand relief of poor neighbors.

The Rule of Modesty was keyed to the concept of hierarchy in a somewhat different way. Because her husband was "known in the gates" and sat "among the elders of the land," the virtuous woman of Proverbs was entitled to dress in "silk and purple" and to make herself "coverings of tapestry," but she did not take these visible emblems too seriously, knowing even as she adorned herself that "beauty is vain." In towns like Ipswich, ordinary women violated the Rule of Modesty by wearing clothing above their status. Silk scarves, for example, were reserved for women whose husbands were worth at least £200. It was not just the threat of sexual impropriety which made modesty a female virtue, but the secondary position of women in the public world. They were to reflect but never to assert status, demonstrating a supportive demeanor in speech, in manners, and in attitude, as well as in clothing.

Because the boundaries of authority and responsibility were

largely defined by custom rather than law, casual watching-and-warding by neighbors was far more significant to most women than the power of magistrates. The close association of women in the premodern world was both conservative and supportive, reinforcing the traditional distribution of authority even as it guarded against its abuse. For colonial women, having the "character" of a good wife was as valuable as having a good lawyer might be today—as the stories of Frances Quilter, Patience Denison, and Elizabeth Hunt show.

FRANCES QUILTER'S HUSBAND, Mark, had a reputation in Ipswich for drinking and losing his temper and, as a result, had been the butt of roisterous humor in the tavern on training days. His own lapses in public dignity may have made him overly conscious of his authority at home.[22] In March of 1664 he was fined for striking his wife and for hitting a neighbor. The incident with the neighbor occurred on a morning when Rebeckah Shatswell had come to the house to "sit and work" with Goody Quilter "to bear her company." Quilter came into the room and demanded something to eat. The exchange which followed emerges vividly from the court record as a triangular dialogue between husband, wife, and neighbor.

"Why are you so hasty?" said the wife.

"It may be that he had not his breakfast," said the neighbor.

"Yes, two hours before he ate meat," the wife countered, but the husband merely groaned, "A poor deal."

"Thus, look here of my pottage," said the wife to the neighbor. "[See] whether I did not boil a good deal of meat."

"It may be you boil a good deal and eat it up yourself," the neighbor answered, whereupon the husband turned upon her.

"Hold your prating," he said.

"I prate no more than you," she replied, when, to her great surprise, he struck her and threw her out the door.[23]

We see the neighbor's role in this family argument changing rapidly. Rebeckah Shatswell had come to the house as a friend; but as the bickering began, her position shifted. Goody Quilter appealed to her first as a defender and then as a judge. She perhaps saw herself as neutral, but to Mark Quilter she was simply an intruder. Even though she supported his right to a good breakfast,

A Friendly Neighbor

he became furious that she was in his house at all. To acknowledge her help would have been to accept her right to intervene in the internal relationships of his family. Horizontal lines between housewife and housewife might form a counterweight to vertical relationships between husband and wife. Mark Quilter's resentment showed that he recognized this—as well he might, for it was the testimony of neighboring wives which eventually brought his conviction in court.

Yet the triangle thus formed was far from simple, as Goody Quilter knew. Attacked by her husband in front of her friend, she became defensive about her cooking. In some sense, neighbors were an informal jury of one's peers. Only by living up to the cluster of responsibilities dictated by custom did one earn the respect—and the potential support—of other women. Paramount among these responsibilities was Industry. The broth left in the kettle was proof that Goody Quilter had not wasted her morning.

The case of a wayward wife from nearby Topsfield gives additional evidence of the way female neighbors enforced this rule. The clinching point in the case against Faith Black seems to have come from Goody Hobbes, who testified that Faith was away from home so much that she had neglected her washing and failed to feed her swine. When the charitable—or meddlesome—neighbor added the husband's shirts to her own wash and carried food to the pigs, all the thanks the wife gave her "was to tell her she did not ask her to do it."[24] This foolish wife lost her case long before it reached the court.

Although the Rule of Industry affected all women, the Rule of Charity was especially important for a wealthy woman like Patience Denison, the wife of the Major-General. Mistress Denison was the second daughter of Dorothy and Thomas Dudley and the sister of the poet Anne Bradstreet, but her modest reputation in colonial history was achieved through her struggles with a servant named Sarah Roper. In March of 1665 the Denisons prosecuted Sarah, who had apparently been stealing from family supplies for more than a year. Most of the stolen provisions had found their way into the kitchen of an impoverished young wife of the neighborhood, Mary Bishop. At this time her husband, Job, may have been at sea. She perhaps lived in part of a house owned by Thomas Bishop just opposite the meetinghouse, or she may have rented a small dwelling owned by a fisherman named Robert Dutch in the block behind the Denison property.[25]

Whatever its location, Mary Bishop's dwelling was within handy reach of Sarah Roper. When Goody Bishop lacked milk to make a posset, Sarah brought it to her. When her brother came to town, Sarah provided beer for his entertainment. Meeting her at the well, Sarah gave her cider from the Denison cellar and on other occasions apples for her children, suet for pudding, and pork. In return Goody Bishop gave Sarah some mackerel, a common grade of fish which she said they did not have at the Denison house.[26] Like friendships between other women in the same community, the bonds between Sarah and Goody Bishop were cemented with small favors. The difference, of course, was that Patience Denison supplied the goods.

Mary Bishop's defense before the court is revealing, not so much of her own situation as of the community norm of charity which underlay her plea. She begged clemency on account of her low condition, another woman testifying that the Bishop family would have starved on their scanty diet "had not Sarah Roper helped them with provisions." Such testimony carried a subtle reproach to Mistress Denison. More pointed was the evidence of another neighbor who said she had heard Sarah Roper call her mistress "an old Jew and hobling Joane."[27]

What is most instructive about this case is not the thievery of the servant but the reluctance of the mistress to invoke the law. Sarah Roper carried away more than £10 in household provisions and clothing before she was finally prosecuted in Ipswich court. The Denison household was a wealthy one, yet Patience Denison knew exactly what she owned and what was missing. In court she gave an itemized list of everything Sarah Roper had taken from her, from a coif worth one shilling to apple and chicken pies worth ten. Sarah was a brazen thief, not content to fill a teacup or a pocket. In one year she carried away nine bushels of wheat, trading it to neighbors for clothes and shoes.[28] Dependent on her servant, Mistress Denison may have found it easier to ignore her misbehavior than to do without her. Yet Sarah's slander of her mistress suggests that there was more to the story than that.

As a wealthy and socially prominent member of her community, Patience Denison—like her mother, Dorothy Dudley—was expected to be "a friendly neighbor pitiful to poor." Sarah

Roper suggested that she was in fact stingy, "an old Jew" insensitive to the serious distress of her near neighbor Mary Bishop. As a household administrator, Patience Denison was supposed to be in firm command of her establishment, "to Servants wisely aweful, but yet kind." According to Sarah, she was really little more than a "hobling Joane" incapable of dealing with flagrant misbehavior in her own kitchen and pantry. Thus, to prosecute Sarah Roper—to reveal the full range of her servant's manipulations—was to expose her own inadequacies. Measured by the ideal, she had failed. Had she really been "charitable," "wise," and "kind," none of this would have happened.

Patience Denison eventually prosecuted her servant and collected damages. But as long as Sarah Roper remained in the neighborhood—in fact, as long as her reputation survived in the memories of Ipswich housewives—Patience could never be entirely rid of her. Nine years later an Ipswich busybody named Elizabeth Hunt suspected Sarah of stealing her bodkin* after it fell to the floor during church. Although the bodkin was retrieved, Goody Hunt continued to press the grievance. Standing by the gate of the Denison house, she told another neighbor that she had been inside to talk to the Major-General about it, but that he would have nothing to do with it even though he was a magistrate. Sarah Roper could not come there to be examined, Goody Hunt reported, because Mistress Denison was "afraid of her."[29]

Patience Denison's troubles with Sarah Roper not only demonstrate the importance of the Rule of Charity, they also reveal the difficulties experienced by the New England gentry in maintaining a system of deference inherited from the Old World. Even in a town like Ipswich, which was probably as stratified as any in New England, status was never assured. Men and women knew each other too well. Within a few hours conversations held in the big houses could find their way across the back fence to the smaller houses nearby.[30] Pushy folks in some of those smaller houses— women like Elizabeth Hunt—were ready to exploit the weaknesses of their betters.

Elizabeth Hunt's own story is closely linked to her husband's

---

* Goody Hunt's bodkin was probably a large blunt needle used for lacing bodices or pulling drawstrings through clothing. No seventeenth-century bodkins survive in New England collections, though silver bodkins occasionally appear in probate inventories.

resentment of the Ipswich gentry. When Daniel Denison ordered the troops to clear brush on the militia field on training day, Samuel Hunt led a small rebellion, insisting that the Major-General had no right to demand such common labor. He picked a fight with another gentleman, Samuel Appleton, over the ownership of a horse. In the court actions which resulted, a rumor surfaced that Nathaniel Browne had boasted he would soon down Appleton because he worked for Hunt, who "kept them like lords for they wanted neither for meat nor drink." Similar pride was evident a few years later when Hunt, negotiating the marriage of his daughter, boasted that he would give her "as good a portion . . . as any man In Ipswich should give any of their daughters Except four or five."[31] Samuel Hunt was laying the foundations of a prosperity which in the next century would give his section of the neighborhood the name Hunt's Cove.[32]

The Rule of Modesty prevented Elizabeth Hunt from such direct and open competition. She had clear ideas about what was appropriate for a woman in her position, as well as obvious insecurities. She knew what was happening in every house in the neighborhood and she testified in almost every case emanating from her section of the town, but she was careful to tell the court, with some officiousness, that a certain bit of information had come from a housewife named Margaret Lambert who had appeared quite unexpectedly in her kitchen "on a sleeveless maid's errand, which was to get some scouring sand."[33] She wanted the court to know that she was above the common tale-carrying of an ordinary wife.

When Elizabeth lost her bodkin, she imagined the servant Sarah Roper "picking her teeth" with it.[34] She recoiled from contact with the now ignominious Sarah, yet the social structure of colonial Ipswich, which put Sarah's father, Walter Roper, on the same level as Samuel Hunt, placed the two women within a few inches of each other in the meetinghouse. Struggling to keep her baby quiet during the sermon, Elizabeth had given him the bodkin much as a mother today might hand a child her car keys or a bracelet. When it dropped to the floor at an awkward angle, she was unable to retrieve it. She said Sarah picked it up. Sarah said it fell into the wide cuff of her sleeve, that she didn't find it until she got home, and that she sent it back promptly the next day. What might have been an innocent accident became in Elizabeth's mind an affront to her dignity.

If her husband's social status gave Elizabeth Hunt little opportunity to become "known in the gates," she was certainly visible in the house of the Lord. That her struggle with Sarah Roper occurred in the meetinghouse tells us much about the female world of colonial Ipswich. It is difficult for twentieth-century minds to comprehend the custom of "seating" the meeting, yet not until the period of the revolution did the majority of towns in New England abandon this visible ratification of hierarchal values.[35] Although a few men—and more women—challenged their own place within this system, they did not challenge the system itself.

Elizabeth Hunt's loss of her bodkin was one of many incidents originating in the Ipswich meetinghouse, including a number of actions involving seating. One of the first controversies is known only through a slander case which ended in the county court. A group of young blades in the town composed a satire which they circulated among the haymows. Entitled "O ye brave Undertakers & gallery makers," it apparently referred to a proposal initiated by a few of the solid freemen of the town to build a gallery for their wives. The refrain, which is all that is preserved of the poem, not so subtly slandered the social ambitions of the goodwives on the south side of the river. Although the clerk cautiously left off the names in the first line of the refrain, it is not too difficult to supply appropriate substitutes.

> *Set aside Mistress [Symonds and Denison]*
> *[For] Goode Rust, mother Woodward & Ann.*
> *Pray find me such three again if you can.*[36]

There is no way of knowing if Symonds and Denison are the missing surnames in the first line, but they fit the crude meter and rhyme as well as the theme of the satire. A town wag who wanted to poke fun at petty pride among the women of the congregation might well invoke the apparently untouchable eminence of the chief gentlewomen of the town.

The predominance of women in meetinghouse controversies can be explained in both psychological and practical terms. Women lacked visible emblems of status. Since the meetinghouse was the one public arena open to them, it is hardly surprising that they acted out their search for position there. On the other hand, their physical position in the building was quite literally an uncomfortable one. In towns like Ipswich, with a young and growing population, they were almost unbearably crowded. Their smallest children sat on their laps or wedged in beside them, while their older daughters perched on improvised benches crammed into the aisles. Their husbands' benches were surely as hard and perhaps just as narrow, but men did not have to cope with wriggling distractions. It is little wonder that a woman like Elizabeth Hunt might succumb to the temptation to push and shove when her neighbor's daughter once again jammed her chair hard against the end of the bench. "Take notice of Goody Hunt," Thomas Knowlton cried aloud from the gallery—as if a dozen of her nearest neighbors had not already recorded both the pattern and the meaning of her behavior.[37]

In 1681 Samuel Hunt was among eight successful petitioners who sought liberty to "raise the hindmost seate in the norwest syde of the Meeting House two foote higher than it now is, for there wives to sitt in."[38] As the first families of the town began to sit together in pews, the distance between wealthy women and women of ordinary status became even more pronounced. If they could not sit with their husbands in a walled-off space, ambitious matrons like Elizabeth Hunt could at least sit together in elevated dignity.

IPSWICH REPRESENTS one form of community organization in northern New England, a stratified nuclear village with a strong church and a court at the center. Such a setting facilitated friendships among women, but it also undermined privacy, nurtured gossip, and reinforced the patriarchal authority of public institutions. Only further study of the spatial and social organization of neighborhoods can tell us how other forms of settlement affected women. Yet scattered evidence suggests that the underlying patterns of neighborliness which we have found here were not limited to a single time or place.

The Rule of Modesty determined that women elsewhere who became involved in squabbles over the selection of a minister or the placing of a meetinghouse would act by indirection. The Rule of Charity dictated that mistresses of the largest houses in the frontier towns would suffer "garrison crowds" during prolonged Indian conflict. Most widespread of all was the Rule of Industry. Though it may not be so recognized, that Rule still operates in some New England towns three hundred years later in the widespread female habit of knitting in public meetings. Such a practice surely goes back to a time when a woman's diligence was known and judged by all her neighbors. Carrying her "knitting work" about with her, a maidservant or a fishwife demonstrated the old proverb, "A man works from sun to sun, but a woman's work is never done."

Chapter Four

PRETTY GENTLEWOMEN

A CENTRAL ISSUE in the interpretation of early American huswifery is compressed in a letter which Benjamin Franklin wrote in 1727 to his younger sister, Jane, who was about to marry.

> I have been thinking what would be a suitable present for me to make, and for you to receive, as I hear you are grown a celebrated beauty. I had almost determined on a tea table, but when I considered that the character of a good housewife was far preferable to that of being only a pretty gentlewoman, I concluded to send you a *spinning wheel*, which I hope you will accept as a small token of my sincere love and affection.[1]

The stereotypes of "good housewife" and "pretty gentlewoman" were not original with Franklin, of course. Periodical literature of eighteenth-century England and America was filled with similar contrasts.[2] Moralists in every century have preferred "productive" to "ornamental" women. The underlying assumption is that the two roles are incompatible, that a woman must give up the homely duties of kitchen and barnyard to acquire the refinements of the parlor. Consider the nursery rhyme:

> *Curly locks, curly locks, wilt thou be mine?*
> *Thou shalt not wash dishes nor yet feed the swine,*
> *But sit on a cushion and sew a fine seam,*
> *And feed upon strawberries, sugar and cream.*

Dainty food, soft cushions, and curled hair typify the decorative frivolity conveyed in the phrase "pretty gentlewoman."

In northern New England, in the years between 1670 and 1730, table linens multiplied, forks appeared where none had existed before, rooms became crowded with chairs, and the incidence of looking glasses increased tenfold (see Table 3). Had

Table 3. Selected Items in Essex and York County Probate Inventories[1]

	1670	1700	1730
CHAIRS			
Percent of inventories listing chairs			
Essex County	56%	78%	78%
York County	26%	41%	70%
Average number of chairs listed			
Essex County	2	9	17
York County	4	9	9
TABLE LINENS			
Essex County	33%	60%	50%
York County	23%	22%	30%
FORKS			
Essex County	none	3%	20%
York County	none	2%	16%
LOOKING GLASSES			
Essex County	3%	35%	34%
York County	4%	22%	34%

1. See Table 1 for source.

primping and crimping, chatting and tea-drinking replaced the homely duties of kitchen and yard? Had industrious housewives, like "curly locks" in the nursery rhyme, given up their essential work and become ornamental? Not so. For a few women the focus of huswifery shifted, but for almost all women the Rule of Industry prevailed.

A close examination of daily work in the diary of one eighteenth-century gentlewoman shows how themes of gentility intermeshed with industrious housekeeping even for women near the height of polite society in a commercial town. Mary Vial Holyoke was the daughter of a Boston merchant and the wife of a Salem gentleman, Edward Augustus Holyoke, a casual versifier and serious physician who was a member of the town's economic and intellectual elite.[3] The Holyokes enjoyed the barbecues, dances, teas, and "turtles" of the Essex County gentry, yet each of the four major housekeeping roles is clearly apparent in Mary's diary, as this selection of entries from the 1760s shows:

Service and maintenance: "Washed." "Ironed." "Scoured pewter." "Scowered rooms." "Scoured furniture Brasses & put up the Chintz bed & hung pictures." "Burnt 5 Chimnies." "Opened cask of Biscuit." "Began a Barrel of flour." "Began upon 22 lb. of chocolate." "Dressed a Calves Head turtle fashion."

Agriculture: "Sowd sweet marjoram." "Sowed pease." "Sowed colleflower." "Sowed 6 w[ee]ks beans." "Pulled first radishes." "Set out turnips & stumps." "Cut 36 asparagus, first cutting here." "Bought 11 Ducks." "Hen began to set." "Bought a pig to keep, weighed 12½ lb." "Bought of Wm Williams a Doe rabbit . . . she brought forth 6 young ones 3 of which died."

Manufacturing: "Killed the pig, weighed 164 lb. Aetatus 11 months." "Salt Pork, put Bacon in Pickle." "Put Bacon up chimney." "Put Beef in Pickle." "Preserved quinces. Made syrup of cores and parings." "Made two Barrels of Soap." "Filled Bed." "Made mead." "Bottled wine, 6 doz." "Preserved Damson, a week too late." "Made the Dr. six Cravats marked H." "Quilted 2 [petti] Coats since yesterday 11 oClock A.M." "Made 5 shirts in a fortnight for ye Doctor, Besides other things."

Trade: "Bought salmon." "Bought tea 1 lb." "Laid in 77 lbs. of butter for the winter in November." "Bought 9 lb. Candles." "Bought sheets." "Bought Bengall gown, plates and Cruets." "Bought a Baize Coat." "First began to take milk at Jno. Felt, 3 pints per Day." "Bought linnen for the Doctor."[4]

The diary shows the persistence of common chores in a sophisticated Salem household of the mid-eighteenth century. If nothing else, it demonstrates that the elaboration of the house might simply mean more work for the housekeeper. Mary Holyoke washed and ironed, but she also polished brasses and hung pictures. Even in this urban setting she was intensely involved in agriculture. In one year she cut 1,836 heads of asparagus from May 10 until June 10! She did not indicate whether she served it, sold it, pickled it, gave it away, or buried it in the cellar in a crock of clarified butter as one ancient cookbook recommended.[5] But she was obviously proud of her productivity. Her involvement with barnyard animals is perhaps more surprising. She did not keep a cow, but she found it profitable to raise her own pork as well as poultry and rabbits. Surplus fruit, large quantities of meat, and excess fat determined that she would be a manufacturer as well. Her autumn schedule included many of the tasks common to rural women a hundred years before. Because she lived in a seaport, she could purchase provisions as well as some items of clothing, but this abundance of consumer goods simply created higher standards without really relieving her of responsibility. She purchased gowns and sheets, but she also stitched her husband's shirts and embroidered his cravats.

Mary Vial Holyoke was a "good housewife." She undoubtedly had servants, yet the form of entry in her diary demonstrates that she considered scouring, salting, planting, plain sewing, and ironing as *her* work, whether or not she took every stitch or covered every seed herself. She was also a "pretty gentlewoman." She did not spin, and she frequently sat at tea with friends. Clearly, the two roles which are set in opposition in Franklin's letter to his sister Jane were quite compatible in real life. Pretty gentlewomen simply refined the skills which all good housewives shared. To a knowledge of plain sewing and common cookery they added a concern for grace and style. Mary Holyoke was a gentlewoman not just because she had wine and silver on her table but because she was interested enough in the fine points of cooking to "dress" a calf's head "turtle fashion" rather than simply dropping it into the pot. Her gentility determined that she would spend at least some of her time updating and remodeling her clothing, that she could afford to send a piece of silk to England to be dyed and "water'd with large water," and that she would know how to monogram as well as construct her husband's scarves.

Embellishment. Refinement. Polish. These are the key motifs. Ursula Cutt, a New Hampshire widow who died a century before Mary Holyoke, was a gentlewoman not only by virtue of her late husband's high position in the province, but because of the kinds of things she kept in a chest of drawers in her Portsmouth house. Her probate inventory, taken in August of 1694, allows us to rummage among her belongings, at least in imagination.

In the upper drawer of her chest was a mounted "pin quishing" (cushion) with its own little drawer beneath containing silver thimbles and an English half-crown. Twelve dozen silver and gold breast buttons, a spoon, a pair of "agget pendents," and remnants of stitching and sewing silk were kept beside it. Perhaps the silk had been used for the "fine wrought Coverings for Cushins not made up" which were listed elsewhere in her house.

Her second drawer also held jewelry (a necklace of "smale Seed perle" and four gold rings) plus some of her best "wearing linen," cambric aprons, fine sleeves, caps, and neckerchiefs. It may have been a while since she had sorted to the bottom of this drawer—her old "knitt wascot" was clearly "moth eaten," though still worth ten shillings.

In the third drawer were remnants of old silk and several small swatches of silver lace, perhaps the ends of that which trimmed her blue satin petticoat.

The fourth drawer was stuffed with cloth and clothing of all descriptions, from a length of homespun wool to "One Tufted holland Cloak with silver Clasps." A red baby blanket and a tiny cloak lined with silk may have been sentimental keepsakes.

Such a woman was distinguished from the common sort by wealth (silver, gold, and pearls), by specialized skills (embroidery silk and fine wrought cushions), and especially by an attitude, an enlarged sense of her own person (fine sleeves, laced petticoats, a tufted cloak). The obvious luxury implied by this assemblage of fabrics and trinkets should not mislead us, however. Mistress Cutt was killed by Indians while haying on her Dover farm.[6]

"Curly locks, curly locks, wilt thou be mine?/Thou shalt not wash dishes nor yet feed the swine." Our first response to the stereotypes posed in the nursery rhyme must be a simple denial. Gentility and industry were quite compatible. A pretty gentlewoman might "feed upon strawberries" (and "olives" of beef and calf's-head jelly!) but not without effort.

We cannot so summarily dismiss the comments of men like Franklin, however. Considered as opposing tendencies rather than as absolute categories, the stereotypes of "good housewife" and "pretty gentlewoman" have considerable validity in northern New England. On one level they suggest important contrasts between Country and Town, differences which became more pronounced in the course of the eighteenth century. On another, they point to crucial psychological issues. The gentry were just close enough to the wilderness to flaunt their civilization, yet many were near enough to middle-class (and often Puritan) origins to be anxious about their own gentility. Both the geographic and the religious inheritances of early New England give deeper meaning to the stereotypes.

ELIZABETH SALTONSTALL of Haverhill was the wife of the most prominent man in her town. Nathaniel Saltonstall was a magistrate and a militia commander; he was also the son of one of the few titled settlers of Massachusetts. Yet in this frontier town in the last decades of the seventeenth century there was little opportunity for genteel pretensions.

Fortunately, Mistress Saltonstall was still relatively young and energetic, and she had been trained by a sober mother to value industry more than gentility. Still, she knew the responsibilities of her class. When her only daughter, sixteen-year-old Elizabeth, had an opportunity to accompany her father to Boston in the spring of 1684, she could not keep her at home. The dairy season was upon them, the garden needed planting, but Elizabeth also needed cultivation. The little boys were still at home, after all, and Betsey Warner was a good maid.

The mother's plans soon went awry. Within a few days of Elizabeth's departure Betsey Warner's mother called her home—the family was sick and needed help. "Were it not that I aime at your good I should not be willing to deny myself as I do," Mistress Saltonstall wrote her daughter late in May, urging her to improve the time that had cost her mother so dearly.

> I have put all the silk I could find in a box and sent it with your other things. Intreat my cozine Clark if she can to procure you some silk. We will willingly satisfy her for it

and for her paines in teaching you. It would be a very great trouble to me you should misuse your precious time or any way mispend it. Consider what a precious talent time is and what a strict account you must another day give for it.[7]

If Elizabeth could not help with the churning in Haverhill, then her mother insisted that she at least sit on a cushion in Boston and learn to embroider.

Within five years, Elizabeth had married a young minister of Ipswich, Patience Denison's grandson John. In Mistress Saltonstall's view, her daughter embarked upon housekeeping with more enthusiasm than judgment. The servant problem might be no better in Ipswich. "Your father tells me when he was last att Ipswich you were thinking of hireing cows which I am truly troubled att," she wrote.

> You have those neer you that are better able to advise then I am but you will certainly find great inconvenience to take much businesses upon your hand and forced to hire all your help. . . . If it be not done allready you may be sencible by your own experience how unsteady servants are therfore little incouragements to keep a great dairy.

In a postscript the mother added, "I have according to your desire sent the flax and hemp seed but almost wish I had not. . . . you will find it difficult to hire help in season."[8]

When John Denison died shortly after the birth of a son, Elizabeth married Rowland Cotton, the minister at Sandwich. Now her mother's letters from Haverhill would be directed to Cape Cod—but the same themes would persist, and when King William's War penetrated the northern frontier, the complaints grew more insistent.

In the late summer of 1694 Haverhill was under siege. "Our house is filled Top-full, and but one roome left free for a Stranger," Nathaniel Saltonstall wrote the Cottons on August 23. Ten days later Elizabeth scratched a hasty note to her daughter. Sixty persons were billeted in the house, she said, as well as "ould Jersey." By October the family was still in "garison crowds; and more than a little . . . busie about Cyder, and winter apples." With all those folks around, there was plenty of help for common chores. As winter settled in, however, farmers' wives and their children went home, though the soldiers stayed. The family had been preserved from both the French and the Indians, Nathaniel wrote to Rowland Cotton in February, but "yet have the cumber and trouble to my only Maid, i.e. Wife, dayly to be cook and to our great charg to provide billets for 4 men posted with me."[9] Young women who might otherwise have helped in the Saltonstall kitchen were probably at home helping their own mothers feed soldiers—or perhaps just trying to catch up on work neglected during the autumn alarm.

Elizabeth Saltonstall not only had difficulty playing the role of "pretty gentlewoman," she also had trouble doing the ordinary cooking, sewing, washing, and churning expected of a "good housewife." She had few of the privileges, yet most of the responsibilities, of gentility. Because her husband was militia commander, she was responsible for billeting soldiers. Because her house was one of the largest in the coastal town, she had to open it to strangers. Because her daughter was destined to be a gentlewoman and her sons to graduate from Harvard, she had to part with them when they might have been of most help. At least one of her sons was glad to be away from home. Writing from Cambridge to his sister in Sandwich, Richard Saltonstall said, "Last week we heard from Haverhil, all Well and in health, but much thronged with Children and Lice; which discourages our taking a Journey thither."[10]

Mistress Saltonstall complained, but she apparently never questioned her duty, though late in autumn, after the Indian alarms were over and the lice and children removed, she balked at carrying on alone as mistress of the manor while her husband took a journey south. Nathaniel wrote to the Cottons that he was sorry he wouldn't be able to visit them at Cape Cod. A Thanksgiving had been appointed, he explained, "and, if I had withdrawn, my wife would not have provided any entertainment, which I was very loth should be omitted; because I have more than . . . one friend in Haverhill."[11] Because her husband was a convivial man as well as a magistrate, Elizabeth Saltonstall could not neglect normal hospitality even after an autumn of abnormal exertion.

In comparing the life of Elizabeth Saltonstall with the life of

Mary Holyoke, the crucial variable is not economic productivity but social complexity. Elizabeth Saltonstall was enmeshed in communal obligations which both increased her burdens and diminished her opportunities. In contrast, Mary Holyoke's life seems simple. She wrote about friends in her diary—but not about neighbors—and she never mentioned her servants. The difference is chronological as well as geographic. When compared with Hannah Grafton or Patience Marston, Salem gentlewomen who lived fifty years before, Mary Holyoke's life still seems narrow. There is no evidence, for example, that she was ever involved in her husband's work, though that is partly explained by the fact that for Edward Augustus Holyoke a profession—medicine—had replaced the collection of public and private enterprises which usually engaged a gentleman. The role of housewife dominates the Holyoke diary because the roles of deputy husband, of mistress, and of neighbor are missing.

All of which suggests that the first specialized "good housewives" in New England were "pretty gentlewomen" of mid-eighteenth-century towns. Such a conclusion must be tentative, since historians as yet know very little about the development of domesticity in America. Although several scholars have begun work on probate records, promising to give us a clearer understanding of changes in material culture in this period, no one has given much attention to social issues, including one of Elizabeth Saltonstall's most pressing problems—the disappearance of maids, a theme which appears over and over again in documents from rural New England. Mary Holyoke's silence on that subject indicates that in her circle servants had either become steadier (an unlikely conclusion) or were more easily replaced (a better possibility). In pre-revolutionary Salem, slaves and an increasing supply of poor men's daughters seem to have given new authority and decreased visibility to the title of mistress. Stretching for position, the coastal gentry had pulled away from the tradition of village interdependence which had placed Sarah Roper in the kitchen of Patience Denison, which had filled Elizabeth Saltonstall's beds with strangers, and which to the end of the century continued to define the lives of women in country towns.

For women like Mary Holyoke, this narrowing of roles was accompanied by a heightening of the ceremonial meaning of housekeeping, a phenomenon which historians can glimpse in increased attention to the rituals of the table and the garden, but especially in needlework. When Curly Locks found a minute to sit down on a cushion and sew a fine seam, she turned to pastoral motifs, demonstrating gentility by idealizing huswifery, embellishing her fancy furniture with country milkmaids or spinners at their work.[12] Like Franklin's wheel, these pretty pictures paid homage to the interdependent world of the Country as they demonstrated the new opportunities of the Town.

Sometime before 1782 Ruth Belknap, the wife of the minister at Dover, New Hampshire, responded to such fantasies with a little poem entitled "The Pleasures of a Country Life . . . written when I had a true taste of them by having no *maid*." Because it so vividly portrays the continuity of female life in rural New England, it is worth quoting at length.

> *Up in the morning I must rise*
> *Before I've time to rub my eyes.*
> *With half-pin'd gown, unbuckled shoe,*
> *I haste to milk my lowing cow.*
> *But, Oh! it makes my heart to ake,*
> *I have no bread till I can bake,*
> *And then, alas! it makes me sputter,*
> *For I must churn or have no butter.*
> *The hogs with swill too I must serve;*
> *For hogs must eat or men will starve.*
> *Besides, my spouse can get no cloaths*
> *Unless I much offend my nose.*
> *For all that try it know it's true*
> *There is no smell like colouring blue.*
> *Then round the parish I must ride*
> *And make enquiry far and wide*
> *To find some girl that is a spinner,*
> *Then hurry home to get my dinner. . . .*
>
> *All summer long I toil & sweat,*
> *Blister my hands, and scold & fret.*
> *And when the summer's work is o'er,*
> *New toils arise from Autumn's store.*

> *Corn must be husk'd, and pork be kill'd,*
> *The house with all confusion fill'd.*
> *O could you see the grand display*
> *Upon our annual butchering day,—*
> *See me look like ten thousand sluts,*
> *My kitchen spread with grease & guts,—*
> *You'd lift your hands surpris'd, & swear*
> *That Mother Trisket's self were there.*
>
> *Ye starch'd up folks that live in town,*
> *That lounge upon your beds till noon,*
> *That never tire yourselves with work,*
> *Unless with handling knife & fork,*
> *Come, see the sweets of country life,*
> *Display'd in Parson B [elknap's] wife.*[13]

The parson's wife was exaggerating, of course, poking fun at pastoral conventions. That she had time to rhyme her frustration suggests that her problems were neither as serious nor as prolonged as those of Elizabeth Saltonstall, yet the two women would have recognized each other.

IN A REGION settled by evangelical Protestants and eventually shattered by revolution, sharp contrasts between "good housewives" and "pretty gentlewomen" cannot be entirely explained in terms of geography or economics. In an analysis of the journal of Esther Burr—a daughter of Jonathan Edwards, the famous theologian and preacher of western Massachusetts—Laurie Crumpacker has described the ambivalence of one New England woman toward housework. "I must submit," Burr wrote, complaining of her domestic duties. "My time is not my own but Gods." Her burdens were genuine, yet Crumpacker suggests that some of her problems, including her inability to keep a maid, may have derived in part from impossible standards and from her own need to spend herself in service. She patterned herself after the industrious housewife of Proverbs whose candle burned far into the night and who nevertheless rose before dawn.[14]

Think for a moment of Elizabeth Saltonstall confined with her

Jersey cow and lice-infested neighbors in a garrison in Haverhill, dutifully mixing bread and scouring pots, all the while complaining about the unreliability of servants and thanking God for her preservation from the enemy. Mistress Saltonstall would have understood the central message of the dozens of Indian-captivity narratives published in these years: the Lord gives no trial to the faithful that will not in the end prove a blessing. If the world was a wilderness and life a pilgrimage, then huswifery was a laborious but essential calling. In various modes, this psychology of the "good housewife" survived the colonial period in New England, though it was continually threatened and sometimes infused with the rival psychology of the "pretty gentlewoman" who saw the earth as at least potentially a garden, life as art, and huswifery as a means to more gracious and comfortable living.

Philip Greven has recently attempted a major analysis of cultural conflict in revolutionary America in terms of temperament, stressing the continuity of "evangelical," "moderate," and "genteel" personality types from the seventeenth through the nineteenth centuries.[15] One need not accept Greven's precise formulations to recognize the utility of his approach even in a study of housekeeping. Two sets of documents dating from the middle of the eighteenth century show strikingly different attitudes toward the most ordinary of a housewife's tasks—providing suitable clothing for her children. Mary Holyoke of Cambridge, the future mother-in-law of the Mary we have met, was obviously a "moderate" in Greven's terms. Mary Gilman of Exeter was an "evangelical."

On May 1, 1755, Mary Holyoke's husband, Edward, wrote to their "dear Child" Edward Augustus Holyoke of Salem. Augustus, who was then in his late twenties, was about to be married, a circumstance which had sent his mother back and forth to Boston almost daily, hastening from tailor to dry-goods shop and then to her married daughter for consultation. Engaged in the important business of dressing her son, Mrs. Holyoke was too busy to write. Her husband, who was then president of Harvard College, was not. "Your Mother desires me to write you what she hath already done in your Affairs," he began, carefully detailing each item his wife had purchased and her reasons for doing so. She had found cloth and trimming for a coat, but had been unable to secure any blue satin. Perhaps this was just as well, for "Mr Loughton where she bo't the Cloth saies that he reckoned a white Sattin wou'd suit the Colour of the coat better & be much more genteel." She had purchased four pair of cotton stockings, though "as to silk stockings, she cannot light of any, but what very ordinary, besides your Sister Mascarene saies you had better not have any, for that they are not fashionable, & People in the highest dress wear no other than Cotton."[16]

For Mary Holyoke of Cambridge, gentility was an easy expectation. For Mary Gilman of Exeter, New Hampshire, it represented a spiritual threat. On January 7, 1753, Joseph Gilman, a young clerk in the countinghouse of a Boston merchant, wrote to his mother asking for stockings, shirts, and "britches." At fifteen, Joseph was discovering for himself the cultural chasm between Country and Town. His own anxieties were focused upon clothes. In August he had written for shirts—one a week simply wouldn't do—and had even suggested having a broadcloth jacket made by a tailor and if possible a "handsome" pair of black breeches. "I do not desire you to send my homespun Cloth coulerd Jacket if you do I shall not wear it," he had fussed. In September he again requested shirts, perhaps with little result, for in November's letter he moderated his demand for "seven good Shirts bag Holland sleeves." "I do not care whether my Shirts are bag Holland or no if they will wash white, nor do I care how few Shirts I have so I can have a clean one when I want it," he told his mother. Since she had been "blamed by some for giving me too good Cloaths," he assured her that he shared her values, that he only desired to "dress neat and Clean but not fine." But by January his frustration was obvious. What was suitable for Exeter simply would not do in Boston, a fact his mother seemed not to understand.

> If it would be of any service I would send home one of my Shirts that I have wore a week and tried to Keep clean as far as it Lay in my power; Pride is not the occasion of my writing thus for I seriously declare I never took Less pains to dress than I now do, I am forced to go with holes In my Stockings very often.

He would be grateful for half a dozen good worsted stockings. As for shirts, if his mother couldn't afford Holland, then checked would have to do.[17]

Joseph's struggles to achieve dignity continued. By summer he seems to have settled on checked shirts, but he vowed never again to wear shoes made in Exeter. "I scarce Ever saw a Worse pair . . . than the Last you sent me," he wrote. Lest she imagine that pride was at the root of his continual demands for stockings, he couched June's request in terms good housekeeping could hardly deny: "my feet Sweat so that when I have Wore a Pair of Stockings three or four days they are Stiff that I can Scarce Weare them."[18]

There were obvious economic differences between the two pairs of mothers and sons. Joseph Gilman was descended from two of Exeter's most prominent merchant families, but he was still a young apprentice and his mother a widow.[19] Augustus Holyoke, on the other hand, was already established in a profession. The difference in world view, however, is even more apparent. The elder Holyoke was a genial minister whose personal diary includes notes on candle-making but nothing on the spiritual state of his youthful flock. Nicholas Gilman, Joseph's father, had been a troubled evangelical whose search for salvation had triggered one of the most ardent "awakenings" in New England. Edward Holyoke lined up his children annually to record their weight; Nicholas Gilman continually tested his sons' growth toward conversion.[20] Little wonder that Joseph defended himself against the charge of "pride."

Significantly, Joseph Gilman's conflicts with his mother centered on clothing. From the days of the Puritan "round heads," differences in apparel and hair-styling had symbolized deeper commitments. New England was periodically rocked by conflict over changes in fashion. As late as 1752 church members in Newbury met together to discipline a brother named Richard Bartlett who refused communion with the church "for no other reason but because the Pastor wears a wigg."[21]

Women's clothing aroused even stronger feelings. One of the first attacks on female fashions in New England was written in 1647 by Elizabeth Saltonstall's grandfather Nathaniel Ward, whose *Simple Cobler of Aggawam* insisted that Zion's daughters had already been disfigured by French fashion, which "trans-clouts them into gantbargeese, ill-shapen-shotten shell fish, Egyptian Hyroglyphicks, or at the best into French flurts of the pastery."[22]

If we could somehow walk into an eighteenth-century meetinghouse and see all of the inhabitants of a town dressed in their best and seated by rank, we would probably learn more about cultural and social divisions than by months of shuffling town records. Even after a century of supposed "levelling" and long after the sumptuary laws were abandoned, clothing carried subtle clues to values and status. These have been only partly transmitted in written records. We know, for example, that in 1772, before her marriage to William Pepperrell, Mary Hurst shocked her country cousins by appearing in York in "fashionable clothing,"[23] but what was the exact nature of her offense? Was her gown cut too low? Was the fabric too sumptuous? Or—scandalous thought—had she succumbed to the vanity of a "hoop-petticoat," a novelty singled out for attack in the Boston press that very year? "Is not Pride of Apparel an Evidence of a proud Heart?" the anonymous author had thundered.[24] The opposite of Franklin's "good housewife" was not just "gentlewoman" but a "pretty gentlewoman." Clothes distinguished the better sort from the commonalty, but they also distinguished the proud from the virtuous.

In the next fifty years that ancient sin of pride would acquire political connotations. When the "Daughters of Liberty" brought down their spinning wheels from their attics, they were responding to a moral imperative as well as to a practical need.[25] Abandoning their "top knots of pride," they renounced the luxury of a corrupt England, demonstrating that the descendants of the saints had not forgotten the lesson of Bathsheba, "She looketh well to the ways of her household, and eateth not the bread of idleness."

One antidote to the sin of pride was industrious labor—what could be more chaste, modest, and productive than homely spinning, the necessary occupation of the poor and the young? An alternate remedy was exemplary piety, which in Puritan tradition meant serious reading and writing as well as prayer. In New England the chief exponent of this view was Cotton Mather.

The text for his *Ornaments for the Daughters of Zion*, first published in 1691, was verse 30 of Proverbs chapter 31: "Favour is

Deceitful, and Beauty is Vain: but A woman that feareth the Lord, she 'tis, that shall be praised." Mather upheld the expected social roles described in the myth of Bathsheba. But he also found room in his text to enlarge the intellectual and spiritual potential of women, insisting that though women might not speak in the church, "yet our God has Employ'd many Women to write for the church, and Inspir'd some of them for the Writing of the scriptures." Among those scriptures, of course, was Proverbs 31, which Puritans attributed to Solomon's mother, the godly Bathsheba.[26]

From the earliest years, godly women had been enjoined to read, to meditate, and to write. With the appropriate education, a very few women polished their piety in publishable prose or verse.[27] The most notable example, of course, is Anne Bradstreet, whose first book was published in 1650. Bradstreet recognized that she was doing something unusual when she wrote in the preface, "I am obnoxious to each carping tongue/Who says my hand a needle better fits." Those "carping tongues" did not belong to the Puritan intelligentsia of northern New England, however. Bradstreet's poems were presented to the world by a Newbury minister, her brother-in-law John Woodbridge, and prefaced by commendatory verses from half a dozen other males, including Nathaniel Ward, Bradstreet's former neighbor in Ipswich, who seems to have been relieved that she had not joined those "French flurts of the pastery" he so deplored.[28] That few female writers matched her achievement is hardly surprising. As John Woodbridge reminded readers, *The Tenth Muse* was the work of a woman esteemed for the "discreet managing of her Family occasions . . . these Poems are the fruit but of some few hours, curtailed from her sleep and other refreshments."[29] Even as an antidote to pride, serious writing might compete with industrious housekeeping.

The relationship between moral values and material culture is subtle, and it deserves further study. It is important to remember, however, that "pretty gentlewomen" might be every bit as religious as "good housewives," though their piety would turn on different issues. The Rule of Modesty sustained Mary Gilman's zealous thrift and encouraged Anne Bradstreet's spirituality; but the Rule of Charity allowed women like Mary Belcher, the wife of the Massachusetts governor, or Mary Pepperrell, the wife of Sir William, the hero of Louisburg, to enjoy their splendor in good conscience as they turned their beauty and their bounty toward uplifting the ministry. Genteel allegiance bolstered the ministry; ministerial approbation ratified gentility.

This symbiotic bond is hinted at, though seldom elaborated, in the dozens of funeral sermons preached for affluent women by grateful pastors. In acknowledging Mary Belcher's charitable activities, Thomas Prince said that her heart was "soft and tender" toward the "afflicted and needy"—including ministers in distress.[30] A drunken shoemaker from Portsmouth put it more bluntly. The Reverend Mr. Moody had two special friends in the town, he said, Mr. Fryer's wife, who "supplied him with Ribbin or trimings for his cloaths," and William Seavy's wife, who "supplied him with coks and hens for to feed ungodly gutts."[31] Mary Pepperrell's devotion to the Kittery Point church and its pastor, John Newmarch, was well known. After Sir William's death in 1759, she built an imposing mansion directly across the road from the meetinghouse, in that one act reinforcing both the gentility which separated her from her neighbors and the piety which joined them. In the blaze of revolution the Pepperrell holdings were confiscated as Tory property. Visible godliness as well as age may explain why Mary was allowed to remain in her house though her grandson, the second Sir William, was forced to flee.[32]

As we have seen, the myth of Bathsheba encompassed the productive roles of housewives and deputy husbands, the social roles of mistresses and neighbors, and the intellectual and spiritual roles of committed Christians. Little wonder that the thirty-first chapter of Proverbs became a favorite text for expanding upon the virtues of the ideal wife. Scriptural models can mean quite different things to different people, however, as we are reminded by a letter which Governor Belcher of Massachusetts wrote in August of 1732 to his son Jonathan, who was then studying law at the Middle Temple in London.

Having heard that Jonathan wanted to marry, the Governor hastened to show his displeasure, closing his letter with a little essay on the nature of a good wife, whose qualities, he reminded Jonathan, were "elegantly described in the 31. chap. of Proverbs, which you wrote out in short hand in your infant day. Pray, read it often, when you have a mind to be marry'd."[33]

The Governor did not leave his son's interpretation of scripture to chance. Not only did he urge Jonathan to make out a detailed list of expenses required in the first year of marriage, but he went on to list for his son the five qualities he considered absolutely essential in a wife. A suitable wife, he wrote, must possess "Strict Vertue" and "Good Nature." She must be "Agreeable (no matter whether beautifull)" and have "Passable good sense (no matter whether over-quick & sharp)." She must also bring "a Plentifull fortune." Lest Jonathan overlook the importance of the last-named quality, his father elaborated and defended it. "A man will soon find himself miserable that makes money his first & principal choice," he wrote. "Yet the other four characters won't do without it. . . . if God please to spare your life, save your vertue, & bless your studies, I hope you will in due time lay 'em in the opposite scale to a lady of 10,000 sterling pounds, with all the other qualifications I have mention'd." Having made his message transparent, the Governor returned to religion in a postscript:

> Lest you shou'd not take the pains to read the 31 chap. of Prov. my clerk had transcrib'd from the 10 ver. & it's inclosed.

He apparently found nothing ironic in the opening passage of that scripture: "Who can find a virtuous woman? for her price is far above rubies."

There is more at issue here than one man's ambivalence—or hypocrisy. The Governor's peculiar mixture of materialism and religion was symptomatic of a larger conflict in New England. Entering a transatlantic scramble for profit and patronage, Belcher still clung to old securities, to New England cider and turnips on the table, to thrift and Bible-reading, and to filial obedience and feminine piety.[34] For him, the "31 chap. of Prov." had none of the specific connotations that we have elaborated. He was not concerned about the religious convictions of Jonathan's future wife, even less so about her housekeeping skills—in his mind "passable good sense" was sufficient. What he really feared was the disruptive power of sex. Youth, distance, and an attractive young woman might undermine both his fatherly authority and his fond hopes for Jonathan.

The Governor's letter shows the way in which idealized notions of marriage might become entangled in the strictures of a property relation. Beneath that, it reflects a quite human tension between youth and age, between the mystery of physical attraction and the demands of social order. As Belcher (and King Solomon) knew, Bathsheba was an Eve transformed.

Part Two

EVE

*And the Lord God said, It is not good that the man should be
alone; I will make him an help meet for him....*
*And the Lord God caused a deep sleep to fall upon Adam, and
he slept: and he took one of his ribs, and closed up the flesh
instead thereof;*
*And the rib, which the Lord God had taken from man, made he
a woman, and brought her unto the man.*
*And Adam said, This is now bone of my bones, and flesh of my
flesh: she shall be called Woman, because she was taken out
of Man.*
*Therefore shall a man leave his father and his mother, and
shall cleave unto his wife: and they shall be one flesh.*
*And they were both naked, the man and his wife, and were not
ashamed.*

GENESIS 2:18, 21–25

*And the man said, The woman whom thou gavest to be with
me, she gave me of the tree, and I did eat.*
*And the Lord God said unto the woman, What is this that thou
hast done? And the woman said, The serpent beguiled me,
and I did eat.*

And the Lord God said unto the serpent, Because thou hast done this, thou art cursed above all cattle, and above every beast of the field; upon thy belly shalt thou go, and dust shalt thou eat all the days of thy life.

And I will put enmity between thee and the woman, and between thy seed and her seed; it shall bruise thy head, and thou shalt bruise his heel.

Unto the woman he said, I will greatly multiply thy sorrow and thy conception; in sorrow thou shalt bring forth children; and thy desire shall be to thy husband, and he shall rule over thee.

And unto Adam he said, Because thou hast hearkened unto the voice of thy wife, and hast eaten of the tree, of which I commanded thee, saying, Thou shalt not eat of it: cursed is the ground for thy sake; in sorrow shalt thou eat of it all the days of thy life. . . .

And Adam called his wife's name Eve; because she was the mother of all living.

GENESIS 3:12–17, 20

Chapter Five

THE SERPENT BEGUILED ME

IT MIGHT HAVE BEEN a Restoration comedy.[1] In the spring of 1663 John Rolfe, a Newbury fisherman, went off to Nantucket, leaving behind a comely and "merily disposed" young wife named Mary. Being "a verie loving husband," Rolfe arranged for Mary to "live Cherfully as he thought and want for nothing" in his absence. Betty Webster, a single woman in the neighborhood, agreed to stay with Mary. Betty's stepfather, Goodman John Emery, promised to be a father to both. But Rolfe's careful arrangements proved a snare. No sooner had he sailed out of Newbury harbor than two strangers from old England sailed in. Henry Greenland and John Cordin, physicians and gentlemen, came to lodge at the Emery house.

Mary confided to Betty Webster that "Mr Cording was as pretty a Carriadg man as Ever shee saw in hir life." But Greenland proved more interesting still. He was uninhibited by the pious manners of the Newbury folk. At supper, before Goodman Emery could half finish prayer, "Mr Grenland put on his hatt and spread his napkin and stored the sampe and said Com Landlord light supper short grace." Mary was both enticed and troubled by his attentions. When he pulled her toward him by her apron strings, she resisted at first, only giving way, as she said, "to save my apron." One minute she rebuked him for acting "an uncivell part." The next she was laughing and eating samp with him out of one dish and with one spoon.

Late one night Betty was in bed with Mary, who was nursing

her baby, when Henry Greenland knocked on the window. Frightened, the women made no answer. "Bettye, Bettye," Greenland called. "Will you let me stand here and starve with the cold?" Betty answered that they were already in bed, that they would not let him in, that they were afraid of him. When he continued to plead, protesting that he "would doe them noe hirt, but desired to smoke a pipe of tobacco," Betty let him in. Still in bed, Mary told her to rake up the fire to give Mr. Greenland some light. While the maid bent over the hearth, Greenland pulled off his clothes and climbed into bed with Mary, who fainted.

"Sir," cried Betty, "what have you done? You have put the woman into a fitt."

"The Devell has such fitts," said Greenland, scrambling out of bed. "It is nothing but a mad fitt."

"What offence have I have given that you should speke such words?" Mary exclaimed. Seeing that his conquest was conscious, Greenland jumped back into bed. "Lord help me," she cried.

At that moment Henry Lessenby, a neighbor's servant, just happened to walk by. He had earlier observed Greenland's attentions to Goody Rolfe. Hearing the cry, he ran to the Rolfe door and knocked loudly. "Lye still," whispered Greenland, "for now there are two witnesses, we shall be tried for our lives." But Lessenby was not to be discouraged by silence. He climbed through the window, stumbled into the room in the dark, and felt his way to the bedside. In the dim light from the fireplace he discerned a gentleman's clothes on a box by the bed. Reaching for the pillow, he felt a beard. Just as he suspected, it was Greenland.

Lessenby might have raised a commotion, but he chose instead to act the part of the stage servant who, loving a secret, is drawn through vanity or cupidity into the intrigues of his betters. As he later reported it, "The woman and I went adore [outdoors] to Consider what was best to be done so we thought becas he was a stranger and a great man it was not best to make an up Rore but to let him go way in a private maner."

Here the plot calls for deeper entanglements, for pacts between the gentleman and the maid, half-kept promises whispered on the doorstep in the dark, and finally the return of the cuckolded husband. But this little drama was not enacted on the London stage but in a Massachusetts village. In this case the young wife was rescued by an old wife, the husband was avenged, and the denouement was played in the county court. Goody Rolfe had a pious mother and an observant sister. At meeting on Sunday, Sarah Bishop saw that Mary had been crying and alerted their mother.

Goody Bishop visited the Rolfe house the next morning. As she approached, she met a boy rushing out with a glass—to get liquor for Dr. Greenland, he said. For two hours she sat in the house, watching and observing and waiting for Greenland to leave. Finally she had a chance to question Mary, who seemed to fear telling her mother all that had happened. Mary admitted that the gentleman had "with many Arguments inticed her to the act of uncleanness," but she insisted that "God had hitherto helped her resist him."

"Will you venture to lay under these temptations & concealed wickedness?" exclaimed the mother. "You may Provoak God to Leave you & then you will come under Great Blame."

"I know not what to doe," Mary sighed. "Hee is in Creditt in the Towne, some take him to be godly & say hee hath grace in his face, he have an honest loke, he have such a carrige that he deceive many: It is saide the Governer sent him a letter Counting it a mercy such an Instrument was in the Country, and what shall such a pore young woman as I doe in such a case, my husband being not at home?"

Goody Bishop was troubled. "These things are not to bee kept private," she insisted. "Goodman Emery beeing grand Jury-man must present them." But when confronted, Goodman Emery proved unwilling to act the part of moral guardian. (Had he seen too much "merriness" on Mary's part?) He promised to keep closer watch on Greenland, to lock up the hard drink, and to see that the Doctor stayed home when half drunk, but he felt matters were best kept quiet for the moment. He could see no harm done.

Goody Bishop was not to be soothed by promises. On her way home she encountered *Goody* Emery and explained to her all that had happened. The wife proved more sympathetic than the husband. Together the two women returned to the Rolfe house, pressed Mary and Betty further, and concluded that Greenland's actions had been "more gross" than they had first believed.

"I dare not keep such things as these private upon my owne head," said Mary's mother as the two women parted.

"Doe wisely," answered her friend.

That night, having asked for God's direction, Goody Bishop revealed all that she knew to a "wise man" in the town, asking for his advice. He directed her to the magistrates. Henry Greenland was tried by jury at his own request, perhaps counting on his good reputation in the town, but was convicted of attempted adultery and fined the whopping sum of £30. The citizens of Newbury supported the pious mother against the dazzling stranger. John Rolfe returned from Nantucket avenged.

To understand this village morality play, we must determine the historical meaning of the characters. That they do not represent the classical stage triangle—husband, wife, and lover—is in itself significant. What can we make of a plot which casts a mother as moral guardian, a dashing Englishman as assailant, and a pretty young bride as victim?

One obvious interpretation would make Puritanism the real protagonist.[2] Surely Goody Bishop represents the community surveillance characteristic of the rule of the saints. As Mary Rolfe's mother, she upheld a morality thundered from the pulpit and enforced by the court. As for Henry Greenland, the libertine Englishman, he was a Thomas Morton (or Tom Jones) caught in a society he did not understand, incriminated as much by his attitude as by his acts. How many of his reported boasts—that it didn't matter that he had a wife in England, that Mary need not worry about consequences, that he could afford two wives—were in jest? He insisted that he meant no harm, but in Newbury his carefree words condemned him. In this view, Mary Rolfe hardly matters. The real conflict was between two cultures—Puritan Massachusetts and Merry England.

Yet a close examination of the case suggests that the most serious division was not between the town and the stranger but within the community itself—and perhaps in the mind of Mary Rolfe. Dragged into court by outraged neighbors, John Emery angrily reported that before the fateful night someone had put "fig dust" (tobacco shavings) and pebbles in Greenland's bed. Had Mary Rolfe surreptitiously invited the pretty gentleman to rap on her window and ask for a light? Had Betty Webster or someone else in Emery's family been playing tricks on them both?[3]

Since the 1930s, discussion of sexual behavior in New England has focused on the relationship between religion and repression. Despite the efforts of Edmund S. Morgan to dispel the stereotype of the "sad and sour" saints, historians continue to ask, "How 'Puritan' were the Puritans?"[4] Michael Zuckerman insists they were hostile to the flesh.[5] Philip Greven says that some of them were.[6] For our purposes, the question is badly put. To understand the historical drama in Newbury, one must give less attention to ideology than to gender, taking the characters pretty much at their surface value. Goody Bishop was an old woman. Mary Rolfe was a young woman. Henry Greenland was an aggressive male. The really crucial issues are exposed in the action itself, with all its confusion and apparent inconsistency. Mary Rolfe was obviously attracted to Greenland. She was also afraid of him. She openly flirted with him. At the same time, she was troubled by her own feelings and by the potential consequences of her behavior.

Her dilemma was created by the coexistence in one rural village of a hierarchal social order (by no means limited to New England), a conservative religious tradition (not exclusively Puritan), and sex-linked patterns of sociability (rooted in English folkways). All three elements determined her behavior. Accustomed to deference—to her mother, to her husband, to the selectman next door—she was easily dazzled by the genteel appearance and apparent good name of Greenland. What right had she to question his behavior? Though taught to fear God, she had not yet acquired the kind of confidence in her own sense of right which propelled her mother to challenge both a popular gentleman and a respected neighbor by bringing the case to court. Finally, in her easy compliance with Greenland's initial advances, Mary Rolfe was responding to a lifetime of instruction in femininity. Massachusetts girls, like ordinary Englishwomen everywhere, knew how to light pipes for strangers.

KEITH THOMAS HAS argued that the double standard in sexual relations is but one manifestation of a hierarchal system which included not just the subordination of one class to another but the subordination of female to male. Thus, from medieval times "the absolute property of the women's chastity was vested not in the woman herself, but in her parents or her husband."[7] In these terms, Henry Greenland's pursuit of Mary Rolfe was not just an attempted seduction, it was a trespass upon the "property rights" of John Rolfe, who in fact successfully sued Greenland for damages soon after his return from sea. (There was no question, of course, of *Mistress* Greenland suing anyone, even though she too arrived in New England not long after the case came to court.[8])

Throughout the Christian world the property concept of chastity was challenged by a religious concept which upheld the value of marital purity and premarital fidelity for both sexes. Potentially at least, this opened the way for a more egalitarian legal system, though in Massachusetts reliance on the Mosaic law created some strange contradictions. Following Leviticus 20, the Laws and Liberties of 1648 established the death penalty for adultery, yet defined the crime according to the marital status of the woman, effectively reinforcing the old notion of a man's property rights in his wife.[9] A married man who engaged in sexual relations with an unmarried partner risked only a fine or a whipping for fornication. A married woman who did the same risked death. The inequity could work the other way, of course. A single man who engaged in sexual relations with a married partner risked death; a single woman who did the same risked only a fine or a whipping—and pregnancy!

In practice, adultery was such a heinous crime in the Bay Colony that convictions were rare.[10] Married folk of either sex were usually punished more or less equally for the lesser crimes of "attempted adultery," "uncleanness," or "lascivious carriage." In prosecuting fornicators, Massachusetts courts moved even closer to a single standard. A woman's accusation, especially if witnessed by the midwives at the time of delivery, was sufficient to convict a man, all his protests notwithstanding.[11]

The legal record is quite clear—in sexual matters, as in most other areas of life, New England women were subject to men, though entitled to protection. The more difficult question is determining how all of this translated into gender roles, which of course were enacted not in court but in the intimate arena of ordinary life.

Sharing rooms, beds, benches, trenchers, and even spoons, ordinary New Englanders had little opportunity to develop the elaborate sense of personal space so essential to "polite" interaction. Chairs were rare. Bedrooms hardly existed. Although in some families the parents' bedstead was curtained for warmth or privacy, it almost always occupied "public" space.[12] In many dwellings, as in Mary Rolfe's, the front door opened on a bed.

Sexual experience had not yet acquired the ceremonial sanctity of a separate setting. Even if the notion had suggested itself, there was little possibility of segregating sex in the larger sense from the daily round of life. Procreation was everywhere, in the barnyard as well as in the house. Since sleeping quarters were crowded and darkness provided the only privacy, many children must have gained their first awareness of copulation from half-muffled sounds and shapes in the night. For a wife there might be advantages to all this crowding. When Abigail Willey of Oyster River wanted to prevent her husband from "coming to her," she planted her two youngest children in the middle of the bed, rather than pushing them to one side as usual. The night John Bickford slept with her mother, seven-year-old Judith Willey told a New Hampshire court, the bed "crakled" so she could not sleep.[13] Goody Willey's extramarital affair was deviant, but the context in which it occurred was not.

There were proprieties, of course. A respectable woman did not undress before her male servants, nor did she lie under the covers with a man not her husband, but she might sleep in the same room with either.[14] She did not sing and drink with strangers in the tavern, though out of common hospitality she would certainly smoke at her own hearth or doorstep with any of her husband's friends.[15] She did not sit on her neighbor's lap or kiss him in the barn, but with good conscience she could share his horse.[16] Lynn folks were shocked when Goody Leonard stood laughing at the millpond where a group of servants were skinny-dipping, forcing the "more modest" of the men to put on their shirts in the water, letting them drop "by degrees" as they came out.[17] But relatives at Ipswich as well as friends at the Isles of Shoals were just as surprised at the jealousy of William Row, who became angry if any man "saluted" his wife with a kiss, a custom which was apparently as acceptable in New England as in old.[18] Even the sermon literature stressed the affability of the good wife, a quality expressed in the very word "consort." From childhood, daughters were taught to please, to smile and fetch and carry, to stand on the table and sing.[19] If for some women affability translated into accessibility, the distance was shorter than we might think.

Such evidence is easily misinterpreted, however. Twentieth-century readers, enjoying the "earthiness" of seventeenth-century court records, may mistake verbal openness for an easy and matter-of-fact attitude to the flesh. The opposite was often nearer the truth. In premodern societies sexual tensions are close to the surface and frequently vented in bawdy stories or in epithets hurled across a fence in anger. To impugn a person's sexual integrity was a particularly potent form of slander in early New England, suggesting that the values enshrined in formal law were widely acknowledged but tenuously held.

How else can one explain the "presentation" in York County Court of Goody Mendum of Kittery, whose crime consisted of calling Mistress Alice Shapleigh "a pedlers Trull"? In a less close-knit society a wild accusation flung at the wife of a town official would hardly deserve the dignity of attention. In seventeenth-century Kittery it called for a forced retraction, not only in court but in church.[20] Because this was a society which still depended primarily upon external rather than internal controls, many New Englanders responded not so much to guilt as to shame. The opinion of one's neighbor was everything. As Goody Bishop expressed it, a body might as well take an axe and knock one of her cows on the head as to take away her daughter's good name.[21]

Whore. Jade. Bawd. Strumpet. Trull. Such words came quickly to the tongues of village gossips. They meant everything and nothing. Certainly there were loose women in most country towns, women like the widow Sarah Stickney of Newbury, who had more than one illegitimate child and little reputation to lose. When Samuel Lowell rode by in a cart, she called, "A you roge, yonder is yor Child under the tree, goe take it up and see it," an action that did not prevent her from successfully suing for child support from John Atkinson, a married father of nine. When Goody Atkinson railed at Sarah and called her "an impudent baud," she spat in her face.[22] In their wider application, however, the epithets turned not on specific behavior but on an underlying ambiguity surrounding sexuality. This is partly explained in religious terms. For Calvinists, the old proverb "There but for the

Grace of God go I" had a literal meaning.[23] Because the potential for evil was innate, lust might break out anywhere. But for many New Englanders, religion was but a thin overlay on a traditional fatalism, an inability to see oneself as in any sense a shaper of events. Such an attitude affected both sexes, of course, but in the traditional world fatalism and femininity were powerfully linked.[24]

The serpent beguiled me, and I did eat. New England ministers did not berate women for the sin of Eve. In fact, in referring to the transgression in Eden they almost always spoke of the "sin of Adam," perhaps unconsciously assuming male pre-eminence even in evil but at least sometimes intentionally countering the ancient misogyny.[25] Eve's sin was in one sense hardly a sin at all. Her transgression was an inevitable consequence of her nature—weak, unstable, susceptible to suggestion. She was "beguiled."[26]

There was no question of one sex being more or less sinful than another. Outside of family and community government, males were carnal, sensual, and devilish. Puritan writers were amazed at the sexual restraint of Indian men, who never raped their captives. They could only attribute this amazing preservation of New England women to divine intervention.[27] No, both sexes were culpable. But they were different. Men required restraint, especially when drunk. Women needed protection, not because they were innocent but because they were not. They were physically and sexually vulnerable, easily aroused, quick to succumb to flattery. Widows were considered especially susceptible to temptation. Their humble—and frequent—confessions in court and church reinforced folk wisdom: "He who wooeth a widow must go stiff before."[28]

As might be expected, the vocabulary describing the sexual misbehavior of women was richer and more direct than that for men. Even the epithets *cuckold* and *pimp* turn on female rather than on male promiscuity. The opposite of *whore* was *rogue*, a term which mixed sexual and more general meanings.[29] For a woman, sexual reputation was everything; for a man, it was part of a larger pattern of responsibility. A *whore* bestowed her favors indiscriminately, denying any man exclusive right to her body. A *rogue* tricked or forced a woman into submission with no regard for consequences. The words mirror traditional gender relationships. A woman gave; a man took. Because the female role was in its nature more ambiguous, less clearly active without quite being passive, a woman could lose her reputation simply in being attacked. "Whore! baud!" Patrick Morrin shouted at Mary Water when she ran from the house after an attempted assault.[30]

So Mary Rolfe smiled when Henry Greenland pulled on her apron strings. She ate out of his dish and laughed at his jokes, and perhaps enjoyed the game of conquest and resistance. When the plot grew more serious, she found herself confused. To call for help would be an admission of complicity. Who would believe her story against a man in credit in the town, especially when everyone knew she was young, pretty, and "often merrily disposed"? Her only recourse was to petition the court and confess herself "a poor young woman and in an aflicted Condition." The same vulnerability which led to her trouble might save her from it.

If the role of Mary Rolfe was clear, so was that of Goody Bishop. She had earned her position through experience. In New England, ultimate authority to police sexual behavior was given to men—to justices, juries, ministers, and elders. In reality, primary responsibility for controlling female sexuality was in the hands of women. The formal role of midwives in fornication cases grew out of a larger and more pervasive system of informal justice. Just as Goody Bishop instinctively turned to Goody Emery in determining her course in response to Henry Greenland, so older women throughout New England acted as advisers, counselors, and ultimately as judges, though sometimes their visible role was intentionally muted.

In September of 1664 Elizabeth Perkins, Sr., and Agnes Ewens of Topsfield sent word to the Essex County Court that "they did not desire to testify but would depose if called." They explained that

> what had brought them forth was the busy prattling of some other, probably the one whom they had taken along with them to advise a young woman, whose simple and foolish carriages and words, having heard of, they desired to advise better. . . . They desired to be excused from testifying because what was told them was a private confession which they had never to that day divulged, and the woman had never offended since that time but had lived gravely and soberly.[31]

In this case the two women assumed a kind of "professional immunity" from the inquisitions of the county officials. Their consciousness of their own importance is striking, but the role they had played was not unusual.

A hierarchal social structure which made female chastity the property of men, a religious tradition which demanded morality from both sexes, and patterns of feminine behavior rooted in traditional fatalism and in the rhythms of village life—against this backdrop men and women in northern New England played out an old drama of conquest and seduction.

Gorgeana, Province of Maine, 1650. For more than a year Jane Bond had been troubled with "fat Robert," who came to her house on at least four occasions when her husband was away "to the East." The first time he "strived with her but hardly knew hur boddy fully." Six months later he came again. When he tried to crawl through the window, she opened the door and let him in. "Robert Collins leave my company and medell not with me," she told him. "If not I will make you a shame to all New England." But though she tried, she "could not save hir selfe." Whether this had anything to do with alcohol is not clear, but when he came the third time at twilight and sat on her doorstep, she would not open the door. "I would have given you some drinke," he said. She answered, "I know not what is in it." About midnight on a May evening as she was making a cake to leave with her children, who would be alone the next day, Collins again came to the door, this time pushing the door almost off the hinges. He asked her to move her youngest child out of the bed and lie with him. She refused. He forced her.

"Put your finger but a littell in the fier you will not be able to Induer it," she told him, "but I must suffer eternally." Then she added, "You burn in your lust."

The next day Jane went to her neighbor Mary Tappe. Her heart was heavy, she was troubled to be so much alone, she said, and she was afraid to live so. Someone had been at her house the night before.

"It might be cattle," the neighbor answered.

"Noe," Jane said, "it was not cattell." Who then had been

there? Jane simply repeated over and over again, "Alase I am but one, I dare not reveale it."

"Why did you not cry out?" Mary asked.

"Alase," she answered. "I may Cry tell my hart ake."[32]

Salem, Essex County, 1672. Elizabeth Goodell was careful to tell the justice of the peace that the language and actions of her brother-in-law John Smith "were such as most tend to the way of his calling in dealing with Cattel and not so like unlawful dalliances tending to uncleanness." No attempted rape—just continual and persistent annoyance. The record is never more specific, but the unbrotherly kisses, the meaningful looks, and the well-placed pats are easy to picture. These "assaults" and "affronts" had been going on for years, ever since her son Zachary was a little boy. Smith approached Elizabeth at her sister's house when he was there digging a well, at Giles Corey's house while Goody Corey was bringing in the linen from the bushes, and once at her own house on the Lord's day while her husband was at meeting. He became so insistent as they rode together to his wife's lying-in that she was forced to jump from the horse. Working in a swamp near her dwelling, he called for fire. When she refused to stay and smoke with him, he chased her up a hill.

Why didn't she complain? A male neighbor testified that he had come into the room after one alleged assault. If there was really a problem, she should have said something then. All he could see was "laughing and smoking."

Female neighbors said that Elizabeth was afraid. She told them that Smith was "an ugly rogue" and she was frightened that if she told, he would kill her or her children or "hurt her creatures." Even if he were tried and convicted, she explained, "what a sad life should I have with my Husbands relations."[33]

Kittery, York County, 1710. When John White, the tinker, came to Mary Jenkins' house asking to borrow a canoe, she was glad to see him. Her husband, Rowland, was frequently at sea and she was afraid of Indians, who had taken captives in her own neighborhood. She told White that if he would stay the night, she would go with him to Mr. Kelley's house in town to get the canoe. He stayed. She sent to a neighbor's house for a pipe and tobacco, and the two of them sat up most of the night talking and smoking, "on two chairs," she said. Near morning he threw her on the bed and said he would "have his will of her," keeping his face so close to hers she could not scream. "I was in Souch a fit," she told the court, "that I do not know all hee dead or how Long hee Stayed."

About daylight Mary's mother knocked on the door. White answered. "Your Daughter would not Lett me come away," he explained. "She was afraid of the Indians."

Goody Muggeridge worried. Mary had given birth to an illegitimate child before she married Jenkins as his third wife. She urged her daughter not to tell her husband of White's visit. Knowing he "did not allow of any man to Be att their house affter it was Night," she was afraid he would "Go Neare to Kill her." Mary decided upon half-truth. When Jenkins returned, she told him that "The Tinker Lay att there house the Night before," but that Goody Pope also lay there, that White had refused the women's offer to give up the bed, that he had slept on chairs, and that he was "an honest and civil man." At a neighbor's house next day Jenkins casually engaged Sarah Pope in conversation and found she had not slept with his wife. When Goody Muggeridge came to the house later, she found her daughter sitting under a tree. She refused to go inside, saying "she wished her selfe Dead her husband had soe Kikt her and hurt her."[34]

DESPITE DIFFERENCES in circumstances, in place, and in time, the three stories illustrate common themes. In each case a woman advertently or inadvertently encouraged her aggressor. In each case she found herself unable to complain. Her fears were complex. There was the danger of beating but also the larger threat of disrupting the hierarchy of relations in which she found herself. Behind that was a deep sense of complicity in the crime.

The stories are grim in the telling, but they do not end here. When Jane Bond broke her silence, she found she was not alone. The record does not explain exactly how Robert Collins came to trial. In the formal record male witnesses predominate, as was frequently the case, but the triggering event seems to have been that first tentative confession to Mary Tappe. When questioned, six-year-old Henry Bond revealed that "fat Robert" was the man who had been with his mother. Once word was out, Henry Norton, who lived in the house next door, remembered hearing a strange sound in the night. Robert Knight thought that he had heard one too. Goody Knight was sure she had seen someone go by the house early in the morning; she thought it was Robert Collins. Pleading "not guilty," Collins was tried by jury, acquitted of the "forcement," which might have brought death, but sentenced to the extremely harsh punishment of "forty stripes but one," the maximum corporal punishment ever administered in New England. In addition he was fined £10, half to go "to the cuntrey," half to Nicholas Bond.[35]

The role of neighborhood women is even more prominent in the case of Elizabeth Goodell. Bit by bit, she too began to talk—to her sister, to her husband, and to trusted friends. Their advice was mixed. Some suggested a private hearing, some a formal complaint. Elizabeth went "down to towne to acquaint Major Hathorne with it but was discouraged by others and being foolish & not acquainted with the law, did forbear." While she hesitated, the scandal quickly and inexorably "spread abroad." Within a few weeks the magistrates were summoning her. Thus, without filing a formal complaint and perhaps without quite consciously meaning to do so, she had brought John Smith to court. She told the magistrates she was sorry about the gossip. She repented of speaking "foolishly vainly or slitely of such matters" and acknowledged it "a dishonor to the Sect of women," but she could not "wrong the truth." She hoped her brother-in-law would not "suffer more than he hath deserved." The court sentenced him to be whipped on the next lecture day.[36]

The outcome of the third case was quite different. Although Mary Jenkins finally convinced her husband that John White had forced her, she could not convince the court. Her first mistake seems to have been in violating the trust of the female community by lying about the presence of Sarah Pope on the fateful night. When the story became known, Mary Rice and Sarah Keene went to Mary and pressed her for details. They later reported the entire conversation to the magistrates. In examination Goody Keene had been as relentless as any state prosecutor. She focused upon the "fit" which Mary had described in her complaint. "Were you sencable when the Tinker was in the vary act?" she asked.

"No," Mary replied. But she insisted that "By what he said and the Circumstances affter ward" she knew that he had raped her.

Keene admonished her for attempting to take away a man's life without better proof than her thoughts. "Did hee Ly with you after you where in your fitte?"

Mary said, "No."

"Then . . . he Never Lay with you atole," Keene answered. "For you said hee did not Ly with you before your fitte Nor after your fitte and in your fitte you whare not Sencebel hee laid with you." Mary Jenkins and John White were *both* sentenced to fifteen stripes at the post.[37]

In each case the role which the neighbor women performed was traditional. In New England, however, this role had been reinforced and strengthened by the involvement of the county courts. This is why the position of young women like Mary Rolfe cannot be understood without examining the position of older women like Mary Bishop. Older women derived their authority both from their established position in the community and from gender. They not only understood enticement, they also knew its consequences—as no magistrate could. Proved in life, they were capable of recognizing and of judging sin. Experience—not innocence—was the supreme female virtue in rural New England.

This chapter began by considering history as drama. It is perhaps appropriate that it should end by examining fiction as history. The eighteenth century has often been considered a pivotal point in the transformation from external to internal controls of sexual behavior. By the end of the seventeenth century in New England the authority of the county courts to enforce morality had already begun to slip. Fines replaced whippings, and convictions failed to keep pace with the growth in deviant behavior. Although churches continued to demand confession for fornication from members, their jurisdiction was narrow. At mid-century, family government was also under strain as parents lost the ability to control the timing of marriage for their children. The last years of the eighteenth century and the first years of the nineteenth saw the creation of a system of repression based upon internalized guilt.[38]

At the heart of the so-called "Victorian morality" which replaced the old "Puritan repression" was an altered concept of female sexuality. Man continued carnal, sensual, and devilish, but Woman assumed an active role as purifier of society. Female chastity became the touchstone of public virtue, purity the radiant light of the home. One of the most potent emblems of this transformation, as many historians have recognized, was Samuel Richardson's novel *Pamela*. Richardson took an old theme, the seduction of a maidservant by her master, and created an epic of middle-class morality. By resisting the increasingly frantic advances of Mr. B, the lovely Pamela won his admiration as well as his love.

Critics continue to argue over the meaning of the story. Was Pamela really as innocent and as artless as she appeared, or was she simply a shrewd bargainer who knew how to play her virtue as the ultimate trump, refusing to become a mistress until she had become a bride? Esther Burr (the daughter of Jonathan Edwards) didn't like the novel. She couldn't understand how a virtuous woman could marry her oppressor, a man who had not only kidnapped her but attempted to rape her as well.[39] Most modern readers probably share Burr's perception. In the eighteenth century, however, *Pamela* was wildly popular, especially among readers of an emerging middle class. It represented problems and solutions which they could understand and share. Keith Thomas may be right in suggesting that one consequence of the elevation of female chastity was the "total desexualization of women," and in arguing that Richardson exemplified this phenomenon in his creation of an idealized heroine who was "delicate, insipid, fainting at the first sexual advance, and utterly devoid of feeling towards her admirer until the marriage knot was tied."[40]

Such an analysis reads backward toward *Pamela* from the nineteenth century. The novel takes on a different significance, however, if we read forward from the seventeenth-century folk world which we have described. Significantly, the three main characters in the long Lincolnshire section of Richardson's novel, like the three main characters in the Rolfe-Greenland story, are a young woman, an old woman, and an aggressive male.

The climactic struggle of the novel is between Pamela and her "rough-natur'd Governess," Mrs. Jewkes, the old housekeeper who has been paid to watch over Pamela after she has been kidnapped and eventually to deliver her up to the lecherous master. As Robert Erickson has shown, Richardson drew upon the rich lore of English midwifery and witchcraft in creating the character of Mrs. Jewkes, playing upon the role of the old wife as a woman who mediated at the mysteries of creation and of death, and who, in traditional society as well as in literature, was capable of expanding "into a figure of great autonomous power."[41] In that final fateful scene in Lincolnshire, Mrs. Jewkes and Mr. B both stand over a prostrate Pamela, whose virtuous fainting has ironically vanquished them both.

When this scene is set against the real-life dramas from northern New England, its meaning becomes startlingly clear. Pamela's triumph was not in retaining her virtue but in seizing responsibility for her own behavior. Facing the tempter, she was not beguiled. If chastity was property in Richardson's novel, it belonged to the heroine, not to her father or to any other man. Using her own assets, Pamela won the title of wife. But victory over the sensual advances of Mr. B was achieved only by overcoming the governance of Mrs. Jewkes, who had failed in her role as protector. It is as though Richardson were saying that the lore of the old wife was insufficient to protect a young woman in the changing world of the eighteenth century. Bereft of parents and of guardians, she must acquire a new world of values, breaking out of the ancient community of women into the sequestered paradise of an idealized marriage.

Chapter Six

CONSORT

From the time of Paul, Christian writers have used the story of Eden to justify a wide range of attitudes toward women. A Dominican theologian, referring to Genesis 2:21, said that because Eve was taken from Adam's side when he was asleep, women's moral capacity was obviously inferior to men's. In contrast, celebrants of the Virgin seized upon God's promise in Genesis 3:15 that the seed of the woman would eventually bruise the heel of the serpent. Protestant reformers tended to reject both extremes. Woman was neither a temptress nor a goddess, but a wife. For them the crucial scripture was Genesis 2:18, "And the Lord God said, It is not good that the man should be alone; I will make him an help meet for him."[1]

Historians continue to argue over the significance of this domesticated Eve. Certainly Protestant attacks upon monasticism did much to counter the old charge of pollution. "Women are creatures without which there is no comfortable Living for man," exclaimed New Hampshire's John Cotton in a sermon entitled *A Meet Help*. Cotton insisted that only blasphemers "despise and decry them, and call them a necessary Evil, for they are a necessary Good; such as it was not good that man should be without."[2] Yet the very language of the argument shows its limitations. Protestantism destroyed convents as well as monasteries, giving every woman only one choice in life, to provide a "comfortable Living for man."

Since that is what most women have always done, the practical significance of the problem may be limited. In theological terms, however, there is more to be said. Though the word *meet* in Genesis 2:18 is often corrupted to *mate*, as in the folk term *helpmate*, it is an adjective, not a noun. Eve was to be a help *fitted* to Adam. Now, the crucial question is what constituted this fitness? Was it simply her sexual nature? Obviously, in biological terms Eve was the completing half of Adam. But she was more than that. As William Secker explained it, God made Eve a "parallel line drawn equal" to Adam, taken not from the head "to claim Superiority, but out of the side to be content with equality."[3] The word *equality* is in Calvin's own commentary on this passage. Eve's meetness lay not just in her ability to provide progeny but in "an affinity of nature." Like Adam, she was created in the image of God.[4]

Most ministers, like Calvin himself, carefully distinguished between spiritual and civil equality. Reformed Protestantism combined a radical theology with a conservative social system, simultaneously releasing and containing two powerful sources of female power. Eve's sexual nature was a "necessary Good," but must be restrained by marriage; her spiritual equality was ordained of God, but could not be allowed to disrupt a civil order of "external connexions and social propriety" in which females were subject to males.[5] In Christianity, sexuality and spirituality had always been in tension. In early New England, at the highest level of self-conscious culture, these two values were uneasily linked in the consort's role.

"A WOMAN OUGHT TO BE a meet help for a man," Faith Black's neighbors told an Essex County Court. Despite the scriptural allusion, they were not thinking of theology but of practical matters. Faith had gadded about, neglecting her wash and forgetting to feed her swine. What was worse, she was too friendly with John How. Yet there were extenuating circumstances. Daniel Black was a violent man, given to fits of rage and jealousy. On one cold day he had sent his wife to the field for a scythe even though she was ill. The magistrates resolved the problem by putting both in the stocks for an hour, then telling them to go home and live peaceably.[6] The civil law demanded obedience from a wife and kindness from a husband—no more than was to be expected in any relation of unequals.

The Christian ideal required more. Certainly a woman was to obey—to do the wash, to go to the field if necessary, to do whatever else her husband required. The great God decreed it. But the subjection of wife to husband was never to be confused with the subjection of child to parent or of servant to master. "The submission here required," wrote Samuel Willard, "is not to be measured by the Notation or import of the Word itself, but by the Quality of the Relation to which it is applied."[7] Reciprocal affection transformed commands into helpfulness and obedience into support, creating consort from discord, harmony from difference.

Over and over again New Englanders heard the love of man and wife compared to the bond between Christ and the Church. Although the analogy obviously ratified the authority of men over women, ministers seldom explored this implication, preferring to draw upon the emotional dimension of marriage to personalize the believer's relationship with Christ. Such a comparison idealized the spiritual oneness of husband and wife. In some sermons it elevated the physical oneness as well. The converted Christian was safe in the arms of a "Head, and Husband, and Saviour," wrote John Allin.[8] Cotton Mather pushed the image even further in a sermon based upon John 14:20, "At that day ye shall know that I am in my Father, and ye in me, and I in you." The covenant of grace, he explained, "appears under the Character of a Marriage, because from this Time, there is an Union, and not only a Legal Union, but also a Vital Union, between the Redeemer and the Believer."[9]

In such sermons ministers were not advancing new ideas about the relation of husbands and wives; they were drawing upon familiar human experiences to help their listeners understand a difficult religious concept. An audience which did not in some sense idealize the marital relation would not have grasped the metaphor.

Within marriage, sexual attraction promoted consort; outside marriage, it led to heinous sins. For this reason female modesty was essential. A good wife was to be physically attractive (the Reverend John Pike of Dover referred to his wife as "the desire of mine eyes"), but she was not to expose her beauty to every eye. At

The frontispiece from Thomas Firmin's *Proposals for the imployment of the poor*, London, 1681, portrays a goodwife at her flax wheel. Note the verse from Proverbs.

Courtesy Folger Shakespeare Library

In seventeenth-century ...sachusetts, an ordinary woman ...ht have been fined for wearing ...ilk hood like this one. As the ...n's clothing shows, bowknots ...lace were badges of class, not ...der. From "a scarce print by ...arshall" in Joseph Strutt, *A ...mplete view of the dress and ...bits of the people of England*, London, 1799.

...urtesy Special Collections, Dimond ...rary, University of New Hampshire

Title page to Anne Bradstreet's *The Tenth Muse*. For Puritan writers of either sex, anonymity was a virtue, though it was especially appropriate for women. "I am obnoxious to each carping tongue/ Who says my hand a needle better fits," Bradstreet wrote.

Courtesy Collection of American Literature, Beinecke Rare Book and Manuscript Library, Yale University

Sampler, c. 1665–1670, by Mary Hollingsworth of Salem. Although embroidery was a more common expression of gentility than poetry, few women left either behind them.

Courtesy Essex Institute, Salem, Massachusetts

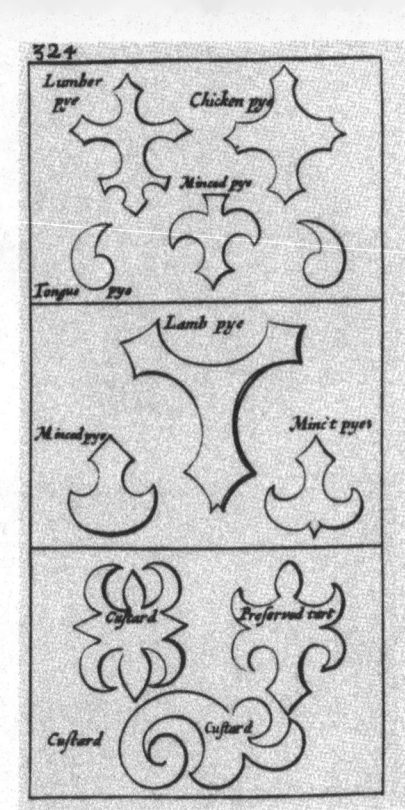

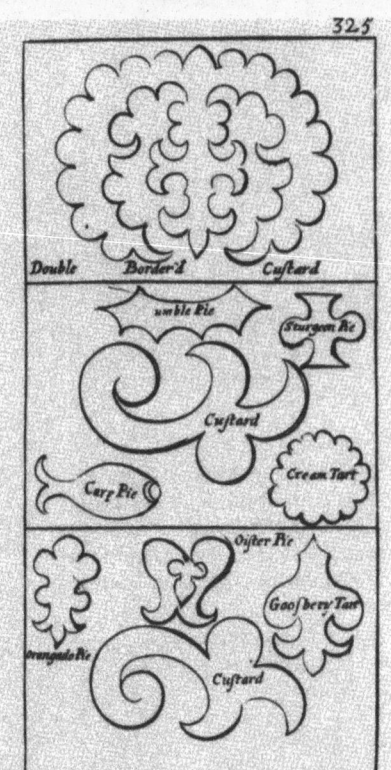

Most female art was as perishable as these pie crust vents from a seventeenth-century English cookbook.

Courtesy Bodleian Library, Oxford University (Douce P 412)

This pocket was pieced together from small scraps of fabric and then embroidered, demonstrating the thrift as well as the skill of its unknown maker.

Courtesy Strawbery Banke, Portsmouth, New Hampshire

"With half-pin'd gown, unbuckled shoe,/ I haste to milk my lowing cow." Ruth Belknap satirized the pastoral ideal as portrayed in this needlework chair seat, Boston, c. 1745–1765.

Courtesy The Henry Francis du Pont Winterthur Museum

Margaret Prince of Gloucester, though pregnant, carried clay from the harbor to daub her unfinished house. The wattle-and-daub wall fill in the contemporary Giddings-Burnham House, Ipswich c. 1680, is shown by a vertical cut in the exterior clapboards.

Photo David McLaren Hart

Mary Rolfe and Henry Greenland ate corn porridge called "samp" out of one bowl and with one spoon. This wooden scoop and samp bowl are from late-seventeenth-century New Hampshire.

Courtesy Woodman Institute, Dover, New Hampshire. Photo Yvette Croteau

This flatiron was found on the site of the Otis Garrison in Dover, New Hampshire. Perhaps it was used by Grizel Otis before her unexpected journey to Canada.

Courtesy Woodman Institute. Photo Yvette Croteau

In northern New England, more women used hoes than spinning wheels. Gardening was a necessity for housewives, and field work always a possibility for deputy husbands.

Courtesty Woodman Institute. Photo Wm. Pride Kelly

In this exquisite needlework panel by Mary Dodge Burnham, handsome gentleme[n] pay court to lovely ladies in a fanciful garden. Newburyport, c. 1725–1760.

Courtesy The Henry Francis du Pont Winterthur Museum

In a less skillful piece by Mary Sa[rah] Titcomb, the gentleman is Adam a[nd] the lady is Eve, though it is somew[hat] difficult to tell them apart! Newbury, c. 1760.

Courtesy Wadsworth Atheneum, Hartfo[rd] Connecticut

Crewelwork bedhangings attribute[d to] Mary Bulman of York, Maine, c. 1[...] unite evangelical piety with the l[ush] imagery of eighteenth-century domesticity. The poem around t[he] valance is by Isaac Watts.

Courtesy Old Gaol Museum, York, Ma[ine]

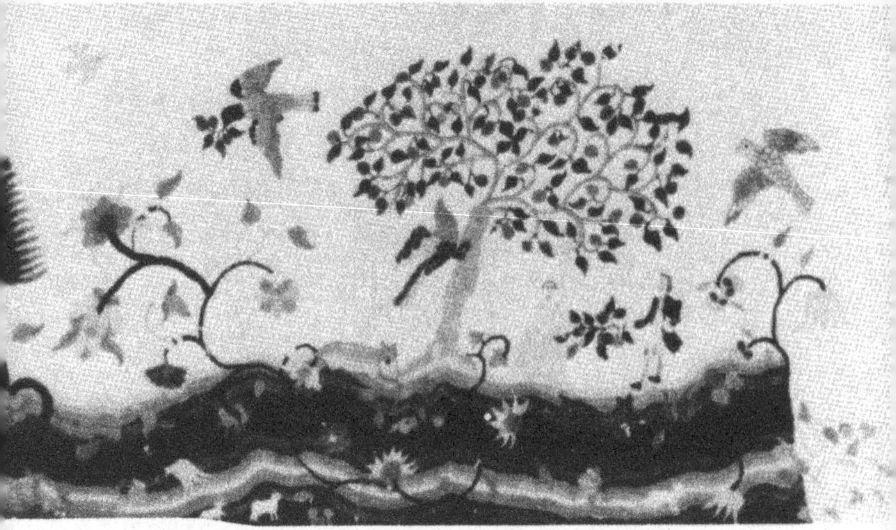

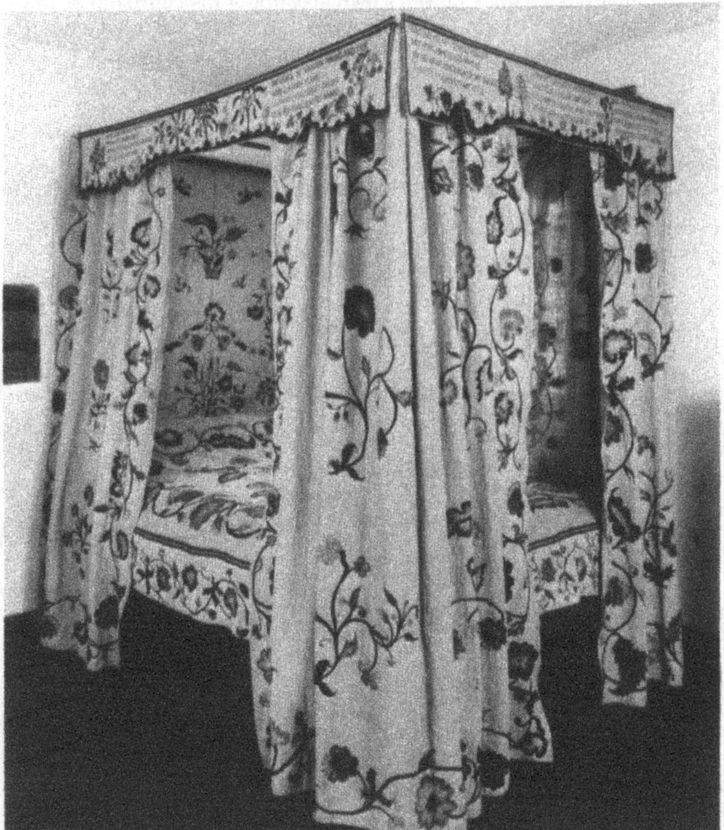

This drawing illustrates Ashley Bowen's own account of his courtship of Dorothy Chadwick. "Will thee Consent to be my bride," he asks. "Sir, I have not that Desirde," she answers.

Courtesy Marblehead Historical Society. Photo Peabody Museum of Salem

John Greenwood's portraits of Catherine and John Moffatt of Portsmouth, c. 1745, reflect an old notion of husband and wife as "yokefellows." Mistress Moffatt's cap and her book by Isaac Watts connote piety.

Courtesy The Society of Colonial Dames of America in New Hampshire. Photo the Currier Gallery; Frank Kelly, photographer

John Smibert's portraits of Elizabeth and Daniel Oliver of Boston, c. 1730, illustrate a more common mode. Though then fifty-one years old and renowned for her wisdom, Mistress Oliver was painted in the garb of her youth. Mary Hurst Pepperrell was educated in the Oliver home.

Courtesy the Oliver family. Photo the Frick Art Reference Library

Flowing tresses and a low-cut gown were the usual emblems of genteel beauty in the eighteenth century, as in this painting of Mary Pepperrell attributed to John Smibert, 1735.

Courtesy Mrs. Arthur L. Shipman, Jr. Photo the Frick Art Reference Library

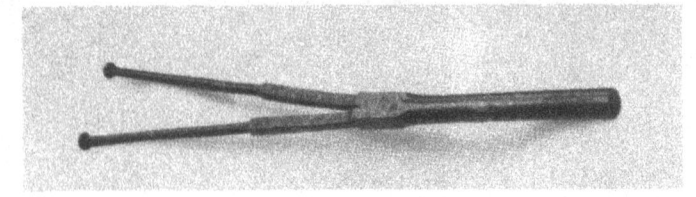

Flowing tresses required a curling iron. This one is from eighteenth-century New Hampshire.

Courtesy Woodman Institute. Photo Yvette Croteau

Detail of mantelpiece.

The mantelpiece in the council chamber of Governor Benning Wentworth's house in Portsmouth draws upon familiar imagery. It was carved about 1750 from a pattern-book design by Inigo Jones.

Courtesy Wentworth-Coolidge Mansion, Portsmouth, New Hampshire. Photo Yvette Croteau

John Greenwood's portrait of
Abigail Gerrish and her
grandmother Abigail Gerrish, c.
1750, beautifully portrays the
theme of perpetuity in New
England culture. The full glory
of motherhood came in old age
when a woman might see her
children's children.

Courtesy Essex Institute, Salem, Massachusetts

Hannah Grafton kept her baby's go-cart in an upstairs chamber
near her spinning wheel. This picture of a go-cart in action, from
an early children's book, appears in Alice Morse Earle,
Child Life in Colonial Days, 1899.

A NARRATIVE,

OF THE

CAPTIVITY,

Sufferings and *Removes,*

OF MRS.

Mary Rowlandson,

Who was taken Prisoner by the Indians, with several others, and treated in the most barbarous and cruel manner by those vile Savages. With many other remarkable events during her travels.

Written by her own Hand, for her private Use, and now made Public, at the earnest Desire of some Friends, and for the benefit of the afflicted.

HAVERHILL, *(New-Hampshire)* PRINTED and SOLD, by NATHANIEL COVERLY and SON, near the Court-House. [Price One Shilling.]
GREAT ALLOWANCE BY THE GROSS OR DOZEN.

Mary Rowlandson's captivity narrative, first published in 1682, was reprinted eleven times in the eighteenth century. This edition appeared in New Hampshire in 1796.

Courtesy Special Collections, Dimond Library, University of New Hampshire

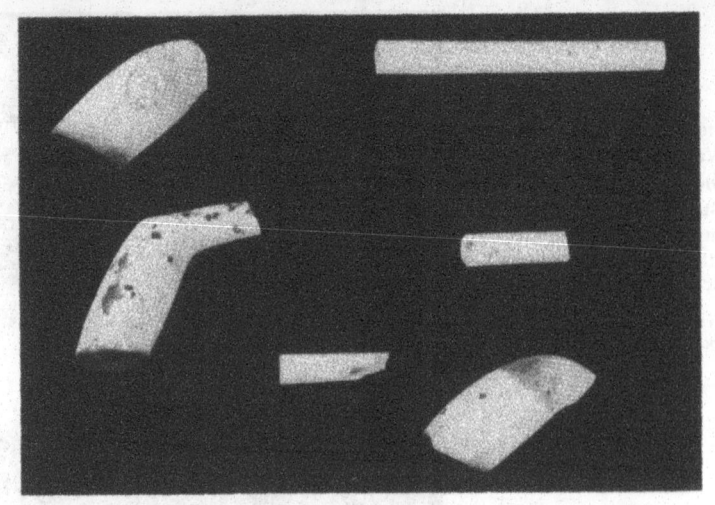

In captivity, Rowlandson gave up smoking, "though formerly when I had taken two or three pipes, I was presently ready for another." These clay pipe fragments, c. 1650–1710, were excavated at the Old Parsonage, Newington, New Hampshire

Courtesy Archaeological Research Services, University of New Hampshire. Photo Wm. Pride Kelly

This plan of Montreal published in London in 1760 shows the hospital and convent which nurtured the New England captives.

Courtesy McCord Museum, McGill University, Montreal

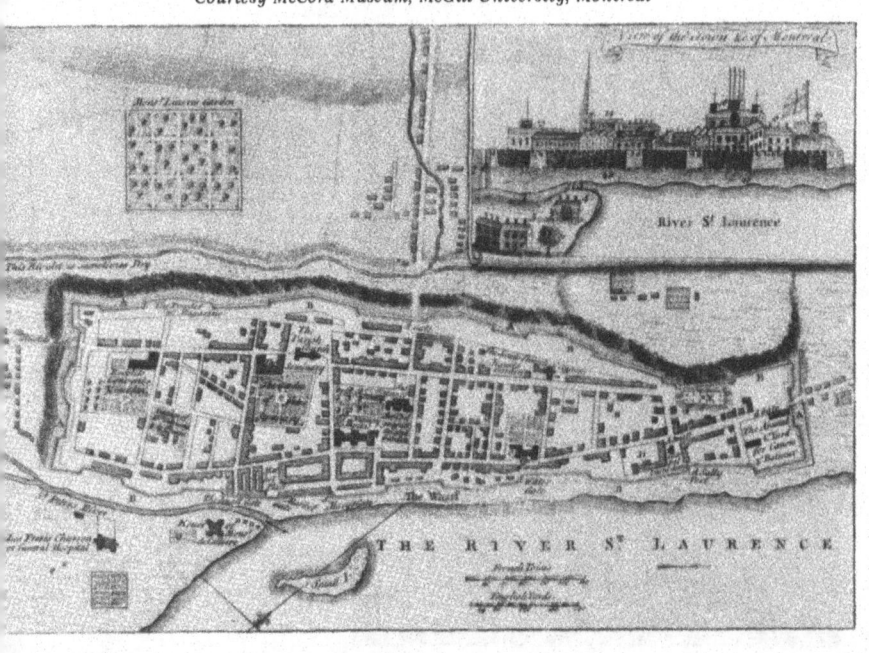

Esther Wheelwright, captured in Wells, Maine, in 1703, later became superior of the Ursuline convent in Quebec. She corresponded with her mother and in 1761 sent her this portrait.

Courtesy Massachusetts Historical Society. Photo George Cushing

This illustration of "Siamese twins" from the 1806 New England edition of *Aristotle's Masterpiece* shows persistence of seventeenth-century notions. The caption reads: "Nature to us sometimes does Monsters show,/ That we by them may our own mercies know;/ And ther by sin's deformity may see/ Than which there's nothing can more monstrous be."

Courtesy The American Antiquarian Society

Joseph Green, minister at Salem Village, died young, his "breasts full of milk." Because breasts signified the milk of the Gospel, breastlike gourds might appear on the gravestones of either men or women. Mary Cutler's stone by Joseph Lamson of Charlestown is a particularly beautiful example of this motif, though similar images can be found in coastal burying grounds as far north as Portsmouth, New Hampshire.

Photo Daniel Farber

"Soul effigies," typical of northern New England carvers, symbolized hope of the Resurrection. A stone for Alice Hart of Ipswich, carved about 1700, uses birds to signify the soul's flight to God, much as Anne Bradstreet did in her poem for her children.

Photo David Watters

Lydia White's stone, Haverhill 1732, contrasts the dead body, represented by the two tablets of the Law, with rosettes symbolizing the Resurrection.

Photo David Watters

Keys symbolized the authority of a housewife over the internal economy of the family. This rust-encrusted key was found on the site of the Otis Garrison, Dover, New Hampshire.

Woodman Institute. Photo Yvette Croteau

Hannah Duston and her daughters, like many other women of their time and place, could not sign their names. These "marks" are from the Essex County probate records.

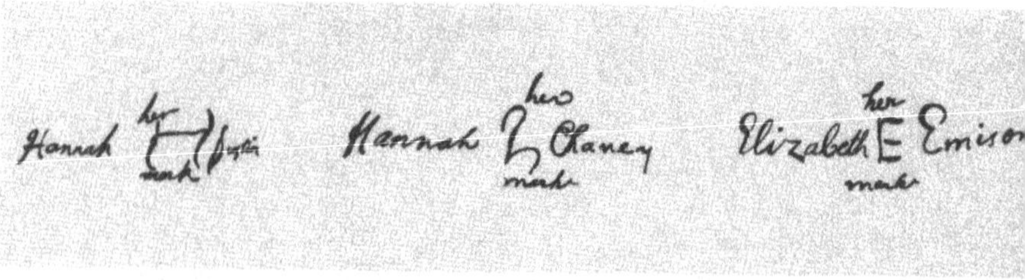

her death in 1681 Mary Mansfield of Salem had five "neckcloths" to tuck into the bosom of her "sad colored gown" and eleven caps and coifs to cover her hair.[10] A bared head was as immodest as a bared bosom. "For if the woman be not covered, let her also be shorn," the apostle Paul had written.

Nor was love within marriage without its dangers. To place too great an emphasis upon the emotional dimension of the relationship was almost as bad as ignoring it altogether. Husband and wife could never forget that they were wedded to Christ before they were joined to each other.

"Ms Mechison tells me often she fears that I love you more than god," Mehitable Parkman wrote to her husband, Deliverance, as he prepared to sail out from Salem harbor in June of 1683. Mehitable was worried about her husband's health (he had not felt well when he left home), and she was anxious about the dangers of "the sea & enimys," but she was also concerned about her neighbor's remark. It put her "in mind of that cripptr [scripture] he that loves father or mother more than me is not worthee of me." She closed her little missive with a prayer, "oh my Dear pray that we might live more by faith on jesus Christ that soe we may be prepared for a better life," then handed the messenger a more tangible token of her devotion. "I sent you a bucket of the bust sucrye of strabyrs by Mr Bedel I beeg your exceptance of my love thear in."[11]

Affection, piety, and a bucket of strawberry preserves! Mehitable Parkman's letter summarizes the Puritan doctrine of marriage as well as any sermon. It also shows the social context in which such doctrines thrived. If a young wife faltered, there was usually an old wife to remind her of her duty. Mistress Mechison may have been thinking of the dangers of the sea as much as of religion when she cautioned Mehitable to moderate her affection. Should Deliverance fail to return, faith would be a stronger support than love.

The role of consort was based on a doctrine of creation which stressed the equality of men and women, an ideal of marriage which transcended legal formulations, and a concept of love which was spiritual, yet fully sexual. But in a fallen world, as even the most idealistic minister knew, marriage might bring discord rather than harmony. "It is most of all to be lamented, when Consorts can not make a Consort, but cease to be Desirable unto one another," Cotton Mather wrote.[12]

In church and in court New Englanders were told that the first remedy for marital conflict was individual reformation and self-control. In cases of severe disruption, however, divorce was at least a possibility. For Puritans marriage was not a sacrament but a civil contract between two individuals, and, like other contracts, it could be broken. In the seventeenth century, county and general courts in Massachusetts dissolved marriages on grounds of adultery, desertion, neglect, and cruelty. Although records are incomplete, women seem to have sued more frequently and more successfully than men. This advantage was lost in the eighteenth century as the governor and council assumed more uniform jurisdiction, but in either century, though rare, divorce was available to both sexes and to all classes, as it had never been in England.[13]

The lives of two of Dorothy Dudley's daughters illustrate the potential for both harmony and discord in marriage. Anne Dudley was married while still in her teens to Simon Bradstreet, her father's assistant in the household of the Earl of Lincoln. When the Dudleys and the Bradstreets moved to New England in 1630, Sarah Dudley was still a child. Eight years later she married Benjamin Keayne, the son of a Boston merchant. Anne Bradstreet's harmonious marriage is known through her poetry; Sarah Keayne's stormy divorce is glimpsed through scattered letters.[14] The two sisters show in radically different ways how spirituality and sexuality combined in the consort's role.

During her early years in New England, Anne Bradstreet wrote three verse epistles addressed "to her Husband, absent upon Publick employment." Though published after her death, these are private poems, love letters in every sense of the term. The first begins with a fervent invocation to the missing spouse.

> *My head, my heart, mine Eyes, my life, nay more,*
> *My joy, my Magazine of earthly store,*
> *If two be one, as surely thou and I,*
> *How stayest thou there, whilst I at Ipswich lye?*

The compounding of epithets in the first couplet builds toward the emotional outburst in the second. How *could* Simon stay away?

The next lines introduce an elaborate astronomical conceit which continues to the end of the poem.

> *I like the earth this season, mourn in black,*
> *My Sun is gone so far in's Zodiack,*
> *Whom whilst I 'joy'd, nor storms, nor frosts I felt,*
> *His warmth such frigid colds did cause to melt.*
> *My chilled limbs now numbed lye forlorn;*
> *Return, return sweet Sol from Capricorn.*

Sexual imagery permeates almost every line. The poet's children become "those fruits which through thy heat I bore"; her breast "the welcome house of him my dearest guest." A closing allusion to Genesis completes the image, returning to the ideal of oneness with which the poem began.

> *Flesh of thy flesh, bone of thy bone,*
> *I here, thou there, yet both but one.*[15]

All three letters can be read as secular poems, yet the surface is misleading. As Rosamund Rosenmeier has demonstrated, the dominant images (the sun in the first two poems, the deer, dove, and fish in the third) are all typological. Bradstreet was not just likening her husband's love to Christ's, she was representing both as one.[16] In such a marriage, sexuality and spirituality were joined in perfect harmony.

In Sarah Keayne's marriage the two elements were in radical disjunction. The first hint of trouble came in a letter written from England in March of 1646. Sarah had accompanied her husband to London and had apparently become intoxicated with the religious enthusiasm released by the Civil War. "My she Cosin Keane is growne a great preacher," Stephen Winthrop wrote his brother. By November Sarah was back in Boston without her husband, being admonished by the First Church for "hir Irregular Prophesying in mixt Assemblies" and for "Refusing ordinarily to heare in the Churches of Christ."[17] The second charge is puzzling. Was she staying away from meeting? Or blatantly ignoring the sermon when she got there?

Soon more troublesome letters would arrive from London. In

March Benjamin Keayne wrote to his father-in-law, Thomas Dudley, declaring his intention never to live with Sarah again. The fault was not his; she had "unwived herself." To his former pastors, John Wilson and John Cotton, he was more explicit. "[I have] hazarded my health & life, to satisfy the unsatiable desire & lust of a wife that in requittal impoysoned my body wth such a running of a reines that would, if not (through mercie) cured, have turned unto the ffrench Pox." Keayne was certain his wife had committed adultery, "For it is cleare & unfallible case that no poyson can be received from the bodie of a woman, but what shee first has received from the infected body of some other." He assured his ministers that he himself was innocent of sexual misadventure, never having given "the due benevolence of a wife" to any other woman in the world.[18]

Unfortunately, we do not have Sarah's side of the story. There must have been some room for doubt, since her father managed to get a divorce through the General Court, though shortly afterward Boston's First Church excommunicated Sarah for failure to answer the earlier charges and for "odious, lewd, & scandalous uncleane behavior with one Nicholas Hart of Taunton, an Excommunicate person."[19] The charge of "unclean behavior" would seem to corroborate Benjamin's accusation, though such evidence must be approached with great caution. Attacks upon religious dissenters frequently included charges of sexual irregularity, as though disruption of one social boundary inevitably entailed the disruption of another. It would be helpful to know what Sarah had been preaching in those mixed assemblies. Puritan authority (both in New England and in Old) was continuously challenged from its own left flank by men and women who turned spirituality into a weapon for attacking the established order. The First Church was still weeding out Anne Hutchinson's supporters when Sarah came as a young bride to Boston; ten years later the memory of Hutchinson's disruptive teaching still colored the church's response to female dissent.[20] But without further evidence we can only speculate. Sarah may have been visionary, or rebellious, or simply unlucky. Married to a man threatened by her ardor, she fell victim to jealousy, gossip, and a nasty virus.

Sarah's ability to get a divorce should not lead us to overestimate that option in early New England. Her father was, after all, a high official in the colony. Even at that, the divorce caused "not a little discourse" among the godly. Sarah lost the custody of her daughter, but she did win the right to remarry. As the wife of an obscure man named Thomas Pacey, she disappeared from the historical record, her life a muted counterpoint to her sister's radiant song.[21]

Sometime in the 1660s Anne Bradstreet composed a long poem inspired, as she said, by an autumn walk along the riverside near her home in Andover. Contrasting the beauty of the natural world with the uncertainties of human existence, she contemplated the trials of Eve, newly banished from Eden.

> *Here sits our Grandame in retired place,*
> *And in her lap, her bloody Cain new born,*
> *The weeping Imp oft looks her in the face,*
> *Bewails his unknown hap, and fate forlorn;*
> *His mother sighs, to think of Paradise,*
> *And how she lost her bliss, to be more wise.*

This is a harsh vision, far less hopeful than the marriage poems, though rooted in the same theology. Bradstreet understood that without Christ even the joys of human existence were in vain. In the closing stanzas she chastened the merry soul who fed upon the sweets of life, unaware of the sorrow to come:

Fond fool, he takes this earth ev'n for heav'ns bower.[22]

THE CENTURY which brought hundreds of English Puritans to New England was also the century in which an English poet nourished in the same tradition built an epic upon the idyllic marriage in Eden. In eighteenth-century New England the preacher's Eve gradually became Milton's Eve, and Milton's Eve, transmogrified by newspaper versifiers and provincial painters, became the apotheosis of genteel womanhood. Milton's concept of marriage derived from the English sermon tradition, but the visual qualities of his poetry nourished visions which Puritan preaching had tended to suppress. Devout New Englanders knew that God created Eve, but through Milton they could see Adam's wounded side with "life blood streaming fresh" miraculously close and heal as the divine hand fashioned the first woman from the severed rib, creating a creature "so lovely fair/That what seemed fair in all the world, seemed now/Mean."[23] Through Milton the "honourable chastity" of the sermon tradition became the naked innocence of the first parents as Eve's swelling breast met Adam's "under the flowing Gold/of her loose tresses." Through the magic of Milton's poetry the scriptural Eden became a tangible Paradise with nectarine fruits and frisking beasts crowned with a nuptial bower where "each beauteous flower,/Iris all hues, roses, and Gessamin/Reared high their flourisht heads."[24]

On the doctrinal level Milton's description of marriage offered nothing new. The *consort* in Milton's Paradise is very much like the *consort* of the sermons, but the infusion of poetic conventions—the transcendent beauty of the woman, the adoration of the man, the elaboration of the complementary virtues of grace and wisdom, softness and valor—shifted the focus ever so subtly from a harmony built upon sameness to a harmony built upon difference.

In August of 1727 the *New England Weekly Journal* published a long poem in praise of *Paradise Lost.* The poet devoted exactly one and one-half lines to "happy Adam" and seventeen and one-half lines to "heav'nly fair, divinely beauteous Eve."[25] Such tributes were standard in eighteenth-century England and America. In a letter to a London friend Hugh Hall confessed he was in search of a wife, then quoted from *Paradise Lost* to counter a popular satire on marriage.[26] Although ministers continued to intone the old themes of redemption, for some New Englanders the focus of happiness seems to have shifted from Heaven to the outskirts of Salem or Portsmouth. A country estate became an emblem of Eden if not a Paradise regained. Asked to compose some lines on visiting the garden retreat of a young Englishwoman, Benjamin Colman of Boston had written:

> *Such Eden's Streams, and Banks, and tow'ring Groves;*
> *Such Eve herself, and such her Muse and Love.*[27]

Not surprisingly, Colman was the first Boston minister to quote *Paradise Lost* from the pulpit.

After 1730 Eve's image became linked with a new cultural form as the pious gentry of Colman's circle—the Pepperrells of Kittery, the Brownes of Salem, the Partridges of Newbury—began to hang locally painted portraits in the spacious entries of their Palladian mansions.[28] In commissioning portraits, prosperous New Englanders were imitating the English gentry, as the "better sort" had always done, validating social position with material objects, with silver snuffboxes, embroidered waistcoats, and carved furniture. But these portraits did more than ratify status; they gave a new importance to gender.

Seen through the portraits, upper-class women in New England were tiny-waisted, full-bosomed, raven-haired creatures suspended in time. The idealized sexuality of the paintings, like the idealized sexuality of Milton's poem, was conventional. The significance is not in the image itself, but in its use. These sex symbols were real women, circumspect and often demonstrably pious matrons, mothers, and mistresses of houses. When he painted Mrs. Charles Apthorp of Boston with an open copy of *Paradise Lost*, Robert Feke explicitly linked the visual and the poetic image.[29]

A few paired portraits from northern New England convey the old sermon image of marriage, the idea of husband and wife as sturdy mates and fellow travelers on the road to salvation. In several of Greenwood's paintings and in a few of Copley's, man and wife appear in solid oneness, elbow to elbow on their separate canvases, white wig echoed by ruffled cap, his solid ledger by her equally solid Bible. These grave couples are unmistakably "yokefellows" in the Puritan tradition.[30] But such portraits are rare. Far more frequently in the eighteenth century wives were transported to a vaporous landscape redolent of innocence and eternal youth.

Lines from a poem by James Bowdoin perfectly describe the portrait image:

> *Now view the maid, the love-inspiring maid,*
> *With virtue and with modesty array'd . . .*
> *See down her neck the charming locks descend;*
> *And, black as jet, in waving ringlets end:*
> *The jetty locks, as down her neck they flow,*
> *The lovely white to great advantage show.*

> *Her tempting breasts the eyes of all command,*
> *And gently rising court the am'rous hand.*
> *Their beauty and proportion strike the eye,*
> *And art's best skill to equal them defy.*[31]

In this milieu such an image was both sexual and respectable. "Tempting breasts" did not make a maiden any less modest, even though with every breath they courted an "am'rous hand."

The emphasis upon bosoms is part of a larger impulse to idealize and to exaggerate the differences between men and women. In painting as in poetry, the focus was on young womanhood, on the moment of flowering. While young husbands often appeared older than they were, wearing white wigs and buttoning elaborate waistcoats over the crescent-shaped profiles common to middle age, quite the opposite was true for their wives. Unless widowed, middle-aged women retained the raven hair and narrow waists of their youth. Elizabeth Oliver, fifty-one-year-old wife of the honorable Daniel Oliver, eulogized at her death for her prudence, dignity, piety, "wise and faithful Counsels and Admonitions," as well as for her wit, was painted by Smibert in 1729 in the pinch-waisted, low-cut gown of a bride, her uncovered locks cascading to her shoulders.[32]

If eighteenth-century paintings idealized sexuality, needlework from the same period idealized domesticity. In pastoral "courting pictures" embroidered by the daughters of wealthy families, gallant gentlemen pay court to fair ladies in imaginary gardens, often within sight of a carefully stitched country mansion. The designs are thematically linked to other panels and samplers which explicitly portrayed Eden, placing Adam and Eve among the same oversized blossoms, fanciful insects, and a leaping deer. Framed, stretched over the seat of a Chippendale chair, or hung from the frame of a sumptuous bed, these laboriously wrought flowers and birds, fish and fruit proclaimed and embellished the private Paradise for which they were created.[33]

Crewel bedhangings attributed to Mary Bulman of York bring together the old piety with the new sensibility in a richly symbolic way. For five years the embroiderer worked, stitch by stitch transforming her conjugal bed into a rosy bower, embellishing side panels, valence, head cloth, and coverlet with leafy garlands, boldly wrought vines, and extravagant blossoms never seen in any garden in York. In this floral Paradise tiny birds fly to ruffled buds twice their size, while heart-shaped strawberries spring to the height of shrubs. Lest anyone mistake the meaning of her art, Mary worked into the valence a poem by Isaac Watts:

> *Sweet muse descend and bless the shade*
> *And bless the evening grove*
> *Business and noise and day are fled*
> *And every care but love.*
>
> *But hence ye wanton young and fair*
> *Mine is a purer flame*
> *No Phillis shall infect the air*
> *with her unhallowed name.*
>
> *Jesus has all my powers possest*
> *My hopes my fears my joys*
> *He the Dear Sovereign of my breast*
> *Shall still command my voice.*[34]

The theme was an old one: the love between man and woman pointed to the higher love between Christ and the converted Christian, but embroidered on linen it was twice removed from the seventeenth-century sermons where it originated. Translated by Watts into the conventional imagery of pastoral courtship, it was carried by Mary Bulman into the tangible Paradise of an eighteenth-century dwelling. This luxurious bed, though dedicated to Jesus, subtly but unmistakably exalted the earthly kingdom of the woman who created it. Both housewife and Bride of Christ, she left a sermon in flat stitch, an epithalamium in worsted.

In 1750 as in 1650, New Englanders acknowledged the multiple aims of marriage: a good wife provided material, spiritual, emotional, and sexual comforts. Within this common framework, however, the balance shifted. Where seventeenth-century preachers found Eve's "meetness," eighteenth-century poets and painters discovered her beauty. Eve became not so much an emblem of spiritual equality as an image of perfected sexuality. At the same time some New Englanders really did begin to take Earth for Heaven's bower.

. . .

BEFORE CONCLUDING THAT these changes in the image of Eve brought corresponding changes to marriage itself, we would do well to consider two basic factors. First, in early New England as in the present, daily life had a way of intruding upon romance. This is perfectly evident in letters which George Corwin, a Salem gentleman, sent to his wife during the months he was absent with the Louisburg expedition. He had ingested some of the conventions of eighteenth-century romance, but he was a very mortal and somewhat temperamental Adam writing to a very busy Eve. Enclosing a £6 bill as a token of his love, Corwin passionately wished it were in his power to make it six thousand. He also hoped Sarah would remember to pin up a notice at Mr. Sparhawk's church begging prayers on his behalf, and to send butter, cider, and "anything that's good to Eat." Later, enclosing a pistole in gold and a piece of eight for each little one, he wished it were in his power to make it ten thousand. Meanwhile where were the shirts she had promised and the new pair of breeches? Had she been to visit Mr. Lynde? How were the children? Many nights he had dreamt that the baby disturbed his sleep, but "alas I wake, & find no such Pleasure." Why hadn't she written? He knew she had been ill, but when a vessel arrived with no message, he could not help but take it hard—"out of sight, & out of mind, which I am very sorry for." Did he detect a note of complaint in her last letter?

> My Dear I always Remember the regard I stand In both as a Husband & father & am Sure I should never have gone upon the Buisness I am now Engaged In had I not been in those Circumstances If you mentioned yt as Reason to Induce me to Return I am sure you might have omitted it, for no one has or Can have a greater Regard to Both Wife & Children than I have & you may Depend That I shall Return as Soon as my Buisness will possibly Admitt off.[35]

Since real marriage existed outside of Eden in a world where cows had to be milked, wars had to be fought, and mothers had to tend to crying babies in the night, an acceptance of romantic conventions might increase rather than decrease marital tensions. Mehitable Parkman felt forced to moderate her expressions of affection; the Corwins seem to have been compelled to elevate theirs, adding to all the problems of separation the need to continually protest their love.

A second factor demands even further emphasis: Except for the poor, livelihood and inheritance were closely tied. Marriage was never just a private contract between a husband and wife, it was an alliance of families and a linchpin in the social structure. Ironically, property considerations became increasingly important in eighteenth-century New England for the very class which first began to romanticize marriage.

The potential for generational conflict in such a situation is beautifully demonstrated in a series of letters between William Pepperrell of Kittery Point and Samuel Waldo of Boston. Andrew Pepperrell and Hannah Waldo became engaged in 1746, though they were never married. Despite the entreaties of friends and the warmest encouragement of both fathers, Andrew kept finding excuses to postpone the wedding. After one exasperating delay, the elder Pepperrell wrote General Waldo, explaining that his son had been busy outfitting a ship for sea. The General retorted, "I should think that could stand in no competition with the grand affair of a settlement for life, which he has been now two years engaged in."[36] Andrew had become a master at passive aggression, neither opposing nor ever quite managing to fulfill his father's dream. In September of 1750, Andrew's brother-in-law Nathaniel Sparhawk wrote him from Boston, "The country, especially the more worthy and better part of it, are very much alarmed at, and appear quite exasperated with your conduct relating to your *amour*.... [W]hat you may imagine will pass still for a justification of your conduct, that you 'intend nothing but honor in the case and will be along soon' is perfectly ridiculed."[37] That Sparhawk could refer to Andrew's engagement as an *amour* underscores the irony. Here was a society in transition, simultaneously committed to patriarchy and to romance.[38]

There is an appealing though unfortunately undocumented tradition that when Andrew Pepperrell finally appeared for his wedding, Hannah Waldo stood up before the assembled guests and refused him. Whether or not it really happened, the story has a kind of truth. In either system of courtship, romantic or negotiated, a woman's power to act on her own behalf was essentially negative. At most, she could reject the offered hand. Because young women have had so much at stake and so little control over the marriage choice, they have been especially susceptible to fantasy, to imaginative projections of what might be. The Salem witchcraft affair began when pubescent girls turned to fortune-telling, dropping the white of an egg in a glass to ask "what trade their sweethearts should be of."[39] Half a century later, servant girls in a Marblehead boarding house managed to slip "a plate, knife, and fork with a blade bone of lamb tied up in a napkin" under the bolster on Ashley Bowen's bed, coyly asking him next morning to tell of his dreams.[40] For upper-class girls, courting pictures were an outlet for similar fantasies. There is a certain irony in the lush imagery of those embroideries. When girls finally acquired their material Eden, they would spend their days weeding its flowers, feeding its animals, and preserving its fruits. But at least a married woman was responsible for her own garden, as no unmarried girl could be.

Disregarding for the moment issues of cultural change, we can see certain constants in the history of courtship. Romance in the larger sense is not so much the product of poetry as of youth. Parents can uphold the economic and/or spiritual values of marriage because they are detached from the emotional and sexual in a way no young person can ever be. Fantasy was not invented in the eighteenth century, nor did ordinary New Englanders have to rely upon sermons or treatises to learn of its dangers. There were sermons enough in daily life. In seventeenth-century Ipswich, for example, there was poor Rachel Clinton, living in a little house by the river, year after year begging the magistrates for help in securing maintenance from her husband, Laurence, a drunkard and ne'er-do-well. She had married for love, offending her relatives and shocking her neighbors by using a small inheritance to buy his freedom when he was indentured to Master Cross. Because her mother and father were dead, she could follow her inclinations. Parents and young women could take heed. No sooner were Laurence and Rachel wed than her troubles began. He squandered her money and kept company with servant girls, and though she petitioned, the magistrates would hear nothing of divorce. (Bitterness would accumulate. Years later she would be tried, though not convicted, as a witch.[41])

Still, affection was not to be trifled with. In the same neighborhood as Rachel Clinton there lived Sarah Woodward, a young woman who consulted her parents, but tried to ignore her feelings. She had been partial to Joseph Lee, a young man of the neighborhood, when a Maine fisherman named William Row sought her hand. Her parents, having a household of daughters to settle, were impressed with his energy and determination. Making inquiries, they found that he had a good reputation at the Isles of Shoals, where he summered, and seemed ambitious to "emprove his estate." Sarah was at first unwilling to accept the match, but time and persuasion had their effect. The pressures were subtle but real. "Sarah, have a care what you do," her mother cautioned. "If you can love him tacke him: and do not say that I perswaded you; its you that must live with him and not I." Sarah's aunt came to counsel with her, urging her to consider carefully, for it was much better to "breacke of now then after wards." Sarah told her she could love Row "well enough."[42]

Not till the banns were published did Sarah muster the courage to oppose her parents. It was too late. When she found a friend to write a letter breaking off the match, her father intervened. Sarah married the man her parents had chosen. Things went well enough, neighbors said, until Joseph Lee began to frequent the house while William was fishing. When Lee joked about Sarah's husband, she defended him—but half seriously. "Why is he not as other men?" she bantered. "If you have bene a sea man as long as hee you would have had wrinkls in your forehead." Eventually Sarah's aversion to her husband became open. Wounded and jealous, William left. Within a few months Sarah was in Essex County Court on trial for her "dalliance" with Lee.[43]

What had happened? Some neighbors thought it was all Lee's fault—that if he had left Sarah alone, she would have been happy enough. William Hubbard, the town's minister, thought otherwise. Since Sarah had lived many years in his house as a maid, he thought he knew more about her than many others. He and his wife had never approved of the match, "foreseeing what has come to pass." As Puritan teaching expressed it, "They that marry where they affect not, will affect where they marry not."[44]

Sarah's mother and her aunt had urged her to consult her feelings. Yet the ability of a daughter to express and perhaps even to recognize her own feelings depended upon the amount of autonomy she had been allowed in growing up. In a deferential society a young woman who had been used to following her parents' direction might have great difficulty in trusting her own judgment, even when invited to think for herself. Sometimes it was better not to try to think at all, but to let things happen as they would. Rebecca Cantlebury of Salem managed to marry the man of her choice by becoming pregnant. Her mother was furious. Months after the wedding she told a neighbor that her son-in-law was a thief and a rogue, a thief because he had stolen "the best flower in her garden" and a rogue because he had "brought her to shame." Rebecca begged her mother to accept the man "that God had appointed" and insisted she was far more contented with him than with those her mother "nominated unto her." The neighbor agreed, urging Goody Cantlebury to forgive and forget. "By the providence of God they were brought together," she said. "There was no finger of God in bringing them together," the mother countered. "It was the mere act of the devil."[45]

There is evidence that premarital pregnancy increased in every decade of the eighteenth century, peaking just before the American revolution. Perhaps the Devil had become more active—or young people less fearful. More probably, external controls of sexual behavior imposed by church, courts, and parents were breaking down, while the new internalized morality which would become characteristic of the nineteenth century had not yet developed. Daniel Scott Smith and Michael S. Hindus have argued that the custom of "bundling"—sleeping or lying in bed together while fully clothed—which created such controversy in the last years of the eighteenth century, was a "compromise between persistent parental control and the pressures of the young to subvert traditional familial authority."[46]

Perhaps. Yet in most accounts bundling is described as a ritualized form of *courtship*. Marriage, not sociability, was the issue. A daughter who wanted to subvert her parents' authority, forcing a marriage against their wishes, could not be stopped by bundling. "Bastards are not at all times got/In feather beds we know," proclaimed an old ballad titled "The Whore on the Snow Crust."[47] Bundling is more logically seen as an attempt to preserve traditional parental *protection* of daughters in a marriage system which increasingly emphasized sexual attraction. The existence of bundling in rural New England in the last years of the eighteenth century suggests that the focus on female sexuality so apparent in upper-class portraits had its counterpart in the village.

Think of the dilemma which faced parents even in the repressive Puritan world of seventeenth-century Ipswich. They could not turn the important decision of marriage entirely over to their daughter (the lesson of Rachel Clinton), nor, on the other hand, could they ignore her feelings (the lesson of Sarah Row). In a less suspicious, more optimistic rural world, bundling might be a perfect solution. Once the choice of a mate had been made on practical grounds, the young folks would have a chance to consult their affection in a controlled setting. If there was little property to settle, bundling made even more sense. According to the songster, it wasn't the custom which mattered, but the girl:

> *Cate Nance and Sue proved just and true,*
>   *Tho' bundling did practise;*
> *But Ruth beguil'd and proved with child,*
>   *Who bundling did dispise.*[48]

Perhaps Kate, Nancy, and Sue were less easily "beguil'd" because, like Pamela, they had learned to use their buxom beauty as a form of capital. But, unlike Pamela, they were still under parental government. A man who met a maid under the "kivers" in her own house (and not in the woods or a haymow) knew he could be held responsible for his behavior.

AN ANONYMOUS COURTING ballad transcribed about 1786 described the first marriage in Eden in much less idyllic terms than ever appeared in sermons or poems, but it came to much the same conclusion—that marriage was ordained by God from the beginning, and that Eve's transgression in no sense detracted from the ability of a good wife to make a man happy.

> *Adam at first was form'd of dust,*
>   *As scripture doth record;*
> *And did receive a wife call'd Eve,*
>   *From his Creator Lord.*
>
> *From Adam's side a crooked bride,*
>   *The Lord was pleas'd to form;*
> *Ordain'd that they in bed might lay*
>   *To keep each other warm.*

To court indeed they had no need,
  She was his wife at first,
And she was made to be his aid,
  Whose origin was dust.

This new made pair full happy were,
  And happy might remain'd,
If his help mate never ate,
  The fruit that was restrain'd.

Tho' Adam's wife destroyed his life,
  In manner that was awful;
Yet marriage now we all allow
  To be both just and lawful....

Since it doth stand each man in hand,
  To happify his life,
I would advise each to be wise,
  And choose a prudent wife.[49]

A consort was indeed a gift of God, ordained to warm a man's bed and "happify his life."

When Ashley Bowen lay down in his bunk at three in the afternoon a hundred leagues from Marblehead, he imagined he saw a woman sitting on his sea chest. He saw her as clearly as if he had been awake; she had five moles on her right cheek and other distinguishing marks. Weeks later he carried a friend's letter to a shoemaker's shop in Andover and found the very woman he had seen on board the sloop *Olive.* He did not know how to express his joy, which he could only compare to the happiness of Christ's mother when she saluted Elizabeth and felt the Babe leap in her womb. Knowing that Providence had led him to his bride, he did not waste any time finding "fair opportunity to examine her real moles and marks with real sweet kisses of real substance of lips and breasts and all the qualifications a young woman could be endowed with to make a man happy."[50] Though Dorothy Chadwick was already being courted by another man, who had given her his mother's earrings and rings, Bowen persisted. Within a year they were married.

Finding the wife of his dreams was probably as much of Eden as any seaman from Marblehead might expect. For Ashley Bowen marriage was the end of the story. For Dorothy it was only the beginning. In the next twelve years she gave birth to six children, including one sturdy little boy who managed to live six months even though he had been born without a palate and could not suck. In the thirteenth year of her marriage she miscarried her seventh child, then grew ill herself and died.[51] God, who gave her a husband, did not provide a bower.

Chapter Seven

TRAVAIL

MODERN WRITERS sometimes state rather glibly that the only difference between the sexes is that women can bear children while men cannot. In the premodern world this simple fact had enormous consequences. Reproduction was the axis of female life. A fortunate bride not only brought into marriage the pots and sheep and kettles provided by her father, but also a set of "childbed linen" inherited from her mother, a mysterious collection of bedding and apparel which was as much ceremonial as practical. The finest childbed linen was embellished with embroidery or lace, like a best petticoat or pillowcase.[1] The rituals of childbirth testified not only to the separateness and the subjection, but to the mysterious power of womankind.

LABOR AND DELIVERY were central events not only for the mother and baby but for the community of women. Depositions in an Essex County case of 1657 reported a dozen women present at a Gloucester birth. A hundred years later Matthew Patten of Bedford, New Hampshire, recorded the names of seven women gathered in the middle of the night when his wife's travail grew "smart." An eighth neighbor arrived in the morning.[2] But Sarah Smith, the wife of the first minister of Portland, Maine, may have set the record for neighborly participation in birth. According to family tradition, all of the married women living in the tiny settlement on Falmouth Neck in June of 1731 were present when she gave birth to her second son.[3]

It would be helpful to know the rules which governed these assemblies. Were there particular tasks assigned according to consanguinity or status? Who, for example, supported the mother in delivery position? Who changed the linen? Did the midwife, the nurse, or the grandmother receive and wash the child? In this same-sex environment, were there procedures to preserve modesty? Could newlywed women or unmarried girls observe the actual process of birth before they experienced it themselves? On such questions the records are silent. Childbirth in early America was almost exclusively in the hands of women, which is another way of saying that its interior history has been lost. Yet in male diaries and in court depositions for the period there are shards of evidence which occasionally allow the historian to penetrate the silence and to make connections with the experience of women in other centuries and with the ragbag of English folk practice preserved in medical-advice books of the period.

In the nineteenth and twentieth centuries childbirth in America became a private ordeal undergone in the antiseptic sanctity of a hospital. The mother's safety—and presumably her dignity—were ensured by the professional anonymity of the attendants. In the past twenty years this medical sanctuary has gradually been undermined. Today the home-birth movement welcomes not only lay midwives but sometimes children, friends, and neighbors as well, making birth the semi-public event which it was in the traditional world.[4] But there is an important difference. In the past the badge of entry was sex. A shared gender identity shaped each detail of the drama of delivery.

For many women, the first stage of labor probably took on something of the character of a party. One of the mother's responsibilities was to provide refreshments for her attendants. The very names *groaning beer* and *groaning cakes* suggest that at least some of this food was consumed during labor itself. Midwifery manuals encouraged the mother to eat light but nourishing foods—broth, poached eggs, or toasted bread in wine—during labor and immediately after birth. They told her to walk about rather than lie down at this stage.[5]

To relieve discomfort, the women used herbs gathered earlier from the field and garden. Most families had a supply of medicinal and culinary herbs; husbands as well as wives might be involved in their preparation. When Nicholas Gilman of Exeter, New Hampshire, went into the woods to gather betony in May of 1740, he was consciously or unconsciously following the instructions of an English midwifery manual of the seventeenth century, which recommended picking the plant "in its prime, which is in May." Mary Gilman may have processed the herb which her husband gathered, crushing it, clarifying the juice, then making it into a syrup with double its weight of sugar. When she went into labor four months later, she was prepared.[6]

Remedies came from the barnyard as well as the forest. When Cotton Mather's wife was suffering in her last illness, she dreamed that a "grave person" appeared to her and told her that the pain in her breast could be relieved by cutting "the warm Wool from a living Sheep" and applying it "warm unto the grieved Pain." She confided the mystical remedy to her physician, who encouraged the family to try it.[7] The remedy which so amazed Mistress Mather's husband was actually an ancient device for relieving labor pain.[8] It had probably existed in oral tradition long before it appeared either in an English medical treatise of the seventeenth century or in Mrs. Mather's dream. She had perhaps heard it talked about, if not seen it used, at a long-since-forgotten birth.

There is symbolic fitness in the use of new-laid eggs. They were not only served to the mother as food but soon after birth were applied externally, first having been stirred over hot embers in an earthen pipkin, then plastered on a dressing.[9] Most of the midwife's supplies were probably as ordinary. Matthew Patten purchased or borrowed butter immediately before each of his wife's deliveries. This may have been coincidental, but probably was not. Fresh butter, with less savory emollients like hog's grease, was used to lubricate the midwife's hands and to anoint the vagina and perineum to facilitate stretching during labor.[10] For the parturient woman, there was comfort as well as reassurance in familiar things.

But an even more important source of aid came from the attendants themselves. Recent studies of the psychology of birth have shown the significance of emotional support during labor. An informed and empathetic coach is an effective analgesic in helping a woman surmount fear and pain.[11] In delivery there was physical as well as emotional intimacy among the women. A mother might give birth held in another woman's lap or leaning against her attendants as she squatted on the low, open-seated "midwife's stool."[12] In cases of extreme difficulty a draught of another mother's milk was considered a sure remedy.[13] The presence in the room of a lactating woman was useful for another reason as well. A friend or neighbor was probably the baby's first nurse, since the mother's own milk (or colostrum) was presumed impure for several days owing to the "commotions" of birth.[14]

Because the attending women would watch the child grow to maturity, they also represented a kind of insurance that nothing would go wrong in delivery that might result in trouble after. A whole collection of superstitions surrounded the handling of the umbilical cord. It must not touch the floor lest the child grow up unable to hold water. It must not be cut too short for a boy, lest he prove "insufficient in encounters with Venus," nor too long for a girl, lest she become immodest.[15] Delivery was characterized by a succession of gender-infused rituals.

Childbearing in seventeenth- and early eighteenth-century New England differed from today's community-centered home birth not only in the exclusion of males and in the intimacy with the natural world, but in the attitude toward suffering. "Natural" birth in the premodern world was presumed to be both painful and dangerous—as God intended.[16] Pious women like Anne Bradstreet of Andover or Sarah Goodhue of Ipswich wrote spiritual testaments as they faced childbirth, just as men of the same class and time signed wills before embarking on a long sea journey or military expedition.[17] A manuscript record kept by John Cotton of Hampton, New Hampshire, and passed on to his son-in-law, Nathaniel Gookin, shows this theme in two generations of Anne Bradstreet's descendants.

Anne Lake Cotton gave birth to nine children in the twenty years between September 1687 and January 1707. Although she lost her first baby two months before the birth of her second, the next five children survived infancy. Then in quick succession she lost three babies at or soon after delivery. The first of these three children was born on Tuesday and died on Saturday before his expected christening on Sunday. "The name design'd was Samuel," his father wrote, "in remembrance of Gods hearing prayers for his mother, who was wonderfully delivered of him after 11 convulsion fits.... God grant his Mercy herein may never be forgotten, tho Samuel be gone to the land of Forgetfullness!"[18]

Mrs. Cotton was apparently suffering from eclampsia, a severe form of toxemia characterized by dangerous elevation of blood pressure. With modern prenatal care this condition seldom develops to the state of convulsions today, but should it do so, the danger is extreme. Although mothers have been known to recover after as many as two hundred "fits," the prognosis for the infant is grim. Even in relatively recent times perinatal mortality has been as high as forty-five percent.[19] Little Samuel's death is not surprising.

Dorothy, the oldest Cotton daughter, was ten years old when the first of three doomed siblings was born. When the last dead fetus was buried in the garden behind the house, she was thirteen. Just four years later she married Nathaniel Gookin and within nine months was delivered of her own first son. By any statistical standard her childbearing record was remarkable. In twenty-three years she gave birth to thirteen children, losing only one premature baby at birth. But she must have carried into her childbearing years the memory of her mother's suffering. Ten of the twelve entries in her husband's handwriting record some variant of the proverbial "long and dangerous travail."

According to the family record, Dorothy Gookin experienced "exceeding hard & Dangerous Travail," "very long Travail," "very sharp (tho' not long) Travail," "hard Travail," "very hard Travail," and "very hard & dangerous travail." With her ninth child she "fell in Travail and was under very Dangerous Circumstances But it pleased God [in] his Great Mercy to Spare her." Despite these recurrent crises, she outlived her husband, who died the very month their last child was born. The thirteenth entry is in the handwriting of their oldest son: "Saturday Aug. 10, 1734 between 9 & 10 in the Morning after a long & dangerous travail My Mother was delivered of a son."[20]

In historical documents the nature of "travail" is almost always a subjective impression reported by women and recorded by men. Childbirth was not only an emblem of the suffering of Eve—it was a moment of supreme drama. One need not diminish in any way the actual suffering of women to recognize that the expected pain and trial were also a source of attention and sympathy. In the drama of childbirth, husbands were twice removed from the scene. Their sex excluded them not only from direct participation but in a very real sense from active support. In the early stages they ran errands, summoning the midwife and getting supplies, but at the height of the crisis their only real calling was to wait. This is apparent in the diary of Nicholas Gilman of Exeter, New Hampshire, who recorded the events surrounding the birth of his fifth child in September of 1740.

> After the Women had been Some time assembled I went out to get a little Briony Water—Upon My return My Wives mother came to me with tears in her Eyes, O, says she, I dont know how it will fare with your poor wife, hinting withal her extreme danger.[21]

Not only the birth itself but the husband's very awareness of the progress of the birth was controlled by the women in the delivery room.

The diary of Matthew Patten, a farmer of Bedford, New Hampshire, is much more matter-of-fact than Gilman's, yet even his laconic entries reveal a similar management of events. "My wife was Delivered Safe of a Daughter precisely at 12 o Clock at noon after abundance of hard Labor and a great deal of Discouragement and fear of Deficulaty," he wrote, adding, "My Wife and the Women were all a great Deal Discouraged."[22] Momentarily at least, childbirth reversed the positions of the sexes, thrusting women into center stage, casting men in supporting roles.

Christ had likened his own death and resurrection to the sorrow and deliverance of a woman whose "time had come."[23] Travail, the curse visited by God upon the daughters of Eve, was not only an emblem of weakness and sin but a means of redemption. Joy permeated the birth record of Mary Cleaveland of Chebacco Parish in Ipswich, who recorded the birth of each child in her own shaky and unformed hand. "[T]he Lord apeard for me and maid me the liveing mother of another liveing Child," she wrote in October of 1751. For her the entry was formulaic. After the birth of her seventh child she wrote, "The Lord was better to me than my fears."[24] So he must have been to more than one woman in northern New England. Bolstered by scriptures and sustained by their sisters, they labored and overcame.

In no other experience in the premodern world were women so completely in control or so firmly bonded. But it would be a mistake to see early American childbirth as entirely independent of male authority. Two men—the minister and the physician—were at least potential intruders into this female milieu. By the end of the eighteenth century, medical involvement in childbirth would be common in cities, foretelling the "modernization" which would eventually banish the midwife. Before 1750 the authority of the women was secure, though there are telling glimpses of what would come in the activities of two northern New England ministers, men who combined scientific and religious authority.

The most dramatic example of ministerial interest in childbirth comes from the period just after the Antinomian controversy in Massachusetts. In the 1640s, when the two chief female dissenters in the colony, Anne Hutchinson and Mary Dyer, both gave birth to "monsters," ministers and public officials were quick to see the judging hand of God. Little wonder that a scientifically curious minister like John Fiske of Wenham would want to examine an "unnatural birth" reported to him. In 1647, in the presence of three women, he performed a partial autopsy on the body of a stillborn infant, a process which he carefully described in his journal, detailing the opening of the skull and the examination of the "brains, fibres, and blood."[25] He decided that the fetus was basically normal but had been damaged in birth. What had brought him to this home? The fears of the mother? The suspicions of the attending women? Or simply neighborhood gossip? In this case the reason for his visit is less important than the authority which he carried. Learning—the formal book-learning which was denied to women—brought him to the home of the mother. His role here was not to officiate at a birth but to interpret it.

Hugh Adams, physician and minister in Durham, New Hampshire, three-quarters of a century later, went further. Adams, an eccentric who was eventually ousted from his parish, wrote a self-serving memoir after his dismissal in which he claimed to have assisted at the birth of Mary Glitten's first child in December of 1724. According to Adams' account, the woman had been in labor three and one-half days when the midwife, Madame Hilton, summoned him. He rode the seven miles to Exeter, carrying both medicine and the authority of Christ. He began with a prayer, pleading the promise of I Timothy "that the woman shall be saved in child bearing." He then gave her "some of the most strong Hysterick medicines to recall and quicken her labour pains; and Dilated the passage of nature with Unguentum Aperitivum meipsum." That failing, he cried unto Christ and then "proceeded by manual operation" to "move the Babe into a capable posture." Within a minute it was born. Having facilitated the child's first birth, Adams then officiated at its second, baptizing it with the name of Benjamin.[26]

It is astonishing to think of the Reverend Mr. Adams, whose obstetrical knowledge consisted of reading a few English treatises, walking into the midwife's house in Exeter and working a medical miracle, especially one which involved complex manipulation of the fetus, a procedure hardly mastered without practice. There is no way of knowing exactly what happened, but it is clear from the minister's own account that he considered his efforts on behalf of Mrs. Glitten one with the other "remarkable providences" described in his memoir. These included calling down the vengeance of the Lord upon the Jesuit missionary Father Rale, as well as protecting his own sons' lives in battle by the ritual blowing of animal horns. Adams believed that melodious psalm-singing (an eighteenth-century innovation opposed by conservatives) was a direct cause of the success of New Hampshire troops against the Indians![27] It is difficult to know whether his mind-set was that of an eighteenth-century man of science or a seventeenth-century wizard. According to his own account, Adams delivered one other baby. Although the mother survived, the child did not.[28]

Two deliveries hardly constitute an obstetrical practice, and we might dismiss Adams' story if it were not so instructive. His success in the case of Mary Glitten can probably be credited to the encouragement of English medical treatises, his own authority as a man of God, a remarkably inflated ego, and luck. But it is also a reminder of the power of the "learned man" in this society. In a moment of extreme peril the traditional experience of the midwife gave way to the book-learning and professional aura of the minister-physician.

In the development of obstetrics in northern New England, Hugh Adams of Durham stands midway between a scientifically curious minister like John Fiske and a professional physician like Edward Augustus Holyoke of Salem, who by 1755 was regularly consulted in cases of "hard labor."[29] The rapid development of forceps in the second half of the eighteenth century gave the physician a technological advantage he had not had before. By 1800 "male science" had diverged dramatically from "female tradition" and midwifery was under strenuous attack.[30]

But the decline of the midwives in the nineteenth century cannot be attributed solely to the development of obstetrical science. It was also a consequence of the undermining of traditional social relations and the increasing privatization of the family.[31] Midwives were "experienced," whereas physicians were "learned." Because the base of the midwives' experience was shared by all women, their authority was communal as well as personal. In attacking the midwives, nineteenth-century physicians were attacking a system more than a profession. The very intensity of their disdain for "old wives' tales" suggests the continuing authority of the women even in this period of dramatic change.[32]

The diary of Mary Holyoke, whose industrious housekeeping we surveyed in Chapter 4, gives some glimpses of childbearing customs in Augustus Holyoke's own family. Holyoke's long interest in obstetrics may have been stimulated by the death of his first wife in childbed. The recurring trauma of his second marriage was not "hard labor," however, but infant death. Mary Holyoke gave birth to twelve children in twenty-two years, only four of whom survived infancy. Her first little Polly lived four years, her second ten months, and her third, christened for her older sisters on the fifth of September 1767, died four days later. Five other infants died in the first weeks or months of life. One after another, the "dear babies" came and went, while Mary continued to garden, write in her journal, sew cravats for the Doctor, and take tea with friends.[33]

She summarized each delivery in the simple phrase "brought to bed," seldom adding any other details. On September 12, 1771, she was "Brought to Bed quite alone 11 A.M. of a Daughter." Was she literally alone in her house, without the assistance of her husband, a maid, or a midwife? Or was she simply implying that no one from outside the family had arrived in time for the birth? For five of the twelve deliveries she did list the names of two or three women who were with her. "Mrs. Jones" was present at four births, "Mrs. Mascarene" (who was Augustus' sister Peggy) at three, and "Mrs. Carwick" at two.[34] No assemblage of the neighborhood is implied here, just an intimate circle of relatives and friends. There are two explicit references to her husband's ministration near the time of birth. Three days before one baby arrived, "the Doctor" bled her. Two months after the birth of another, when she developed a breast infection, he lanced it. Medical assistance did not banish traditional comforts, however. When Mary developed a "knot" in her breast a few days after the birth of her ninth child, "Nurse anointed it with Parsley, wormwood & Camomel Stewed in Butter."[35]

The diary suggests that in urban Salem, as elsewhere in New England, childbirth remained a central event in the community of women. Mary noted in her diary when her friends were "brought to bed," but among these women a formal "sitting up week" seems to have replaced the hasty gathering in the night still characteristic of rural neighborhoods. On March 3 Mary herself "kept chamber" and the next day was "Brought to bed of Peggy." Two weeks later, when she was ready to sit in a chair and chat, the visits began. On Sunday one friend came, on Monday five, on Thursday two, and during the following week eight more.[36] These women sipped tea and admired each other's gifts, including perhaps a fancy pincushion stuck with the baby's initials or the motto "Welcome Little Stranger."[37] The circle of female support had begun to shrink as the intimate ritual of birth gave way to a more distant ceremony of welcome.

FOR MOST WOMEN, life in the childbearing years was less firmly bound by the agricultural seasons than by personal seasons of pregnancy and lactation, twenty-to-thirty-month cycles which stretched from the birth of one baby to the birth of the next. The "travail" of birth was preceded by the "travail" of pregnancy.

Twentieth-century women would recognize some aspects of seventeenth-century prenatal care. Missing from premodern guides to pregnancy was any reference to weight control, but there were remedies for other common problems. For swelling of feet and ankles, *The Experienced Midwife* offered a lotion of vinegar and rosewater; for pressure pain, it suggested an improvised and probably uncomfortable version of a maternity corset, swathing bands looped around the abdomen and tied at the neck. It had little to say about the most famous of female complaints—morning sickness—though it did note that nausea was a possible sign of pregnancy.[38]

Court records suggest that daily life continued with little interruption for pregnancy. At the same time, they make it clear that pregnant women were endowed with a special status entitling them to deference and protection. The case of Sarah Boynton of Haverhill is instructive. She was probably in her fourth month when Ebenezer Browne came to her yard looking for an ox which her husband had locked up. Sarah ordered Browne off their ground, telling him, "If you will come, you must take what comes, for I will do what I can to hinder you." Browne retorted, "If you were a man as you are a woman I would stave out your braines." Not to be intimidated, she thrust a ladder against the door of the hovel where the animal was kept. When Browne grabbed it and threw it down, the uppermost rung struck her.[39]

In March, Sarah Boynton's husband successfully sued for damages, claiming that his wife, being pregnant, had suffered great pain from her injuries, had been unable to do her work for twenty-six weeks, and had required expensive advice from midwives. Although Sarah Boynton clearly felt it her duty to defend her husband's right to the ox, her pregnancy notwithstanding, her frailness became a key point of the damage claim in court. Ebenezer Browne knew he should not strike a woman, yet he did. His taunt, "If you were a man as you are a woman," implied that Sarah had stepped beyond the bounds which he would tolerate in a male, as though in abandoning feminine weakness she had invited attack. The court, in this case, did not agree.

But what were the limits of male protectiveness? And what was the responsibility of the woman herself for her own health and that of her child? Margaret Prince of Gloucester said she "was as lusty as any woman in town" before William Browne began to trouble her, dropping veiled threats, calling her "one of Goodwife

Jackson's imps," and warning her that the formal complaint she had lodged in court would be the dearest day's work she ever made. She had a difficult delivery and her child was stillborn. In her mind the case was clear: Browne was responsible for the death of her child.[40] She probably implied witchcraft, though not necessarily. Midwifery manuals warned newly pregnant women to avoid all unusual worries and anxieties for the good of the child.[41] In attacking the psychological health of the mother, Browne attacked the baby.

Yet two neighbors, Goody and Goodman Kettle, argued in Browne's defense that there were much more apparent reasons for Margaret Prince's troubles. Not three weeks before her travail they had seen her carrying clay to her house in a bucket on her head. What is more, she had "reached up over the door to daub with clay."[42] They were undoubtedly referring to a folk belief (still held by some women in the middle of the twentieth century) that reaching over one's head in the last months of pregnancy would result in a tangled umbilical cord and the possible death of the child. Goody Kettle said that she had walked home with her neighbor and told her "she did wrong in carrying clay at such a time, but Goody Prince replied that she had to, her husband would not, and her house lay open. She had carried three pails and had three more to carry."[43]

Here was a woman caught between two imperatives—to preserve the safety of her unborn child and to finish her house. Perhaps her behavior was a kind of demonstration of desperation, an appeal for help. She apparently got none. Goody Kettle could offer advice, but, without ignoring her own precepts, she could not offer physical assistance because she herself was pregnant.[44] Angry at her husband, Margaret Prince violated folk wisdom, then turned her anguish at the loss of her child toward William Browne, a troublesome and disrespectful neighbor. Although her husband (perhaps experiencing some guilt of his own) concurred in the accusation, the court was not convinced and the Princes lost their suit.

Because such cases are isolated, they admit only tentative impressions. Yet the kind of conflict Margaret Prince and Sarah Boynton exemplify may have been frequent among women of ordinary status and small means. Folk proscriptions on lifting helped to curb what might have become a dangerous workload in this labor-poor society. Yet, regardless of status, a woman could afford to be pampered only in proportion to the number of other persons available to do her work.

For a gentlewoman, like Mary Gilman of Exeter, relatives and servants might prove as much an added burden as a help. In the spring of 1740 the Gilman family included four children ranging in age from eighteen months to eight years. Mary's mother lived with them, as did a teen-aged cousin, Molly Little. Nicholas' parents and several unmarried sisters lived nearby. Despite all this potential help, it is doubtful if Mary Gilman had much time to put up her feet during the last five months of her fifth pregnancy. One after the other, over a two-month period all four children contracted measles, followed by Molly Little herself. Meanwhile Mary's mother was called away to Newbury to the bedside of a dying father, and Nicholas' mother was totally absorbed in nursing one daughter who was dying and another who was chronically ill. Mary herself took a turn watching her sisters-in-law at night. Nicholas was absorbed with his own spiritual and professional problems. Between bouts of headache and toothache he prepared sermons, spending two to three days a week in his new pastorate of Durham, fifteen miles away. Except for one brief entry noting that Mary herself had broken out with a rash, he never mentions her health in the diary. The first evidence of her pregnancy is the announcement of the birth of a son in September.[45]

Through such records we can barely glimpse the routines, shared anxieties, and supporting female lore which characterized the "nine months travail" which preceded the birth of each child.

"DAUGHTER BEGINS to suckle her little Molly; God make her a good nurse," Benjamin Lynde of Salem wrote in his diary four days after the birth of his first grandchild. Lynde reflected a common attitude in New England—nursing one's own children was both a blessing and a duty.[46] An ordinary woman had no choice, of course, since the only alternative was to hire another mother to do it for her. For all classes in northern New England, maternal breast-feeding was the norm.[47]

Mothers nursed in public as well as in private, sitting on the ground outside the village church as well as at home in their own beds—with or without the presence of visitors.[48] Young mothers learned by observation as well as by explicit instruction how to deal with cracked nipples, sleepy infants, and insistent toddlers. They probably also learned a medley of techniques lost to their more fastidious descendants, including the use of puppies to relieve engorged breasts. At some point they discovered that suckling "suppressed the terms."[49] Whether or not they consciously relied upon this ancient method of contraception, they tuned their lives to the natural rhythms of the reproductive cycle.

That those rhythms did indeed shape female life becomes apparent if we look closely at the reproductive histories of three eighteenth-century women as reflected in their husbands' diaries. Although male diarists seldom wrote about their wives, they did consistently record those female activities which disrupted or affected their own. Simply by correlating the two events most consistently mentioned—births and overnight journeys—one can derive circumstantial, though impressive, evidence of the personal meaning of fertility.

The diaries of Zaccheus Collins, Matthew Patten, and Joseph Green cover large portions of the years of childbearing for each of their wives—fifteen out of seventeen years for Mrs. Green, eighteen out of twenty-one years for Mrs. Patten, and twenty out of twenty-two years for Mrs. Collins.[50] The three families were not only prolific but unusually healthy, exemplifying premodern reproductive patterns in an almost ideal form, with birth intervals averaging twenty-two, twenty-three, and twenty-five months. Elizabeth Collins and Elizabeth Patten each gave birth to eleven children. Elizabeth Green was expecting her ninth child at the time of her husband's death.

The diary of Joseph Green begins in 1700, soon after his call to the ministry in Salem Village, now Danvers, Massachusetts. That of Zaccheus Collins, a Quaker farmer of Lynn, Massachusetts, opens in 1725, while that of Matthew Patten, a founder of the Scotch-Irish community of Bedford, New Hampshire, begins in 1754. In comparison to their husbands, all three wives led sheltered and narrow lives, though each traveled—in her own way and according to her own seasons. As might be expected, Elizabeth Collins, the Quaker, traveled most frequently, sometimes accompanying itinerant Friends who were passing through Lynn on their way to nearby meetings. Mrs. Patten, who lived in an isolated and, in its early stages, frontier community, traveled least. Yet the journeys of all three women fall into a remarkably consistent pattern when keyed to their reproductive histories.

For purposes of analysis, the overnight journeys of the three wives can be divided into three periods: a period of "Pregnancy," beginning 280 days before the birth of each child; a period of "Infancy," from birth to ten months; and an "Interim" period, a variable span from ten months after the birth of the last child to 280 days before the birth of the next. (See Table 4.) For all three women, the greatest frequency of travel was in the so-called "Interim" period. For two of the three women, "Infancy" was clearly a more serious restraint than "Pregnancy." To grasp the significance of these rather limited facts, we must look at each period in greater detail.

It is hardly surprising that pregnancy restrained travel. What is surprising is the number of times all three women undertook journeys in the middle trimester. The most adventuresome trip Elizabeth Patten ever took was during the fifth month of her tenth pregnancy when she went by horseback alone the more than eighty miles to Boston to sell cloth and thread. Matthew, who was usually responsible for such ventures, was heavily involved in harvesting at the time.[51] Elizabeth Collins took a number of journeys early in the sixth month of pregnancy. In March of 1731 she spent almost two weeks in Haverhill and Newbury, presumably visiting relatives. In April of 1741 Zaccheus took her and her sister-in-law

Table 4. Incidence of Travel During Pregnancy and Lactation[1]

	Pregnancy	Infancy	Interim	All
Elizabeth Collins	.185	.044	.229	.142
Elizabeth Green	.105	.016	.225	.102
Elizabeth Patten	.11	.071	.266	.129

1. I arrived at the numerical index by dividing the total number of overnight journeys by the total number of months in each stage.

to Boston, returning for them three days later.[52] Elizabeth Green completed two journeys in the seventh month, both of them to nearby Wenham, where her parents lived. Joseph's diary entry for June 8, 1710, is quite explicit about the fact that they shared a horse.[53]

All three women, however, remained close to their homes during the last two months of each pregnancy. This seems to have been true even when unusual circumstances might have impelled them to travel. Late in September of 1755 Elizabeth Patten remained in Bedford while her husband attended her own father's funeral in nearby Londonderry. She was just one month away from the delivery of her fourth child.[54] Pregnancy may have been a "nine month sickness" as the midwifery manual said, but these women were slow to succumb. A more dramatic restraint on travel is apparent in the next period—the first ten months of each baby's life. This is undoubtedly related to lactation, which in many ways placed more demands on the mother than pregnancy. Although a woman might leave her infant for a short while, perhaps relying for an occasional feeding upon a neighbor who was also nursing, she could not travel far or long without taking the child with her. Mrs. Green and Mrs. Patten occasionally traveled with infants (James Patten was baptized in Londonderry, New Hampshire, at the age of seven months while his parents were visiting there).[55] But all three mothers avoided traveling during the third quarter of their child's first year. One reason is obvious. Compared with a newborn infant, a baby seven or eight months old is simply not very portable, being both heavier and more active. If he or she were still dependent upon mother's milk, the only practical solution was to stay home.

But for all three women, the most significant pattern is not the restraint on travel during pregnancy and infancy but the sudden jump in activity after the tenth month of each baby's life. For Elizabeth Collins, this is especially dramatic. For six of the nine babies mentioned in the diary, her first journey after birth was between ten and fifteen months. For the other babies, the second journey after birth fell into this same crucial period. A similar pattern is discernible for Mrs. Green. The timing suggests some connections with weaning, a possibility confirmed in Joseph Green's diary entry for April 12, 1702. Green noted that on this day he took his wife to her parents' home in Wenham, then "came home to wean John," who was then seventeen months old.[56]

There is supporting evidence in less-detailed diaries of the period for the idea of the "weaning journey." From January 1740, when Nicholas Gilman began his daily diary, until late in August of 1741, his wife, Mary, apparently never left Exeter, New Hampshire, where they lived. This period included the last eight months of her fifth pregnancy and the first year of their son Josiah's life. But just before Josiah's first birthday she took an unexplained three-day journey alone to her grandmother's home in Newbury, Massachusetts.[57] There is a similar example in the almanac diary of Edward Holyoke of Salem. In January of 1730 his wife made a two-week visit to her parents' home in Ipswich. Their child was then sixteen months old.[58] The evidence is circumstantial but suggestive.

Supposing New England mothers did leave home to wean their babies, what might this mean? Did maternal absence mean abrupt and traumatic weaning? Was it a manifestation of a repressive and potentially pathological approach to child care? Some historians might argue that it did. Noting the pervasiveness of oral themes and anxieties in the historical record of New England witchcraft, John Demos has speculated that "many New England children were faced with some unspecified but extremely difficult psychic tasks in the first year or so of life."[59] James Axtell has pointed to John Winthrop's simile for his own conversion: "I became as a weaned child. I knew I was worthy of nothing for I knew I could doe nothing for my self."[60] Certainly the sudden disappearance not only of the breast but of the mother herself might present severe difficulties for the infant.

Yet the Winthrop quotation cuts in two directions. It documents the child's sense of loss, but it does so from the parent's point of view. Discounting the unlikely possibility that John Winthrop remembered his own weaning, we find him describing the feelings of the child as he perceived them from the outside. The situation he described may indeed document parental harshness, but the *description* of the situation suggests considerable empathy. Winthrop did not focus upon the behavior of the child, its crying or its demands for its mother, but upon his perception of its interior state, its feeling of helplessness.

Now, the really crucial problem for our purposes is the response of parents to this perceived state. How can parents who understand and sympathize with a child's need deliberately deny it? As the scripture says, "What man is there of you, whom if his son ask bread, will he give him a stone?" Setting aside for the moment unconscious motives, we can say that loving parents will deny a child's need for only two reasons: either they lack the ability to satisfy it or they believe that denial will result in long-term good. In the crisis of weaning, mothers and fathers were obviously in quite different positions because one could supply the demand, one could not. Assuming that in colonial America both parents believed that rather sudden weaning was for the ultimate benefit of the child, the withdrawal of the mother made perfectly good sense.

This would be especially so if the parent who *could* supply the need might be tempted to do so. In the words of an eighteenth-century Maine minister, the converted Christian learned that Christ was "as willing to feed him with his Flesh and Blood; as ever Tender Mother was to draw out her full & aking Breast to her hungry, crying child."[61] Abrupt or sudden weaning would be as painful for the mother as it was difficult for the child. The discomfort would be both physical and psychological, as the mother thwarted both the impulse to relieve her breasts and the desire to nurture her crying child. This denial of the maternal role may well have reduced *her* to the state of psychic helplessness characteristic of a weaned child. Hence her own trip home to mother.

The facts fit together neatly—rather too neatly perhaps. Although there is circumstantial evidence for a more widespread practice, there is only one fully documented example of a "weaning journey" in the diaries under investigation—that of Elizabeth Green, who remained at her parents' home in Wenham in the spring of 1702 while her husband returned home to wean sixteen-month-old John. Even this event can have more than one interpretation. On the one hand, the mother's journey can be seen as a drastic measure, an abrupt and psychologically disturbing end to infancy. On the other hand, at sixteen months little John might already have shown clear independence and a loss of interest in the breast. Nursing may have been confined to one or two brief feedings, perhaps at night or in the early morning when it was easier for the mother to bring him to bed than get up and prepare other food. The journey of the mother may have been simply the ritual termination of an already waning stage, an experience made more pleasant for both mother and child by the active interest and involvement of the father.

Yet disturbing questions remain. If the stage of weaning was not marked with anxiety and potential conflict, why did the mother find it necessary to leave? Was she in fact acting counter to her own instincts? Did Joseph Green's diary entry mark the eventual triumph of a husband over the prolonged, and to him perhaps disturbing, intimacy of mother and child? Or was it that Mrs. Green simply did not trust her own resolve? Did she believe herself incapable of surmounting that "softness," that excessiveness of maternal affection so mistrusted by ministers? Was her dependence on John perhaps an even greater issue than his dependence on her? Little matter, perhaps, for within a few months there would be another infant in the house and the whole cycle would begin again.

PREGNANCY, BIRTH, LACTATION—these three stages in the female reproductive cycle established the parameters of life in the childbearing years. One need not exaggerate their importance or describe women in bondage to the curse of Eve to recognize that these personal seasons might shape the smallest details of daily life—when to lift a heavy wash kettle or daub the chinks of a house, how far to go from home in quest of butter or yarn, whether to travel to Newbury meeting, mount a neighbor's horse for a trip to Boston, or stay at home and brew beer. Each cycle of reproduction was marked by epicycles, recurring patterns of restraint and release, pain and deliverance, sorrow and celebration. All of these were summarized in the word *travail*, a term which connoted not simply pain but *effort*, especially strenuous or self-sacrificing effort.

"O my children all, which in pains and care have cost me dear," Sarah Goodhue began a long passage of advice to her offspring. In *The Four Ages of Man* Anne Bradstreet put a more detailed description of maternal effort into the mouth of a child.

> *With tears into the world I did arrive,*
> *My mother still did waste as I did thrive,*
> *Who yet with love and all alacrity,*
> *Spending, was willing to be spent for me.*

> *With wayward cryes I did disturb her rest,*
> *Who sought still to appease me with the breast:*
> *With weary arms she danc'd and By By sung,*
> *When wretched I ingrate had done the wrong.*[62]

Eve's badge of sorrow might reinforce cultural notions of the weakness or vulnerability of women, but it might also become an instrument of female power. Suffering in childbirth could arouse the sympathy and protective instincts of husbands, but, even more profoundly perhaps, the prolonged sacrifices of pregnancy, birth, and lactation might convince religious children of their mother's claims upon them.

In 1701 Samuel Sewall of Boston stood in tearful elegy beside the grave of his mother, one of the first settlers of Newbury, Massachusetts. "My honoured and beloved Friends and Neighbours!" he exclaimed. "My dear Mother never thought much of doing the most frequent and homely offices of Love for me; and lavish'd away many Thousands of Words upon me, before I could return one word in Answer."[63] Sewall spoke of his mother's piety and her industry, but the focus of emotion for this grown man was clearly his own infancy. Spending herself in childbearing, Mistress Sewall had earned the devotion of her son.

Chapter Eight

MOTHER OF ALL LIVING

PERHAPS THERE IS no significance in the fact that Judith Coffin's monument in the old burying ground in Newbury, Massachusetts, is twice as large as her husband's. Nevertheless it may represent some measure of earthly justice meted out by her descendants. In life Tristram had been honored among men. His epitaph highlights a title and a position:

> To the memory of Tristram Coffin, Esq., who having served the first church of Newbury in the office of a Deacon 20 years died Feb. 4, 1703–4 aged 72 years.
>
> > *On earth he purchased a good degree,*
> > *Great boldness in the faith and liberty,*
> > *And now possesses immortality.*

Judith's eminence had been private. Her epitaph celebrates her sobriety and her piety but, above all, her amazing fecundity:

> To the memory of Mrs. Judith late virtuous wife of Deac. Tristram Coffin, Esqr. who having lived to see 177 of her children and children's children to the 3d generation died Dec. 15, 1705 aged 80.
>
> > *Grave, sober, faithful, fruitfull vine was she,*
> > *A rare example of true piety.*
> > *Widow'd awhile she wayted wisht for rest*
> > *With her dear husband in her Savior's breast.*[1]

The key metaphor in Tristram's verse is economic—"he purchased a good degree." In Judith's it is organic—a "fruitfull vine was she." Property versus reproduction—the two markers etch traditional gender distinctions, but with the order of eminence curiously reversed! Still, though Judith's stone towers over Tristram's, there is no explicit concern for balancing a scale. In honoring the wife, the eulogist quietly but unmistakably honored the husband as well. Judith Coffin lived and died the "virtuous wife of Deac. Tristram Coffin, Esqr."; in widowhood she "wisht for rest/With her dear husband in her Savior's breast." Perhaps the monument did not celebrate a woman so much as it celebrated a concept of family that had not yet become the exclusive preserve of women.

For many New Englanders—male as well as female—the values celebrated on Judith Coffin's stone *were* ascendant. She and Tristram inherited the ancient blessing of Abraham, Isaac, and Jacob, living to see their own seed multiply as the stars. Students of politics, economics, and religion have long known that family bonds played a significant part in the external life of the New England colonies.[2] Less clearly understood have been the balances between external and internal values and between masculine and feminine roles. Precisely where in the tents of Israel stood Rachel, Hannah, and Leah? "Honoured mother"—the phrase rings through letters, diaries, wills, estate accounts, and sermons from seventeenth- and eighteenth-century New England. What does it mean? Beneath the frozen sentiment, what were the social, biological, and cultural realities which shaped the maternal role?

FOR PURPOSES OF ANALYSIS, we might distinguish within any single family a "family of property," a "family of reproduction," and a "family of sentiment." Each of these "families" must be approached in a different way. The Coffin family of property, for example, can be discerned in the will which Tristram signed in May of 1703. A family of reproduction can be sketched through the birth and death records of Judith's 177 children and children's children. A family of sentiment, though more difficult to define, can at least be glimpsed in the names which these children bore. By looking at such materials carefully and by relating them to larger patterns for northern New England, we can better understand the concept of motherhood magnified in that intriguing gravestone in Newbury burying ground.

Like other prudent fathers of his generation, Tristram Coffin "purchased" an earthly as well as a heavenly estate, adding additional parcels of land to his original allotment in order to provide for each of his four surviving sons.[3] At their father's death, all four sons, though grown men, remained economically beholden to their father, and each now received clear title to land which he had probably long been farming. James received part of the homestead plus other plots of land in Newbury. Stephen received "housing and upland and meddows with priviligis of Common Rights" in the neighboring town of Haverhill. Peter was given the deed to a farm in Gloucester. Nathaniel, the youngest, inherited his father's "now dwelling house with my barnes and pastuour land a joyning."

Judith Coffin, like many aged widows in New England, received a comfortable maintenance rather than the traditional "thirds." Nathaniel was to "take spesshall care" of his mother to "provid for har in all Respectes." The other sons were to help, paying their brother a fixed sum annually for their mother's support. As for the daughters, their portions had probably long since been paid, perhaps in sheets, kettles, coverlets, or cattle given at marriage. Tristram gave Mary, Judith, and Lydia small amounts of money and promised Deborah twelve walnut trees. He also made a number of small and perhaps sentimental bequests to grandchildren—including three boys named Tristram.

The pattern is familiar: land for sons, movables for daughters, and for widows a carefully defined dependency. "Families of property" in New England, as elsewhere in the western world, revolved upon the orderly transmittal of wealth and livelihood from father to son.[4]

The Coffin "family of reproduction" was far more complex. When Judith Somerby married Tristram Coffin in March of 1653, she was a widow with three young children: Sarah, who was eight, Elizabeth, who was six, and Daniel, who was not yet three. (Another son had died in infancy.) In the next sixteen years Judith gave birth to ten Coffin children, all of whom survived infancy.[5] There is an almost saucy irony in the family name, as though some wind of Yankee humor had swept Puritan Newbury. Death seldom visited the Coffins.

By the time Judith's last baby was born in March of 1669 she already had six grandchildren. From 1677 until her death in 1705—twenty-eight years—at least one grandchild was born in each year. In the most prolific period, from 1686 to 1696, thirty-eight infants were born, almost four a year. Judith's gravestone should probably be taken literally when it says she lived to *see* 177 descendants, for two of her four surviving sons and five of her six daughters remained in Newbury, while the others clustered in nearby communities. The oldest son, James, lived in a house separated from the family dwelling only by the dairy. If Judith made any effort to assist at these births, to help during lyings-in, to watch in sickness, and to assist with the nurture of her grandchildren, as many women did, there was little lull in her mothering. One can imagine her greeting each infant in turn, examining noses and earlobes, cowlicks or birthmarks, searching for characteristics which identified each child as a Coffin or a Somerby or a Knight. Each year her sight may have grown more dim. Near the end these children may have rocked her in the "grandmother's" cradle which still stands in the old house.[6]

The Coffin family exemplifies premodern reproductive patterns under the most favorable of environmental conditions. John Coffin and his half-brother, Daniel Somerby, were killed in King Philip's War, and Enoch died before reaching his teens, but all of the other children lived to marry. Such a demographic profile was by no means unique in northern New England, especially in the seventeenth century, though it coexisted with, and in some communities was superseded by, more traditional patterns of early death and separation of spouses and children.[7] Families like the Coffins thrived in a world in which impermanence was an expectation if not always a reality.

Patterns of property and of reproduction are more easily discerned than the attitudes and feelings which accompanied them. Yet some hint of the Coffin "family of sentiment" survives in the most accessible of historical records—the names which parents gave their children. Surnames reflect the patriarchal and patrilineal structure of New England families. Given names reveal a more complex and varied world, a landscape marked by more subtle metes and bounds. A full exploration of naming patterns could tell us a great deal about family boundaries in colonial America. Even the briefest excursion substantiates two conclusions. "Families of sentiment" were matrilineal as well as patrilineal, and they were oriented toward the past.

In genealogical records an occasional "Seaborn" testifies to the existence of a new world, but most names link to a long chain of progenitors, with each generation turning toward the one just before. But *chain* is the wrong word to convey the complexity of such bonds. Because names came from both sides in roughly equal proportions, each new family symbolically joined two branching families of origin. The genealogist's metaphor is better. In towns like Newbury the roots and foliage of the old families spread luxuriantly until it was difficult to distinguish kin from neighbor.

Were colonial New Englanders conscious of these extended families? Some of them certainly were. In 1722 Tristram and Judith's nephew Stephen Greenleaf decided to tally the descendants of his maternal grandfather, the first Tristram Coffin, who had come to America in 1642 with his widowed mother, his wife, and his five children. Stephen remembered his great-grandmother Coffin. Perhaps his childhood memories helped to focus his genealogical interest on his mother's rather than his father's family. He counted 1,138 descendants, 570 of them tracing to his mother, Elizabeth, or to his uncle Tristram, the two Coffin children who remained in Newbury.[8] For most people the concept of family was probably less expansive, though there is good evidence that consanguinity played a much wider role in ordinary life than it does today.[9]

Among the 142 grandchildren of Tristram Coffin and his sister Elizabeth Greenleaf, eighty-six percent were named for parents, grandparents, aunts, or uncles.[10] In christening their children, parents fulfilled the Biblical command: "Thou shalt honor thy father and thy mother." Almost as frequently they used a name to restore symbolically some lost part of the immediate family. Both impulses are amply illustrated among the grandchildren of Judith and Tristram.

Deborah Coffin and her youngest sister Mary were married on the same day in 1677. Before the year was out, each had a baby girl named Judith. In marriage they had given up their father's name, becoming submerged in new families of property, but in motherhood each had honored her family of origin. The new little Judiths already had a three-year-old cousin, Judith Sanborn of Hampton. Before their grandmother's death in 1704 there would be seven more namesakes—Judith Pike, Judith Clark, Judith Hale, Judith Little, and three Judith Coffins. There were almost as many Tristrams. All but one of the children named a daughter for their mother and a son for their father. The one exception is significant. Nathaniel, the youngest son, heir to the homestead and custodian of the aged mother, the child most visibly bound to the parents, was the only one who did not pass on their names. Perhaps the honored parents were simply too much with him.

But in naming his first son John and the second Enoch, Nathaniel demonstrated a second naming pattern. Both names belonged to brothers now dead. Nathaniel had been six when Enoch died; he was eight when John went off to the Indian wars. Both deaths, coming after two decades without a loss, must have been deeply felt in the family. Lydia's first son, born in 1680, might have been named George for his paternal grandfather or Moses for his father, the usual practice. Instead he too became John. Twelve days later Deborah gave birth to her first son, named for the same lost uncle. The death of John Coffin might not account for every one of the Johns among the Coffin grandchildren—the name is, after all, a common one—but Enoch's death certainly explains the three children by that name in the family. Among the living brothers the names of Peter and Stephen appear but once and those of James and Nathaniel not at all.

Death was only one of many possible motives for singling out a particular name. Three Coffin children named a daughter for Lydia, but only one for Deborah, though the reason is impossible to determine. Did they prefer one sister to another? Or only her name? Nathaniel's first daughter was named Apphia, a name with a curious history in the family. His wife, Sarah, had a stepsister of that name who was about her age. Sarah married her first husband, Henry Dole, at about the same time that Apphia married Nathaniel's brother Peter Coffin. Perhaps Apphia's removal to Gloucester explains why Sarah named her first daughter for the now distant sister. When Sarah married Nathaniel Coffin, this Apphia was just five years old. Within a year she died. When a Coffin daughter arrived four years later, she too became Apphia, in remembrance of her mother's stepsister and her own.

Parents frequently named one child for another who had died. In March of 1696, for example, Deborah's John died at the age of six. When another boy was born nine months later, he received his brother's (and his uncle's) name. Mary had two Josephs; Stephen had two Tristrams; and Peter as well as Nathaniel had two daughters named Apphia. Such a custom may demonstrate indifference to the individual identity of young children, as some historians have suggested, but it also represents a now forgotten way of transcending death through progeny, of extending and enlarging each family's past through a link to the living present. The custom of naming a child for a dead sibling was part of a larger pattern of remembrance. Almost all New England children, whether named for grandparents, parents, aunts, uncles, or lost brothers or sisters, became carriers of the past. Each family existed in the sum of its parts.

"Families of property" were built upon the transfer of land and livelihood from fathers to sons. Within these families women were secondary and dependent. "Families of reproduction" were determined by biological cycles of birth and death. Although Providence, not individual choice, decreed how many children one would have or how long a marriage would survive, women of necessity stood at the physical center of these families, not only in youth but in middle age as the stage of mothering merged with the stage of grandmothering. At the deepest level "families of sentiment" responded to a tension between the felt need to perpetuate the clan and the apparent fragility of any individual. Birth and death, more than any sequence of action in between, directed the focus of feeling.

All three families helped to create the idealized motherhood magnified on the gravestone of Judith Coffin. "Grave, sober, faithful, fruitfull vine was she"—"grave and sober" because she stood at the bridge of life and death, "faithful" because she lived to serve rather than to own, "fruitfull" because in her 177 descendants she had surmounted mutability. Returning to her "Savior's breast," she would live in the memories of her children and her children's children. Defined in private experience and in public pronouncement, these qualities characterized the maternal role in early New England.

WRITING FROM ENGLAND in June of 1688, Muriel Mosely sent word to her brother Nathaniel Saltonstall that his "dear Mother" had died. There had apparently been a breach in the family, a conflict between Nathaniel and his father over property. Despite the problem, Muriel wanted Nathaniel to know that he had lost "a praying mother, a Carfull, painfull, tender hearted, self-denying mother; who did what she could for you, and beyond her power; for she abridged her self of necessarys that she might save a little for you."[11] Saintly motherhood was not invented in the nineteenth century nor in America. It was a theme dear to devout Christians on both sides of the Atlantic. In early eighteenth-century New England it became a favorite theme of the publishing ministry. In a sermon preached at the death of his own mother Cotton Mather went so far as to consider whether the Holy Spirit might be the maternal member of the Trinity. Since there was a Father and a Son, certainly there should be a Mother as well.[12] In a sermon published in 1713 Mather even suggested that through motherhood Eve became an instrument of redemption, "And that brave Woman, being Styled, The Mother of all the Living, it has induced Learned Men to conceive, That Eve was, by being the First of them all, in a peculiar manner, the Mother of all that Live unto God; and that she was on this account (Oh! most Happy Woman!) a Mother to her own Husband, and the Instrument of bringing him to Believe in the Great Redeemer."[13] Two years later Benjamin Colman reversed an ancient metaphor in proclaiming that "Adam bore the Name of the Dying Body, Eve of the Living Soul."[14]

In such pronouncements the idealization of motherhood received its fullest expression. Puritan motherhood was not Victorian motherhood, however. Three crucial factors determined the particular nature of the maternal role in early New England. Mothers represented the affectionate mode in an essentially authoritarian system of child-rearing. Mothering was extensive rather than intensive. Motherhood was still closely keyed to the folk concept of fertility.

Mothers represented the affectionate mode in an essentially authoritarian system of child-rearing. Men like Tristram Coffin presided over a world of finite resources and uncertain need. In any generation, a "family of reproduction" might overwhelm a "family of property." Most men and women had neither the ability nor the inclination to limit the first or to effect dramatic changes in the second. True, there was land beyond Pennacook and Kittery, but there were limits to what could be attained, cleared, and (especially in this era) defended. For many reasons New Englanders also had a deep fear of social disintegration. They cherished stability even when they could not attain it. To provide for succeeding generations but also to protect the needs of the whole, including the aged, the orphaned, and the widowed, patriarchal order was seen as essential. Families could not be fed on sentiment.

In such a setting, mother love or any other form of human love could never be an unqualified good. When they sought a metaphor for spiritual nourishment, ministers frequently turned to mothering and especially to breast-feeding. But such unqualified giving was potentially troublesome in life, an invitation to disorder. "Persons are often more apt to despise a Mother, (the weaker vessel, and frequently most indulgent)," one minister told his congregation. Another explained that "by reason of her blandishments, and fond indulgence" a mother was more often subject to irreverence than a father.[15] Here, then, the valuation was negative. Because indulgence brought its own reward in disrespectful children, maternal love had always to be balanced by paternal government.

This distinction is beautifully developed in the "Valedictory and Monitory Writing" which Sarah Goodhue of Ipswich composed just before her death in 1681. Having a premonition that her ninth travail would be her last, she wrote a long letter of farewell, folding it up among her husband's papers with instructions to open it "if by sudden death I am taken away from thee." Her prescience was deemed so remarkable and her pious resignation so edifying that her letter appeared in print not long afterward. As a document "profitable to all that may happen to read the same," it is surprisingly personal, as long passages of sober advice open into delicate vignettes of seventeenth-century family life. Sarah urged her children to obey and honor their father, "for I must testify the truth unto you, and I may call some of you to testify against yourselves; that your Father hath been loving, kind, tender-hearted towards you all." Had the children any reason to doubt it? Sarah's concern seems to imply that they did. Perhaps a need to govern the growing family, to suppress any tendency toward indulgence in himself, had somehow created an emotional distance between the father and the older children. The mother stood in the breach, justifying and defending the stronger parent.

> You that are grown up, cannot but see how careful your father is when he cometh home from his work, to take the young ones up into his wearied arms, by his loving carriage and care towards those, you may behold as in a glass, his tender care and love to you every one as you grow up: I can safely say, that his love was so to you all, that I cannot say which is the child he doth love best.

The father's instruction, his reproofs, his "laying before you the ill event that would happen unto you, if you did not walk in God's ways" had all been intended for their good, Sarah told her children. How could they forget it? Their godly mother, about to give her life to bring another child into the world, had given them her solemn testimony.[16]

Sarah Goodhue's letter describes a mode of parenting common in early America. Tender nurture and open expressions of affection in early childhood gave way to firm discipline and pious rule-making as the children grew. Parents reinforced their own authority with frequent reminders of the correcting power of God.[17] Although both men and women may have fondled babies, spanked toddlers, and chastened teens, the affectionate side of child-rearing was symbolically linked with mothers, the authoritarian with fathers.[18] It could hardly have been otherwise. Mothers were responsible for the very survival of children in their earliest and most vulnerable years, fathers for the hard decisions of emerging adulthood, the questions of land and livelihood.

When a father was missing, the town fathers stood in his place, sometimes creating visible conflicts between authority and affection as mother love struggled with economic reality. In November of 1670, for example, Wiboroe Gatchell found herself in the stocks for "abusing" Richard Prince and "offering to take away his servant." The servant was Gatchell's own son, an apprentice to Prince.[19] In another case, Thamar Quilter tried unsuccessfully to break the contract which bound her only son, Joseph, to William Buckley of Ipswich. When Joseph became ill, the widow Quilter made frequent visits to his master's house, becoming "greeved to the harte" at conditions there. His room was cold, she told the court, and Buckley was "harsh to him (tho the boy as is well known was in great extremytye)." When Buckley offered to let her take Joseph home, she was at first unwilling, yet with "a mothers bowel yerneing toward my child . . . did not turne him backe; feareing he might perish." Though she insisted that Buckley had been the one to break the contract, the courts forced her to return her son.[20] In apprenticeship cases, affection seldom out-argued authority.

In a more spectacular case, involving young Joseph Porter of Salem, mother love at least tempered justice. In March of 1664 Porter was sentenced to stand in the gallows and then to be whipped, imprisoned, and fined. He might have died. According to a contemporary, "If the mother of the said Porter had not been overmoved by hir tender & motherly affections to forbeare, but had joyned with his father in complaining & craving justice, the Court must necessarily have proceeded with him as a capitall offender, according to our law, being ground upon & expressed in the word of God, in Deut 22:20, 21." The Biblical dictum, never applied in Massachusetts, required death for a stubborn and rebellious child. Porter had not only disobeyed his parents, he had slandered them. He had called his mother "Rambeggar, Gammar Shithouse, Gammar Pissehouse, Gammar Two Shoes, & told hir her tongue went like a peare monger."[21]

Goody Porter's tongue may indeed have run on "like a peare monger." Our concern, however, is not with child-rearing practices as such, but with contemporary perceptions of mothering. In this regard Goody Porter's personality and even her motives are of little consequence. In relation to her own husband she was perceived as "tender." Like Sarah Goodhue, Thamar Quilter, and Wiboroe Gatchell, she represented the affectionate mode in a dual concept of parenting.

Mothering in early New England was extensive rather than intensive. For women like Judith Coffin, as well as for their husbands, there were also tensions between "property" and "reproduction," though these would be focused upon the immediate rather than the future needs of the family—how to keep feathers in beds, fresh milk in porridge, or stockings on multiplying pairs of feet.[22] Only in infancy were children simply children. As soon as they could pluck goose feathers or dry spoons, children were also servants. Hired servants, at the same time, were children, needing clothes of their own, firm discipline, and instruction in the Bible. Mothering meant generalized responsibility for an assembly of youngsters rather than concentrated devotion to a few. If babies were referred to as "it," this was a sign not only of their undeveloped personalities but also of the continually changing but persistent identity of the youngest family member as one infant succeeded another.

Seventeenth- and eighteenth-century households were busy and cluttered places where at any given moment everyone and no one might be watching the children. When Alice Walton came in from the field after taking her husband his dinner, she found her toddler missing. "It was here Just now presently," an older daughter exclaimed. But the mother was too late. The child had drowned in an unfenced water hole. When Thomas Newall's child drowned in a two-foot-deep pit near his house, he sued a neighbor, who had apparently dug the pit for tanning. Other neighbors testified that the tanner had filled in the pit, but that Newall's own son had dug it out again to keep alewives in. His mother testified that the child was out of her sight no more than thirty minutes to an hour. Within the house there were similar dangers. Nicholas Gilman's son Tristram, five and a half years old, fell through a trapdoor in a shop chamber where he was playing. Not long afterward a Gilman cousin "narrowly escaped drowning being fallen into a Kettle of Suds," but was "Seasonably Spyd and pulled out by the Heels." Hannah Palmer's daughter was not so fortunate. While her mother was still lying in and perhaps grieving over the loss of twins born five days before, she fell into a kettle of scalding water and lived but a day.[23]

Open fires, wash kettles, and unfenced streams and ponds competed with measles, whooping cough, diphtheria, and intestinal worms as potential killers, yet mothers had little time to dote upon their children even in the most dangerous age of their life. Some parents dealt with the fragility of life through emotional disengagement, a mode which could lead to indifference if not outright neglect. For other parents, the imminence of death reinforced a concern with the salvation of their growing children. The little Maine boy who refused to go to sleep each night until his mother had heard his prayers may have been precociously pious, as his minister believed, but he had also discovered an effective way to capture and hold his busy mother's attention.[24] For many women, personal piety became a form of nurture. With heavy responsibilities, little time, and few resources, they could at least admonish and pray.

If mothers in early New England did not focus intense care and concern on any one child, they did extend the nurturing role into the community in the support of other women in childbearing, in casual surveillance of one another's children, in the more formal tutelage of servants, and sometimes in the development of neighborhood "dame schools," which were as much systems of communal day care as "schools" in any modern sense.[25] This more general notion of mothering reached into old age. Among the gentry a young man might remember his grandmother as a "tender parent." In rural villages any old woman was a "mother" or a "gammar."[26]

The extensive nature of mothering also helps to account for the existence in rural communities of witches. If a witch was by definition a bad neighbor, she was also a bad mother. Instead of nursing babies, she gave suck to familiar spirits or to the Devil himself. Witchcraft is closely linked with fertility in its larger sense.[27] Witches killed pigs, blasted babies, and cast spells on pubescent girls. Elements of this lore survived in country towns well into the eighteenth century. When Sarah Keene of Kittery discovered what appeared to be an extra nipple under one of her breasts, she worried about it enough to ask her neighbor Elizabeth Pettegrew if she thought it were possible to be a witch without knowing it. Years later the aura of witchcraft still pursued her. When John Spinney was rowing home from the tavern one evening in 1725, he struck at a specter in the water, telling his companions that it was "Mother Kene or the Devil."[28]

Witchcraft belief confirms the social nature of the maternal role. Because women were perceived to have real, though mysterious, power, they could become the focus of communal fear and anger. But it also testifies to the psychological complexity of mothering in this insecure and frightening environment. As Bruno Bettelheim has shown, fairy tales with their wicked witches, cruel stepmothers, and fairy godmothers allow children to separate the tender, all-giving, self-denying aspects of motherhood from the angry, punishing, and revengeful. Only by separating the frightening mother from the real mother can a child feel fully protected by her.[29] In early New England, of course, witches were not fantasies but realities, a measure perhaps of the depth of conflict and need for security in this often incomprehensible world. There should be no surprise in finding witchcraft in the same time and place as idealized motherhood.

Even on the most sophisticated level, the concept of motherhood was closely tied to fertility. Whatever their demographic history, the values of early New Englanders were still planted in a world where most children did not survive. To bear children and, above all, to see those children bear children were accounted rich blessings. Though reproduction was uncontrollable, the source of real tensions for fathers and for mothers, it was also highly valued. To have 177 descendants was to achieve a crown on earth. Aside from any abstract quality of character or spirit, fruitfulness in itself conferred status. This is why the crown of mothering came in old age when a woman might see not only her children but her children's children. "May [you] glorifi the Lord in helping to buld up the house of jacobe yor father," Margaret Thatcher wrote to her ailing and presumably pregnant daughter in October of 1686. Father Jacob was of course the Biblical Jacob, but the spiritual service which this mother rendered began in biological reproduction, though of course it did not end there. Mistress Thatcher hoped to see her little grandchildren become "polished stons" in the house of the Lord. " [T]hem i do hertili inbrace," she wrote.[30]

The births and deaths of grandchildren could touch grandmothers in an especially powerful way, for each one was in some sense a "remainder" of herself. During the diphtheria epidemic of 1735 Deborah Jaques of Newbury went into an upstairs chamber to fetch some candles which were kept in a bushel basket under a bed. As she leaned over to return the basket to its place, she saw what seemed to be a little hand in a striped boy's sleeve, though there was no child to be found in the house. One week following this apparition her grandson Henry died, followed by Ebenezer, and then by Stephen.[31]

Philip Greven has shown the conservative effect which patriarchal longevity had upon "families of property" in early New England. Matriarchal longevity may have been equally important in sustaining and enlarging "families of sentiment." There is suggestive evidence of this in a genealogical record from eighteenth-century Ipswich. Elizabeth Rogers Appleton was fourth in a succession of godly grandmothers descended from Dorothy Dudley. Her grandmother Patience Denison died at seventy-one. Her mother, Elizabeth Rogers, was something of a marvel to her relatives at the age of eighty. Elizabeth herself outlived both her mother and her grandmother, dying in 1754 at the age of ninety-one. Like the Coffins of Newbury, the Appletons of Ipswich were given to counting their progeny, but the demographic profile of the two families is strikingly different.

In the last years of her life Elizabeth summarized the family record which she had kept, interspersing brief sentiments among the names and dates.[32] Only five of her nine children lived to marry, and among these Priscilla died at the age of twenty-eight, leaving only one child, a boy who died himself soon after his tenth birthday. Two of Elizabeth's daughters and the wives of two of her sons lived to the end of their childbearing years, producing twenty grandsons and twenty granddaughters—but fewer than half of these children survived. The grandsons were especially vulnerable, perhaps because of some inherited disorder aggravated by the custom of intermarriage among the Ipswich elite. The family record of Daniel Appleton is especially grim. His wife gave birth to eleven children in the nineteen years between 1717 and 1736. Only three survived. One of these, an unmarried daughter named Margaret, expired at the age of twenty-two, as her grandmother said, "after 4 or 5 years weaknes and languishing." The statistics for Daniel's brother Nathaniel appear cheerful only in comparison. His wife bore thirteen children in twenty-one years. Six survived.

Two themes emerge from Elizabeth Appleton's running commentary on the demographic reversals in her own family history. The first, predictably, is religious resignation. She seems to have been consoled in the belief that her granddaughter Margaret was "under great conviction and received joy and comfort" during the last stage of her illness. But there is anguish as well as piety in the grandmother's reflections, a sense not only of communal but of personal loss as each tender shoot on her vine was blasted. "[S]o it pleased God to take away one after another of my dear children, I hope, to himself," she wrote after the death of a grandchild. When a great-granddaughter died very suddenly at the age of two, she could only note "another bitter bereavement of a dear pleasant desirable grand child."

At the very end of the record Mrs. Appleton brought the two themes together, summarizing her gains and losses and affirming her deepest hopes:

> Hear is an account of all my posterity. 6 sons and 3 daughters, 20 grand son and 20 grand daughters, 58 in all. 33 are gon before me. I hope I shall mett them all att Christ's rit hand among his sheep and lambs. I often look over this list with sorrow but with comfortable hopes that they which are gone are gon to rest and I desire they that survive may remember their creator in the days of thire youth, and fear God betimes.

Elizabeth Appleton considered herself the mother not only of the living but of the dead—of the Margarets, Elizabeths, Daniels, Johns, and Nathaniels who had gone before as well as of those who remained. She could not know with certainty that all had been saved any more than she could be positive of her own election. But family pride as well as religious conviction gave her "good hopes."

In this she was not alone. Long before the Great Awakening, New England burying grounds give evidence of the optimism of orthodox parents, men and women who knew that their children were elected to salvation or damnation by the supreme will of God and that earthly baptism gave no guarantee of salvation. When Samuel Sewall's sister Mehetable died in 1702, her marker confidently promised reunion with "her glorified son William," a child who had died two years before.[33] Three years later Mehetable's nephew Samuel Moody, a staunch Calvinist who preached hellfire and damnation to three generations of Maine children, allowed this hopeful sentiment to be inscribed beneath the winged death's-head on the marker of his infant daughter:

RESURRECTION

To Immortality in spotless Beauty, with all Other Bodily Perfections, after the fashion of Christs Glorious Body, is expected for the Sub adjacent Dust of Lucy Moodey Who was born, & died, July the 6, 1705 Thus Birth, Spousals to Christ, Death, Coronation All in One Day may have their Celebration.[34]

For tiny Lucy, "Spousals to Christ" through baptism could not ensure a crown on high, yet her bereaved parents not only hoped for but expected "Coronation." A family in Heaven enlarged a family on earth.

WE HAVE DESCRIBED an ideal of motherhood which focused upon tenderness, self-denial, piety, and fruitfulness, and which traced a progression from the intense nurturing of infants through the haphazard but pious watchfulness of growing children to an old age characterized by economic dependency, religious resignation, and an absorbing concern with the next generation. All of these themes are realized in a graceful poem which Anne Bradstreet composed for her own children sometime after 1656.

> *I had eight birds hatcht in one nest,*
> *Four Cocks there were, and Hens the rest,*
> *I nurst them up with pain and care,*
> *Nor cost, nor labour did I spare,*
> *Till at the last they felt their wing.*
> *Mounted the Trees, and learn'd to sing.*

The emotions of the mother bird turn on two related issues—her fears for her children and her perception of her own changing role in relation to them. She had done her best, had bred them, fed them, and with her "wings kept off all harm." Now there was little she could do but pray that her children would avoid the "Fowlers snare." Meanwhile she could sit in the shade and sing, contemplating her own flight into that "country beyond sight."

But the poem did not end there. For the aging bird, immortality lay not only in the far country but in her song and in her children's memories.

> When each of you shall in your nest
> Among your young ones take your rest,
> In chirping language oft them tell,
> You had a Dam that lov'd you well.
> That did what could be done for young,
> And nurst you up till you were strong,
> And fore she once would let you fly,
> She shew'd you joy and misery;
> Taught what was good, and what was ill,
> What would save life, and what would kill.
> Thus gone, amongst you I may live,
> And dead, yet speak, and counsel give.[35]

If the poet ignored the threats within the nest itself, the crowding, the screeching, the insistent demands upon the mother bird, she was only fulfilling the highest expectations of her maternal role. An honored mother was fruitful, faithful, tender, and giving. Her chief monument was in her progeny.

Part Three

JAEL

Blessed above women shall Jael the wife of Heber the Kenite be; blessed shall she be above women in the tent.
He asked water, and she gave him milk; she brought forth butter in a lordly dish.
She put her hand to the nail, and her right hand to the workmen's hammer; and with the hammer she smote Sisera, she smote off his head, when she had pierced and stricken through his temples.
At her feet he bowed, he fell, he lay down: at her feet he bowed, he fell: where he bowed, there he fell down dead.
The mother of Sisera looked out at a window, and cried through the lattice, Why is his chariot so long in coming? why tarry the wheels of his chariots?
Her wise ladies answered her, yea, she returned answer to herself.
Have they not sped? have they not divided the prey; to every man a damsel or two; to Sisera a prey of divers colors, a prey of divers colors of needlework on both sides, meet for the necks of them that take the spoil?
So let all thine enemies perish, O Lord: but let them that love him be as the sun when he goeth forth in his might.

JUDGES 5:24–31, *"The Song of Deborah"*

Chapter Nine

BLESSED
ABOVE WOMEN

BY 1698 THE MOST FAMOUS WOMAN in New England was Hannah Duston of Haverhill. Cotton Mather had published her story twice, first in a sermon printed in 1697 and again the next year in his history of "the Long War, which New-England hath had with the Indian Salvages."[1] John Pike, sometime minister to the straggling village of Cocheco (Dover), New Hampshire, may have learned the story first from Mather's accounts, but news of Hannah's exploit probably spread even more rapidly by word of mouth along the military corridors leading into the war-torn eastern parts. To the list of "Observable Providences" collected in his journal for the year 1697 he added:

> March 15.—The Indians fell upon some part of Haverhill, about 7 in the morning, killed and carried away 39 or 40 persons. Two of these captive women, viz. Duston and Neff, (with another young man,) slew ten of the Indians, and returned home with their scalps.[2]

Hannah Duston's deed was spectacular. Five days out of childbed, she had marched a hundred miles into the wilderness and with the help of her companion, Mary Neff, and a boy named Samuel Lennardson had not only killed her captors and escaped but had brought home ten scalps to prove it. Little matter that six of those scalps were of children. Boston acclaimed her a heroine.

When Hannah visited the city in April of 1697, the month after her captivity, Samuel Sewall entertained her; Cotton Mather interviewed her and honored her with a sermon at his church; and the Great and General Court, responding to a petition from her husband, Thomas, awarded her a scalp bounty of £25.[3] Her name and her significance were to extend beyond her own time and place. Canonized in 1702 in Mather's monumental *Magnalia Christi Americana,* she became an American amazon, a defender of Israel, and an archetypal heroine of the New World frontier.

In Cotton Mather's words, Hannah Duston's heroism imitated "the action of Jael upon Siseria."[4] The Biblical image was apt. In Jael, Mather found a model which both justified and elevated Hannah Duston's deed. As recounted in Judges, chapter 4, the tale is a simple one. Jael, the wife of Heber the Kenite, welcomed the enemy Sisera into her tent, fed him, lulled him to sleep, and then murdered him by driving a tent peg through his head. Retold in the Song of Deborah in Judges, chapter 5, it became a narrative and poetic masterpiece, carefully exploiting the contrasting images of the woman as nurturer and killer.

> Blessed above women shall Jael the wife of Heber the Kenite be; blessed shall she be above women in the tent.

As Sisera entered the tent, Jael went beyond the ordinary demands of hospitality, bringing milk and butter when he asked only for water, but once he slept, she acted coolly and with resolution. Putting her hand to the nail, "she smote Sisera, she smote off his head." The poet relished Jael's triumph in the rhythmic telling of Sisera's death: "At her feet he bowed, he fell, he lay down: at her feet he bowed, he fell: where he bowed, there he fell down dead."

Although Cotton Mather lacked the finesse of his Hebrew predecessor, he did grasp the importance for his own story of the contrasting imagery. Hannah Duston had given birth less than a week before her capture and was still attended by her nurse, Mary Neff. Mather highlighted this situation in his account. He described her "sitting down in the chimney with a heart full of most fearful expectation" as the attackers rifled her house and killed her baby. In his description of the captivity itself he again emphasized her femininity, speaking of her "sighs" as well as of her courage. "Like another Hannah," he wrote, she had no recourse but prayer. In this way he prepared for the ironic conclusion,

Hannah's slaughter of the Indians. In the final scene he simply paraphrased the Bible: Duston's Indians "bow'd" and "fell" and "lay down" like Sisera before them.[5]

Mather recognized the chief literary lesson in his model, yet the affinities between the two stories go beyond narrative technique. In both, the heroism of the woman was magnified as a means of rallying and chastising a nation. Jael was instrumental in saving Israel at a time of spiritual and military disintegration. Deborah the prophetess had asked a general named Barak to take ten thousand men and attack the army, but Barak had refused to go unless Deborah promised to go with him. "I will surely go with thee," she answered, "notwithstanding the journey that thou takest shall not be for thine honour; for the Lord shall sell Sisera into the hand of a woman" (Judges 4:4-9). Jael's heroism was a rebuke to Barak, who had been reluctant to defend his nation. Although Deborah and Jael equal any Biblical male in courage and in fierceness, the purpose of the narrative was not to extol the military potential of women. On the contrary, the effectiveness of the narrative rests on an awareness of role contradiction. Because Jael was womanly in the traditional sense—and remained so—her ability to kill Sisera testified all the more powerfully to God's part in her triumph. Her faithfulness was a mirror held up to a flagging Israel.

The Hannah Duston of Mather's story fits this pattern well. In her victory God demonstrated His desire to sustain the American Israel even though many of Israel's children had abandoned Him. Duston became a killer because the moral order around her had broken down. Moving into a vacuum created by war, she did individually what New England had been unable to do collectively. In the sermon which included the first printed version of Hannah Duston's story, Mather made this explicit: "If we did now Humble ourselves throughout the Land," he wrote, "who can say whether the Revenges on the Enemy, thus Exemplified, would not proceed much rather into the Quick Extirpation, of those Bloody and Crafty men."[6]

The seventeenth century was the age of the jeremiad, of fearful pronouncements of an impending judgment, a cataclysm made to seem all the more possible by the prolonged struggles of the Indian wars. It was also an age of biography. Through portraits of meek, pious, and prayerful Christians—mostly ministers but also, to an increasing extent, women—New England's clergymen promoted a vision of a godly New England, a reformed Israel which lived up to the presumed vision of its founders.[7] The real Hannah Duston, the flesh-and-blood woman unretouched for Mather's portrait, fitted awkwardly into this frame, as we shall see. But the drama of her story, as shaped by the Biblical precedent of Jael, fulfilled the dual requirements of "entertainment" and of "holy history" which Cotton Mather set for his *Magnalia*. In its pages, and in histories of New England written in the centuries since, Hannah Duston plays a colorful but minor part.

Looked at from the viewpoint of women's history, however, the story has a larger significance. Without challenging the presumed weakness of women or denying the primacy of the nurturing roles, Mather's account glorified both feminine strength and feminine assertiveness. On one level, of course, Jael was simply acting as a deputy husband. The ability to assume male roles temporarily and then shrink back into submissiveness has been a traditional female quality—especially in wartime. But the myth of Jael goes deeper than that. If woman is capable of assuming male responsibilities in the service of male authority, what is to prevent her from challenging that authority altogether? What contains the immense destructive power beneath the benign feminine mask? Such questions are inherent in the story itself. Even the method of destruction—the nail driven into Sisera's head—is a rude caricature of the male sexual act.

On the surface at least, this was not a problem which troubled Cotton Mather—in itself an important historical clue, for such questions *did* concern writers and popular moralists of the nineteenth century, many of whom went to great lengths to deny the aggressive potential of women. One of the ways they did this was to divide women into pure and untouchable blondes and mysterious and dangerous brunettes, good women and bad women. Nathaniel Hawthorne, who was more critical of this convention than has sometimes been recognized, nevertheless used it in a number of stories. His characterization of Miriam, the dark lady in *The Marble Faun*, is worth examining in some detail for its allusions to the myth of Jael.

Like many of Hawthorne's heroines, Miriam was a woman with a secret. A sinister male figure shadowed her through the streets of Rome, keeping alive haunting images of a troubled past. Miriam longed to rid herself of her oppressor, but because she was a respectable woman (and a character in a Hawthorne novel), she repressed her hatred, venting it only through art in a series of sketches kept in a secret portfolio. One day an innocent young Italian named Donatello came upon her drawings. The first was a sketch "in which the artist had jotted down her rough ideas for a picture of Jael driving the nail through the temples of Sisera." Donatello found it impressive, but he discerned a contradiction in Miriam's conception of her subject. At first she had painted Jael as a figure of "perfect womanhood, a lovely form, and a high, heroic face of lofty beauty,"

> but dissatisfied either with her own work or the terrible story itself, Miriam had added a certain wayward quirk of her pencil, which at once converted the heroine into a vulgar murderess. It was evident that a Jael like this would be sure to search Sisera's pockets as soon as the breath was out of his body.[8]

The reference to money in this passage is telling when contrasted with the story of Hannah Duston, for her motivation for scalping her victims was openly pecuniary. Without scalps, she would have had no proof of her exploit and, as a consequence, no bounty from the General Court.

Such details did not tarnish her heroism in Cotton Mather's eyes. In fact, he was responsible for recording them. But for the nineteenth-century writer, such opportunism was impossible in a true heroine. In Hawthorne's view, Miriam's drawings, "grotesque or sternly sad," brought out the moral "that woman must strike through her own heart to reach a human life, whatever were the motive that impelled her."[9] For Hawthorne, female aggression was simply contrary to nature. He could not sustain the juxtaposition of qualities inherent in the Biblical and in the colonial myth of Jael.

This is more than a literary curiosity. Hawthorne's novel highlights a shift in sensibility of great consequence. Such a shift can be seen even more clearly in nineteenth-century accounts of Hannah Duston. Her story, largely forgotten outside her own community by 1800, was revived by Timothy Dwight in his travel sketches published in 1821. For narrative detail, Dwight followed Mather's account closely, but he introduced an apologetic note foreign to his predecessor. "Whether all their sufferings, and all the danger of suffering anew, justified this slaughter may probably be questioned by you or some other exact moralist," Dwight wrote.[10]

Successive writers followed Dwight's lead. In "A Mother's Revenge" in his *Legends of New England,* John Greenleaf Whittier, a Haverhill son, allowed for the temporary insanity of Hannah. Henry Thoreau simply shifted the emphasis in his narrative from the murder to the homeward flight along the Merrimack River. Hawthorne was more blunt. In an account written in 1836 for the *American Magazine,* he confessed that he admired Thomas Duston, but didn't know whom to dislike more—Cotton Mather or Hannah Duston. "Would that the bloody old hag had been drowned in crossing Contocook river," he wrote, "or that she had sunk over head and ears in a swamp, and been there buried, until summoned forth to confront her victims at the Day of Judgment."[11] Hawthorne obviously had some sympathy for the Indians, yet his aversion to Hannah went deeper. Only a "hag" could have behaved in such an unfeminine manner.

By the mid-nineteenth century Cotton Mather's story had lost its epic dimensions and had become the property of idealized local history and domestic romance, realms in which female submissiveness was assumed. Little wonder that an aggressive and opportunistic woman like Hannah Duston caused discomfort! In the light of this change her story becomes even more interesting for the student of colonial women, raising intriguing questions about the nature of female heroism in early America. Were there other assertive females in the wartime literature of northern New England? Was Hannah Duston's response to captivity unique? Was her capacity for violence in any way symptomatic of larger patterns of female behavior? This chapter will focus on the first of those questions, exploring the theme of female heroism in the ministerial literature of the late seventeenth and early eighteenth centuries.

BY THE TIME Hannah Duston faced the "tawny savages" in her house in Haverhill, war and captivity had become commonplace themes in New England literature. The earliest heroines emerged in the aftermath of Metacom's Rebellion (or King Philip's War) of 1675-76, the first of a devastating series of racial conflicts in New England and one of the most destructive wars in proportion to population in American history. The war began in Plymouth Colony, but soon spread into the Connecticut Valley and eventually sparked a related rebellion in Maine. Before the war's end, fifty-two of the ninety towns in the region had been attacked and twelve destroyed.[12] The power of the Indian rebellion was a surprising and demoralizing blow. At the end of the war, surviving red leaders were either executed or exported as slaves, ending any hope of peaceful coexistence of the two races and creating a legacy of fear and hate which would erupt periodically on the northern frontier in the next century.[13] Ministerial narratives published at the end of the war attempted to derive historical and spiritual lessons from an experience which had left few New Englanders untouched.

For our purposes, the three most important literary documents of Metacom's Rebellion are Increase Mather's *A Brief History of the War with the Indians in New England* (1676), William Hubbard's *A Narrative of the Trouble with the Indians in New England* (1677), and Mary Rowlandson's story of her own captivity, published in 1682 as *The Soveraignty & Goodness of God, Together, with the Faithfulness of His Promises Displayed*. The most important motif in all three is not female heroism but female suffering. This is most pronounced in Mather's history, which invariably depicts women as victims. Describing an attack on a group of churchgoers near Springfield, Mather highlighted not only Indian cruelty but English cowardice. Eighteen well-armed men had fled while two women and their children were captured. "O Lord What Shall I say When Israel turns their backs before their Enemies?" he cried. It was not enough to add that the Indians had killed the babies. Mather heightened the pathos by describing them knocking the infants on the head "as they were sucking their mother's breasts."[14]

The "sucking infant" theme was a popular one with New England writers who wanted to enlarge upon Indian cruelty. The most gruesome example is in Hubbard's description of an attack on Cape Neddick in Maine. "Having dashed out the brains of a poor woman that gave suck," he wrote, "they nayled the young

Child to the dead body of its mother, which was found sucking in that rueful manner, when the People came to the Place."[15] In her story of Goodwife Joslin, Mary Rowlandson used another version of the "outraged maternity" theme. In this case a woman "big with child" was stripped, placed in the center of a band of singing, taunting Indians, then burned.[16] Assaults upon nursing or pregnant women became the chief evidence of Indian cruelty in the narratives, since there were no instances of rape, a fact which clearly astounded white New Englanders.[17]

Though the heroism of white soldiers appears in a few memorable passages in Increase Mather's history, there is no room in his narrative for heroines.[18] For him, the helpless suffering of women served as a measure of New England's spiritual and physical desolation. Hubbard's history of the Massachusetts war doesn't differ from Mather's in this respect, but in his related but separate narrative of Indian conflict in Maine, New England's first frontier heroines emerged. Rowlandson also made use of the passive-victim motif, but she too transcended it, creating a different version of female heroism from the trials of her own captivity. The essential difference between Rowlandson's and Hubbard's heroines—the godly captive and the self-reliant virago—can be seen in contrasting incidents involving an escape by water.

Toward the end of February 1676 Mary Rowlandson was with a group of Nipmuck, Narragansett, and Wampanoag Indians near what is now Barre, Vermont, when they received word that an English force was approaching. The "stoutest" men, Mrs. Rowlandson recalled, went off to hold the English army, while the women and children, the old, the sick, and the lame, "like Jehu . . . marched on furiously." When they reached the Ware River, the women felled dry trees and made rafts to carry them over. Mrs. Rowlandson was terrified, "being unacquainted with such kind of doings or dangers." She accounted it a special favor from God that, sitting on a pile of brush in the middle of the makeshift raft, she crossed without getting wet. Her initiation into wilderness ways was made even more dramatic when a few hours later the same river stopped the pursuing English army. For Rowlandson, the river-crossing was an experience in humiliation, a discovery of her own weakness and vulnerability before God.[19] Her heroism lay in her ability to survive by trusting God.

Hubbard's story of Ann Brackett, though far less detailed, is strikingly different. Mistress Brackett, with her husband, at least one child, and a black servant, had been captured by local Indians led by a man named Simon. When Simon heard of a successful attack on the Arowsick trading house on the Kennebec, he left his captives in a lonely camp on the north side of Casco Bay and went to join in the plunder. Ann Brackett immediately set to work on an "old Burchin Canoe" which she hoped was "an opportunity Providence offered for their escape." Using a needle and thread found in the camp, she repaired the Indian craft and with her family "crossed water eight or nine miles broad" to Black Point, where they were rescued by a ship bound for Piscataqua.[20]

As recounted in Hubbard's history, this story has a fairy-tale quality. One would like to know more about the condition of the canoe and the nature of the repair, but for Hubbard the details were less important than the outcome. He clearly credited Ann Brackett, rather than her husband or the male servant who accompanied them, with the inspiration, the resourcefulness, and the skill which made the escape possible. Unlike Mary Rowlandson, she *was* acquainted with wilderness "doings & dangers." Her heroism lay in self-reliance rather than faith.

In another passage in the same section of the history, Hubbard praised a second resourceful heroine, an eighteen-year-old "Virago" whose unusual courage saved fifteen women and children from an assault by "two cruel and barbarous caytiffes." This unnamed maiden of Newechewanick, "being endued with more courage than ordinarily the rest of her Sex use to be, (the blessing of Jael light upon her) first shut to the dore, whereby they were denied Entrance, till the rest within escaped to the next house, that was better fortified." Though wounded and left for dead, she managed to reach the next garrison, "where she was soon after healed of her wounds, and restored to perfect health again."[21]

Seventeenth-century historians (like some of their twentieth-century successors) drew sharp contrasts between the compact settlements of Massachusetts with their settled churches and presumably Puritan outlook and the straggling plantations of Maine and New Hampshire where colonists came to fish, not pray. It is a short step from these notions to the idea of colonial history as a conflict between inherited religious and communal values and the acquired individualism of a land-rich frontier. Mary Rowlandson and Ann Brackett might represent the female version of this dichotomy. Rowlandson, the God-fearing Puritan, was a transplanted Englishwoman thrust into an alien American world. Lacking experience with the ways of the forest, Rowlandson dismissed it as the domain of Satan's hosts. Brackett, a daughter of the Maine frontier, had inherited wilderness craft as well as wilderness courage. At home in the New World, she relied on herself.

Biographical details for the two women give some support to these stereotypes. Mary Rowlandson was born in Somersetshire about 1635 and migrated to Salem, Massachusetts, as a young child. Though she moved with her family to the new town of Lancaster in her late teens and had lived there more than twenty years when taken captive, her narrative gives constant evidence of resistance to what might be described as "frontier" ways. The passage in which she described her first taste of bear meat in captivity is exemplary: "I have sometimes seen Bear baked very handsomely among the English, and some like it," she wrote, "but the thought that it was Bear, made me tremble: but now that was savoury to me that one would think was enough to turn the stomach of a bruit Creature."[22] For Mary Rowlandson, wild meat was symbolic of a wilderness she feared.

Ann Brackett left no record of her own thoughts or attitudes, yet what can be pieced together of her background contrasts with Rowlandson's. She was the granddaughter of George Cleeves, an independent fisherman and trader who was the first settler on Casco Bay. She grew up in the most remote and sparsely settled spot in New England, the daughter of Cleeves' only child, Elizabeth, and Michael Mitton, who was associated with his father-in-law in fishing and trading.[23] In contrast to Rowlandson, who described keeping "six stout dogs" in the garrison ready to tear apart any Indian who ventured to the door, the Cleeveses and Mittons depended upon daily intercourse with the natives who surrounded and outnumbered them.[24]

We know nothing of Brackett's own religious attitudes, though in reporting her family's captivity her brother-in-law wrote, "The Lord of late hath renewed his witnesses against us & hath dealt very bitterly with us."[25] One need not imagine the inhabitants of the Maine frontier as a breed apart to recognize that the practical experience of the daughter of an Indian trader might differ in significant ways from that of a minister's wife.

The differences between Rowlandson and Brackett are useful in describing the probable range of female response to the wilderness, but they should not be pushed too far. There was no rigid contrast between women in agricultural villages like Lancaster and in outlying plantations like Casco Bay. As Rowlandson's own narrative showed, some of her neighbors enjoyed eating bear, and even within the Brackett family captivity could be interpreted in religious terms. The caution goes deeper than that, however. Although Mary Rowlandson appeared briefly in both Mather's and Hubbard's narratives simply as an object of Indian cruelty, she was neither passive nor helpless. Though she showed no inclination to repair birchbark canoes or engage in hand-to-hand combat with invading Indians, she had her own kind of courage, exemplifying not just heroic faith but a practical ability to survive by placing her huswifery skills at the service of her captors. We will return to Rowlandson's story in Chapter 12. At this point it is enough to note her importance as the first of the literary captives.

Mary Rowlandson's narrative and William Hubbard's history introduced two variants of the frontier heroine: the godly captive and the self-reliant virago. In the next fifty years other writers would develop these two and add a third, the pious Christian who served by simply staying put.

AFTER KING PHILIP'S WAR, New England experienced a decade of peace, but in 1689, with the outbreak of King William's War, local tensions between whites and natives in Maine and New Hampshire were absorbed in what historians have since called "the great struggle for Empire," the conflict between Britain and France for dominance in North America. King William's War (1689–1698) and Queen Anne's War (1703–1713) were largely fought in America by Indians, first Iroquois provoked by the English to attacks on the Canadian frontier, but later and more effectively by various groups of Canadian and Maine Indians, often led by French *coureurs de bois* in devastating raids on exposed outposts in New York and New England.[26]

For twenty years a succession of unpredictable and debilitating attacks on the northern frontier wreaked psychological and physical desolation. The events of these wars provided new material for the Boston press. Ministerial literature of the period was already characterized by a conscious effort to elevate the public image, if not the status, of women.[27] Because Cotton Mather, the chief exponent of the new emphasis, was also the most prominent historian of the Indian wars, living heroines of the northern frontier took their place in these years beside pious Boston matrons eulogized in countless funeral sermons.

The fighting Jaels prefigured in Hubbard's history are the most colorful, if not the most significant, of the heroines. Like "Molly Pitcher," the legendary water-carrier of the Revolutionary War, who fired a cannon in the pressure of a battle, some women learned to shoot in these first French and Indian wars. In describing an assault on Wells in King William's War, Cotton Mather praised the women of the garrison who "took up the Amazonian Stroke, and not only brought Ammunition to the Men, but also with a Manly Resolution fired several Times upon the Enemy."[28]

For every such account which appeared in public records of the period there must have been others which survived only in local tradition or family legend. By the end of the eighteenth century, stories of Oyster River heroines had acquired the vivid detail recorded by Jeremy Belknap, whose information, so he said, was collected from "aged persons" by a descendant of one of the suffering families. According to Belknap, no men were inside a garrison near the house of John Drew when a small party attacked in April of 1706. The women, "seeing nothing but death before them, fired an alarm, and then putting on hats, and loosening their hair that they might appear like men, they fired so briskly that the enemy, apprehending the people were alarmed, fled without burning or even plundering the house which they had attacked."[29] Belknap told of a similar event which occurred at the Heard garrison in Dover in 1712. Again the house was left defenseless when a "woman named Esther Jones mounted guard and with a commanding voice called so loudly and resolutely as made the enemy think there was help at hand, and prevented farther mischief."[30]

These stories fit well with the notion of women as deputy husbands able to step into a void created by male absence and fulfill male responsibilities without in any sense altering the prescribed female roles. The emphasis on male disguise in Belknap's stories is significant. As Mather made clear, firing upon the enemy at Wells required a "manly resolution."

There is no way of knowing if Philip Moodey's mother personally used the half-pound of gunpowder he purchased for her in Nicholas Perryman's store in Exeter in 1722.[31] Since the French and Indian Wars forced greater general preparedness on the frontier, women may have become more familiar with firearms than in earlier wars, and a few perhaps learned to load and fire on their own. In 1724 Samuel Penhallow of Portsmouth described the heroism of an Oxford woman who shot and killed an Indian who was attempting to break through her roof. According to local tradition, she had two muskets and two pistols charged and ready for his three companions.[32]

The question of means may be misplaced, however. The important problem is not whether colonial women had the ability to defend themselves but whether they had the will. There were familiar weapons at hand. Hannah Bradley of Haverhill scalded an attacker with a kettle of boiling soap.[33] Given the impulse, a housewife like Hannah Duston, who had undoubtedly slaughtered chickens and skinned and eviscerated animals, would know how to kill and take a scalp.

Thus, a number of intrepid females living on the frontier of New England in the years after 1689 inherited the "blessing of Jael" first invoked by William Hubbard a decade before. They successfully defended themselves and were praised for doing so. This does not mean that fighting was a typical female response. Like most embattled societies before and since, the villages of Maine and New Hampshire evacuated women and children first and expected men to do the shooting.[34] The heroism of women like Hannah Bradley or Esther Jones represented possibility, not probability. Presumed weak, women on the northern colonial frontier might prove themselves strong.

Even more persistent than the image of Jael was the image of the godly captive. The title page of one narrative, published in 1728, states the common theme: "God's Mercy surmounting Man's Cruelty Exemplifyed in the Captivity and Redemption of Elizabeth Hanson ... In which are inserted, Sundry remarkable

Preservations, Deliverances, and Marks of the Care and Kindness of Providence."[35] It matters little that Elizabeth Hanson was a Quaker or that she lived on a remote farm in a scattered New Hampshire settlement; the purposes of her narrative, to praise God and to promote piety, were those which had motivated Mary Rowlandson fifty years before and which continued to dominate the sermons and histories of Hanson's Puritan contemporary Cotton Mather.

Forced into submissiveness, the godly captive proved her strength by surviving, then gave the credit to God. As in Mary Rowlandson's day, her Indian captors stood for the powers of darkness. Yet in the wars at the end of the century God's enemies had acquired a new and awesome ally. Cotton Mather expressed the ministerial perception of this threat when he wrote in a tract addressed to the inhabitants of the Maine frontier: "We hear of a Vexatious Adversary, Wild Indians, headed and acted by French Papists, breaking in upon you now and then; killing of some, and siezing and snatching away others, for a Captivity, full of miseries."[36] From the perspective of dissenting Protestantism, the Indian-French combination epitomized the twin threats of barbarism and false faith. The ideal captive, then, was a woman like Hannah Swarton, who not only survived the rigors of the wilderness but heroically refused to succumb to the enticements of the "Papists" who rescued her from the Indians.

Frontier women who upheld Protestant piety at home could also become heroines. In his history of Queen Anne's War, Cotton Mather argued that God was punishing all New England in a conflict which afflicted taxpayers, soldiers, and the families of soldiers in communities throughout the land. But he gave particular emphasis to the trials of "our dear Brethren in the Frontier . . . who are Posted in the Valley of Achor."[37] The Biblical allusion was to a traditional Palestinian "valley of trouble" where a disobedient Israelite had been stoned for hiding Babylonish spoils salvaged in the conquest of Canaan. New Englanders who searched for Providential design in every event had ample reason to suspect that God had indeed singled out the eastern parts for a special chastening. With the exception of Deerfield in the Connecticut Valley of western Massachusetts, no other area of New England suffered so acutely in the French and Indian Wars. The vast majority of New England captives taken to Canada between 1689 and 1728 came from the Piscataqua region of Maine and New Hampshire or the isolated plantations along the Maine coast between Wells and Pemaquid.[38]

Some settlers in these parts shared Mather's conception of their danger. Hannah Swarton saw her own captivity as a punishment for her family's negligence in removing from the established community of Beverly, where there was a church and a minister, to the wilderness of Casco Bay, "thereby Exposing our Children to be bred Ignorantly like Indians."[39] John Gyles, a captive of Pemaquid, recalled that after removing to Maine his father had been much troubled by "the Immoralities of a People who had long lived Lawless."[40] Such comments cut in two directions, however. In describing the ungodliness of the Maine frontier, these writers inadvertently testified to the presence there of at least a few articulate settlers of exemplary piety.

John Gyles' memoir paints a vivid portrait of one zealous Maine Protestant, his own mother. He recalled her last words to him as they were separated in captivity: "Oh! my dear Child! If it were God's will, I had rather follow you to your Grave! or never see you more in this World, than you should be sold to a Jesuit."[41] So impressive were her fears that when a French priest offered him a biscuit, he hid it under a log, "fearing that he had put something in it to make me love him: for I was very Young, and had heard much of the Papists torturing the Protestants, etc. so that I hated the sight of a Jesuit."[42] Captivity taught Gyles to respect both his Indian and his French captors, but he did not forget his mother's teachings. When after six years among the Indians he was sold to a French family, he cried in the woods thinking of how his mother had detested "papists."[43]

Neither public officials nor the colonial ministry wanted to see the frontier abandoned. From a military standpoint, the settlements in Maine and New Hampshire were a necessary buffer, a ring of defense against further French incursions onto English soil. From a religious viewpoint, the safety of New England rested in extending the protection of God to the "Valley of Achor." It is not surprising, then, that in the crisis atmosphere of these years some women, especially aged and pious widows, became heroines by refusing to leave their wilderness homes despite the entreaties of friends or relatives.

According to Cotton Mather, Mrs. Elizabeth Heard was miraculously preserved in the Dover Massacre of 1689. She witnessed scenes of desolation which might have overcome a lesser person, but she did not abandon her home in the long war which followed. "This Gentlewoman's Garrison was the most Extream Frontier of the Province, and more Obnoxious than any other, and more uncapable of Relief; nevertheless, by her presence and courage, it held out all the War, even for Ten Years together," he wrote, adding that she resisted the offers of her friends to remove to safety in Portsmouth, "which would have been a Damage to the Town and Land."[44]

Other Bostonians admired the tenacity of frontier women. In 1710 Samuel Sewall of Boston wrote to Elizabeth Saltonstall of Haverhill, who had recently been widowed, praising her for "the Obligation you lay even upon the Province, by denying your self, and continuing to live in a Frontier Town." In Sewall's view, Mrs. Saltonstall's service to the commonwealth was twofold: he admired both her courage and her piety. As he phrased it, her heroism consisted in "venturing to keep Watch and Ward for the Inward Towns."[45] In his letter Sewall mentioned enclosing a book "as a small Token of my Respect." He did not give the title, though it may well have been one of the sermons or discourses for women which Cotton Mather was printing so frequently in these years. Women like Mistress Saltonstall perhaps read as well as inspired the public praise extended to their sex in the first years of the eighteenth century.

IN A FUNERAL SERMON preached in 1728 for Katharin Willard, the wife of Massachusetts' provincial secretary, Mather included a generalized paean to New England women. "There have been, and thro' the Grace of our God there still are, to be found, in many parts of these American Regions, and even in the Cottages of the Wilderness, as well as in our Capital city, those Handmaids of the Lord, who tho' they ly very much Conceal'd from the World, and may be called, The Hidden Ones, yet have no little share in the Beauty and the Defence of the Land."[46] Mather was perhaps thinking of the many women he had praised over the past thirty years in his histories of the Indian wars: the assertive viragoes who physically assaulted the enemy, the pious captives who made a trek to Canada a religious quest, and especially the godly Christians whose homes were a barrier to enemy attack and whose presence provided spiritual insurance of God's care. Hannah Duston of Haverhill, Hannah Swarton of Casco Bay, and Elizabeth Heard of Cocheco served in different ways, but in Mather's view each woman was a defender of Zion.

Wilderness courage and Protestant piety were both important ingredients in the myth of frontier heroism which was born in the narratives of King Philip's War and nurtured in the ministerial histories which followed. In real life the relationship between heroism and religion was far more complex. On closer examination, Hannah Duston's aggression was linked less to a militant Puritanism than to a violent underside in the village culture of New England; Swarton's resistance to Catholicism was less striking than the capitulation of other captives; while Heard's home-bound piety, though less spectacular than either, had a greater significance in the long-range history of New England—a significance discovered, however, not in ministerial narratives but in close examination of female roles in the religious development of the region.

Chapter Ten

VIRAGOES

Boston's North Church, April 1697: Cotton Mather is in the pulpit concluding a sermon on the humiliations which must precede conversion. He pauses, then looks toward the women's side of the meetinghouse, where a housewife from Haverhill sits silent in her best gown and hood. Mather begs his congregation to permit a digression, for before his very eyes is a woman who has known the real humiliation of a frightening captivity among savages. If God could deliver her from an enemy so terrible, surely He might deliver a repentant soul from the greater bondage of sin. Though fainting and weary, still recovering from the birth of a child, God had sustained Hannah Duston in the wilderness and given her the courage to slay her captors. Her deliverance was an emblem for all New England.[1]

Did Hannah look at the pulpit or at her hands as Mather spoke? As she sat in his church that spring morning and heard him "Publickly & Solemnly" and with all his authority as a servant of the Lord Jesus Christ call upon her "to make a Right use of the Deliverance, wherewith He has Highly favoured you," did she think of her sister Elizabeth? Did Mather? Did he remember that other sermon he had preached just four years before? In that age so conscious of family, surely he or others in the congregation must have realized that Hannah Duston, the Indian fighter, and Elizabeth Emerson, the condemned murderer, were sisters. Yet no commentator, from the seventeenth century to the present, has ever linked their two stories.[2] In 1697 Hannah Duston confessed to killing ten sleeping Indians and was proclaimed a savior of New England. Not for a hundred years would anyone question her motivation or her behavior. In 1693 a jury had convicted her sister Elizabeth Emerson of killing her twin babies at birth. Though she denied it, no witness appeared in her favor. The infamy of Elizabeth casts an unexpected light on the fame of Hannah, forcing us to place "heroism" within the wider context of violent behavior.

Hannah Duston and Elizabeth Emerson were both unusual. In their society, as in every other for which information is available, females were less disposed to physical aggression than males.[3] In Essex County in the last years of the seventeenth century, women were assailants in fewer than twenty percent of court cases involving some form of violent behavior.[4] Yet a closer examination of court records from the region suggests that their behavior, though unusual, was unusual in patterned ways. If most women avoided using physical force, a significant and highly visible minority did not. The two sisters touch opposite margins of a larger fabric of female violence in northern New England.

Colonial Americans would never have focused upon a quality such as "violence" in the way we are doing here. For them, there could be no real connection between Hannah Duston and Elizabeth Emerson because they performed in radically different settings. Role was more significant than personality. Some of their contemporaries certainly knew the family connection, but because premodern Americans did not always draw firm connections between external behavior and intrinsic character, they would not have drawn from it the same significance as would a twentieth-century psychologist or, for that matter, a nineteenth-century romantic like Hawthorne. Certain patterns of behavior could be put on and taken off according to circumstances without altering the essential nature of the person; women could act as "deputy husbands" or men as "brides of Christ" without becoming any less "submissive" or "masterful" in other social relations. A psychologist might look for developmental patterns in the Emerson family, a romanticist for some dark secret which might explain a common flaw. Colonial Americans were interested in neither. To understand their perceptions of Hannah Duston and Elizabeth Emerson, we must search for the roles these women filled.

War and infanticide, the most public and the most private of violent acts, describe two extremes of a far more common response to human stress. Violence can be defined as any physical assault upon a person or property. In northern New England a number of almost ordinary vignettes typified the normal range of violent behavior—a master beating his servant, a woman throwing stones at a neighbor's hog, a crowd of young troopers fighting in a tavern, one man tearing down another man's fence. Each incident was defined by the position of the assailant and the victim in a hierarchy of social relations.

Authoritarian violence was employed by a superior to enforce obedience by an inferior—the servant had hidden when it was time to rake hay.

Defensive violence involved direct action against a perceived trespass—the hog had gotten through the fence and was rooting in the corn.

Disorderly violence, often associated with drinking, had no immediately visible objective, yet almost always involved an audience and a bid for attention. It both defined and made bearable the position of an inferior in the underlying order which it attacked—training day had been hard and hot and the rewards few; it was time to let off steam.

Demonstrative violence involved a premeditated assault on authority in an effort to witness an injustice—the fence stood on disputed land.

In colonial America the first two types of violence were seen positively as well as negatively. The essential question was not whether the master had the right to strike the servant or the woman to drive off the pig, but whether the violence used was excessive and whether other, more peaceful means had been available. Here the issue was abuse of, rather than disobedience to, authority. The last two types of violence clearly stood beyond the bounds of law, but even here the aggressor respected the very bounds he violated. If there had been no law against fighting in the tavern nor a proscription against tearing down fences, the aggression would have been without social meaning. All four types come close to what Emanuel Marx has called "social violence"— that is, aggressive behavior by ordinary persons for more or less clearly understood ends.[5]

Viragoes 187

In contrast, *anti-social violence* signaled the aggressor's alienation from the community. Murder or suicide destroyed the social bond rather than simply trying to contain or enlarge it. Such a typology will not explain the origins of violence, but it will help us to see something of its range. A closer examination of each type reveals certain clearly established female roles.

FROM THE WHIPPING POST on the town common to the pudding stick in the hand of a mother, colonial Americans accepted *authoritarian violence* as essential to social order. The most extreme forms of violence were monopolized by the state, which had the power to kill as well as to whip, but masters, mistresses, schoolmasters, and parents had not only the right but the obligation to administer physical correction if needed. As Anne Bradstreet put it, "some children (like sowre land) are of so tough and morose a dispo[si]tion, that the plough of correction must make long furrows on their back, and the Harrow of discipline goe often over them, before they bee fit soile to sow the seed of morality, much lesse of grace in them."[6] Though wife-beating was technically illegal, it too was at least tacitly condoned by the society.[7] In litigation the issue was not the right of the superior to use force, but the appropriateness of its administration. Presented with evidence of a bruised limb or a broken head, the court tended to ask: Did the citizen resist the constable? Was the child or the servant incorrigible? Did the wife provoke the husband?

When neighbors initiated court action against Elizabeth Woodbury for striking Elizabeth Heriden, Heriden admitted that her mistress had "never struck her but two blows in her life, and those might have been given to a child of two years."[8] As the weakest members in the social order, children were probably the most frequent victims of authoritarian violence, though their stories seldom reached the court. Servants account for the largest number of cases, probably because the family bond which often seals even abused family members to silence was missing. Some New England women were fully capable of hurting their servants. In 1666 Judith Weeks of Kittery was "bound over . . . to answere her Confession for Cuttin off her servant Nicholas Woodmans toes."[9] The record does not tell whether her blade accidentally met his bare foot while they were grubbing roots or chopping wood or whether she had deliberately countered a threat to run away with one swift (and eventually fatal) stroke. For a mistress, gross violence was unusual. In dealing with servants, as well as with their own children, women were presumed to be softer than men, though weakness, rather than gentleness, was the perceived difference here. When Thomas Maule and his wife were tried, their servant Joan Sullivan testified that the master used a horsewhip, whereas the mistress simply thumped her and turned her out of doors.[10]

Women could be victims as well as perpetrators of authoritarian violence, though the extent of wife-beating is difficult to measure because wives might fail to press charges even after fleeing to their neighbors for help. Elizabeth Ela ran to William White's house crying that her husband had beaten her and threatened her with a knife. "Alass, poore woman, I am sorry for you," White said. "Sorry," said she, "if you will not entertaine mee & lett mee abide in yor house I will lie in the street in the snow & if I perish, my blood be upon yor head." Other neighbors testified of Goodman Ela's ill-temper and his wife's desperation, but when the case came to court, Elizabeth meekly recanted. If she had "spoke Agenste him: Abowghte his barbarose usage toward me," it had all been in a passion. "I have nothinge Agenst my husband to charge him with."[11]

Guilt as much as fear may have motivated the recantations. Since childhood, colonial Americans had learned that submissiveness to authority and careful attention to duty were the best assurance of good treatment. If their parents or their master beat them, they had probably deserved it. Most assaults upon women seem to have been provoked by some sort of overt challenge to male authority—a widow questioned her son's distribution of resources, a wife refused to feed the pigs or fetch a scythe from the field or she undermined her husband in front of his friends. Robert Holmes quietly described his own situation: "I Being about to corak won of my children my wife indefring to take it aweye and some words she gafe me that stord up my anger and i gafe her several Blows."[12] In his own view, he was not an evil man; he just didn't like to be questioned, especially in front of a neighbor. Magistrates could not condone such behavior; but they could understand it.

For wives and widows, as well as for servants and children, submissiveness was the best protection.

In *defensive violence,* however, wives were in a far more favorable position. As deputy husbands, they could protect their families or property against an intruder, using any means at their disposal—stones, sticks, or pots of boiling water. Some women proved themselves powerful defenders. When Nathaniel Keene complained of Joanna Williams for striking him with a club, she insisted she acted in self-defense. There had been an argument over a boundary. Keene had come to her house while her husband was away, perhaps deliberately. Unable to get help from the neighbors, she had gone to the field, threatening to break his compass if he did not get off the land. Sarah Keene and Elizabeth Hammans, who saw the whole encounter from a distance, described it in court as a kind of slow-motion pantomime:

> and as she Strook him we saw him fall as he was running from her and She also fell and then they got both up & said Keene went from her and She followed him bending of her fist as if she threatened him but the wind blowing, we could only hear her voyce but could not understand what She Said.[13]

Joanna was acquitted.

Trespass is the key motif in most such records. Often the immediate provocation was a runaway pig or cow, though commercial life could also generate conflict. Thomas Maule, the inspector of Salem Market, complained that when he tried to weigh a bag of bread he believed was underweight, the baker Elizabeth Darby "took me by the throat & with her fist punched me in the Breast soe that I was faynt for want of Breath."[14] Specific encounters with neighbors often reached back to a long pattern of conflict involving husbands, wives, and children in various combinations. When Robert Potter tried to take several of Mr. John Hathorne's shoats to the pound, Hathorne struck him with a barrel stave while Mistress Hathorne and their children scratched him and pulled his hair. When Goody Potter joined the fray, Hathorne hit her with a board.[15] A few years later Hathorne was on the receiving end in a similar conflict. When he tried to seize calves and hogs won in an attachment, John Gifford struck him with the stale of a rake and Mistress Gifford bit him on the back of the hand.[16]

Biting and hair-pulling were frequently employed by women against male aggressors, perhaps because they administered considerable pain without a great deal of force. Hair-pulling had symbolical significance in male-female encounters, since most women kept their own hair tucked under a coif or cap and only men let their hair hang free. As witchcraft lore shows, hair (like nail parings or urine) was perceived as an extension of the person and might have magical potential as well.[17] This may help to explain the curious behavior of Mary Tucker. When Leonard Belringer came to her house and asked for a drink, she said he didn't need it and threw him out. Then she followed him to the yard, grabbed him by the hair, and pulled him to the ground, beating his head upon the paving stones until her maid ran for help, fearing she would kill him. One witness saw Mary pull Belringer's hair out and shove some of it in her pocket. When told that was not a Christian thing to do, she flung it away.[18] Would the hair give her additional power over her victim—or was she simply taking a trophy like Hannah Duston?

A woman like Mary Tucker pushed beyond defensive toward *disorderly violence.* Belringer was perhaps a frequent and troublesome customer for her ale or cider. After a hard day she may have been incapable of dealing with his provocations, yet this hardly explains the extremity of her behavior. She was so out of control that even her maid had to intervene, reversing roles for a time with her mistress. Disorderly violence was especially disturbing to observers because it did appear uncontrolled, random, and unprovoked. One man might be sitting "peacably and quietyly by the fire" when another came staggering through the door, struck him, and pulled him into the street.[19]

For males, disorderly violence was often employed to assert or reinforce status within a group. The evening after a military muster or the first night ashore after a fishing expedition were frequent settings. Small resentments or subtle affronts to individual dignity, suppressed in the discipline of training and work, might break out at nightfall, especially under the influence of alcohol.[20] For women, communal enterprise does not seem to have provoked direct aggression, perhaps because group work was more casual and less tightly disciplined, but also because it was often focused on the care of the sick or newborn. There is, however, one fascinating though somewhat obscure incident in the New Hampshire court records: A number of married women were sleeping at the house of Walter Abbott, perhaps taking turns watching during an illness or lying-in, when a disturbance erupted in an outer room. Ann Jones clambered out of bed in time to see Alice Cate and Sarah Abbott down on the floor, both of them bloody. "She hav a most bit of my thum," Abbott screamed. Perhaps too much beer and a chance remark by Sarah Abbott had unleashed her uncontrollable rage. Ann Elliot later testified that she had to "thrust her the said Allies Down before she this Deponent could part them & get her thumb out of her mouth." Alice Cate could only sob that Goody Abbott was the cause of her losing her child.[21]

A look at the overall sample of court cases from Essex County suggests a different and somewhat more surprising pattern, however. Although male aggressors attacked other men in seventy percent of the cases in which they were involved, the much smaller number of female aggressors attacked men equally as often as they attacked other women.[22] Male violence, that is, was apparently more sex-linked than was female violence. Although women were less disposed to use physical force than men, when they did they broke through a powerful gender barrier. Violent men were still men; violent women became superwomen, amazons, viragoes. Bawdry frequently combined with physical aggression in depositions regarding female disorder, suggesting that such women derived their terrifying strength by combining male aggressiveness with the force of female sexuality.

A woman like Elizabeth Fanning both fascinated and horrified her neighbors. A whipping was little deterrent to her "opprobrious, vile carriages." She threw a brick at Henry Luke and went after John Ally with a hatchet, forcing him to leap over a fence for fear of his life. She had even been seen beating her husband, but when he broke his leg, she came to him in a mockingly seductive manner and said, "O pore ould roge, is they leage broke i will leke [lick] it hole."[23] In their outrageous behavior such women compressed two forms of disorder: sex and violence. Surely this is an underlying and perhaps unconscious meaning of the myth of Jael: "He asked water, and she gave him milk; she brought forth butter in a lordly dish. . . . She put her hand to the nail, and her right hand to the workmen's hammer; and with the hammer she smote Sisera, she smote off his head."

Demonstrative violence witnessed an injustice. Through an assault upon a person or property, it appealed to a higher authority, to a court, to the neighborhood, or only to some more exalted sense of justice. On a Monday morning in May of 1674 a widow named Joane Furson, with three married daughters and two of their children, went into a cornfield belonging to Richard Cummings of Portsmouth and began pulling up the new shoots. Neighbors quickly gathered around, amazed and puzzled by what they saw. Though some tried to persuade them to quit, the women continued their work, saying they would set up a wigwam in the field and stay all night. "Is this the way to get your rights?" John Fletcher asked. "Yea," the women answered, "Mr. Comings will not come to speake with us wee desire that he would sue us."[24]

Years before, Cummings had been involved with the widow Furson's first husband in the purchase of land. She was certain that her share had never been sold or conveyed, yet Cummings had refused to listen to her grievance, having sent her a twenty-shilling payment as dower. She and her daughters were convinced that they deserved more and that a direct assault on Cummings' land was the best—and the cheapest—way to advertise their claim. "Mr. Comins may doe what he pleases but wee cannot have Justice for wee have not fatt hoggs & shoulders of mutton & pockets full of money as mr. Comins has to fee great men with," they said. Their dramatic action did bring a suit, though with quite different results than they had expected. The magistrates were far less interested in Furson's claims to the land than in the flagrant destruction of the corn. She and her daughters' husbands were forced to pay the full value of the harvest which the newly planted corn might have yielded, as well as the fees of the court.[25]

Though unsuccessful, Joane Furson's assault on Cummings' corn illustrated the essential features of demonstrative violence. As in disorderly violence, a conscious violation of role boundaries played an important part. The widow's aggression highlighted both her weakness in relation to Cummings and her determination. The stance of the men in her family is particularly interesting here. According to the witnesses, her daughters' husbands stood in the field the whole time, neither helping nor trying to stop the women. "Doe you allow of the womens pulling up the corne?" one neighbor asked. The sons-in-law neither accepted nor denied responsibility. "Lett the women doe what they please wee will stand by them in it," they answered. When Cummings sued, Widow Furson humbly beseeched the court to lay all of the blame upon her. The whole thing had been her idea, she insisted, and her daughters just happened to be with her when she decided to pull up the corn. Unfortunately, the presence of the men in the field made it impossible for them to deny their involvement.[26] The fact that they remained aloof from the actual violence, however, is in itself significant.

Drunkenness or passion might excuse disorderly violence, but a deliberate and premeditated assault upon authority was more difficult to explain. Numbers often provided some safety. Half a dozen outraged farmers pouring out their corn in the constable's yard made the point much more effectively than one—next time the constable would be on time at the landing to collect the county tax.[27] Letting women perpetrate the crime was an even more effective strategy. Because only a deeply felt outrage could call forth feminine aggression, the demonstrative power of the act was increased; because women were presumably weaker than men, the resistance which they met might be less; and, finally, because women were by nature less stable, more easily misled or beguiled, their husbands could pass the whole thing off as a momentary lapse of patriarchal control. Wives could act out a rebellion which men might formally deny. Is it mere coincidence that wives so frequently tangled with constables when they came to collect taxes?[28]

The most dramatic (and certainly the bloodiest) incident of demonstrative violence in northern New England was implemented by a group of Marblehead wives at sunset on a Sabbath evening in July of 1677 just at the end of Metacom's Rebellion. Although the war had wound down in the south, a related conflict had broken out in Maine, where Abenaki Indians had begun to attack Essex County fishing vessels. When a group of local fishermen who had escaped from their captors came into the harbor bringing two Abenaki prisoners with them, a crowd rushed to the waterside, demanding to know why they had left the Indians alive.

The men answered that they had lost all they had in the attack and hoped to realize something from their captives, and that they intended to take them to the constable so that "they might be answerable to the court at Boston." But as they came ashore:

> the whole town flocked about them, begining at first to insult them, and soon after, the women surrounded them, drove them by force from them, (we escaping at no little peril,) and laid violent hands upon the captives, some stoning us in the meantime, because we would protect them, others seizing them by the hair, got full possession of them, nor was there any way left by which we could rescue them. Then with stones, billets of wood, and what else they might, they made an end of these Indians. We were kept at such distance that we could not see them till they were dead, and then we found them with their heads off and gone, and their flesh in a manner pulled from their bones. And such was the tumultation these women made, that for my life I could not tell who these women were, or the names of any of them.[29]

There is a strong suggestion that the women acted as surrogates for the larger community, since no one in that small town was willing to identify or prosecute them. Their violence was demonstrative, directed at the perceived lenience of the magistrates in Boston as well as against the Indians themselves, but in murdering the two Abenaki braves they called upon the even more powerful persona of the disorderly woman. So immense was their rage that no authority could contain them. Boasting that they might kill "forty of the best Indians in the country," they symbolically restored the potency of a frightened and desperate community.

This was not "frontier vigilantism," as one historian has suggested, but an American version of an Old World pattern. Natalie Davis has demonstrated that from the seventeenth to the early nineteenth century the image of the "disorderly woman" sanctioned riot and political disobedience in England. Women were directly involved and even led some of these demonstrations. In others, male leaders assumed female disguise, blacking their faces and putting on women's clothing. Female disguise had both practical and symbolic value. Petticoats and soot were available in almost every house. More important than that, however, such disguise "freed men from full responsibility for their deeds and perhaps, too, from fear of outrageous revenge upon their manhood. After all, it was mere women who were acting in this disorderly way."[30]

The use of disguises in mob violence is a familiar pattern in later American history—patriots dressed as Indians dumped tea into the harbor in Boston, vigilantes with their faces blackened like slaves rid their community of undesirables. The use of female disguise in such riots has not been studied, though there is one fragmentary but fascinating example from northern New England. On September 1, 1719, John Roberts, deputy sheriff of Exeter, attempted to serve a writ on Richard Hilton and was greeted in a time-honored manner. Mr. Hilton seized Roberts by the throat "so hard that he was Licke to have choaked him." Mrs. Hilton "furiously assaulted him," pulled him by the hair, grabbed his writ, and tore it. Two days later Roberts returned with reinforcements and an arrest warrant, but when he approached the house, he saw what appeared to be thirty or forty persons inside, some of the men "in womens Cloaths & others with their faces smuted as black as Negroes."[31] The yeomen of Exeter, like their counterparts in England a hundred years before, knew the power of female identity in demonstrative violence.

Thus, Hannah Duston's heroism belongs to a much larger tradition of violence in northern New England. Raising her hatchet, she defended herself and her companions against a dangerous assailant, enlarging the quite commonplace role of a wife as deputy husband and defender. The mythic power of her act—though of course not its setting—reached toward a much deeper tradition of disorderly and demonstrative violence in both England and America. As an Amazon, she transcended feminine roles without departing from them.

What then of Elizabeth? Hannah's sister was one of eleven persons executed for murder in Massachusetts between 1630 and 1692. Four of those convicted murderers were women, three of the four had killed their own children.[32] The crime of infanticide has had a complicated history. In medieval England it was not considered homicide at all, but was a lesser crime punished by the church courts, which did not distinguish it from induced abortion. By the seventeenth century, both in Old England and in New, infanticide had become not only a capital crime but a crime of the weakest and most desperate of women.[33] In New England, women convicted of infanticide were almost always servants, women on the fringes of society, often Irish, Indian, or Black, the very persons who would have been most likely to have been beaten and abused themselves. Infanticide was a difficult crime to prove, since newborn infants were notoriously fragile. Had there been malice? Neglect? Or simply little breath in the child to begin with? After 1692 the colonial laws were revised to make "concealing the death of a bastard child" punishable by death.[34] In the context of contemporary attitudes toward childbearing, infanticide was not just a cover-up for sexual misbehavior, it signaled a rejection of the entire social and human order. To fail to call the midwives placed a woman outside the community; to become "the butcher of her own bowels" gave the crime an almost suicidal dimension as well.

Yet, curiously, the printed memorials of convicted murderesses show a strenuous effort on the part of the religious community to bring these women back into the circle of human society.[35] God might redeem even the most despicable of his children, but only if they acknowledged their rebelliousness, their disobedience, their depravity—only, that is, if they absolved society of any responsibility for their desperation.

In her confession, taken down in 1735 by York's minister, Samuel Moody, an Indian servant named Patience Boston admitted to having had murderous feelings toward her baby "when I perceived it's crying, and it's taking up my Time to tend it, caused some Uneasiness in the Family." When it died two months later, she felt herself a murderer. Patience's long confession is an almost excruciating account of deprivation and rage, a rage which she finally turned inward, becoming a notorious self-accuser. She was finally executed for pushing her master's eight-year-old child into a well. "I would have killed my Master myself, if I could have done it," she told Moody, adding that when she saw that the boy was dead, "I lifted up my Hands with my Eyes towards Heaven, speaking after this manner, Now am I guilty of Murder indeed."[36]

Elizabeth Emerson was not a servant, but she was an unwed

mother who not only failed to call the midwives but concealed the deaths of her babies as well. She was the fifth (and Hannah Duston the oldest) of the fifteen children of Michael and Hannah Emerson of Haverhill. Her father, a farmer and shoemaker and occasional grand-juryman, had been an early settler of the town. Her mother, the daughter of a baker and the stepdaughter of a miller, had spent her early years in Ipswich and Newbury. Except for the unexpected heroism of one daughter—and the equally spectacular deviance of another—we would know the Emersons as common folk, hard-working, sturdy, and no more or less visible in local records than most of their neighbors. When Michael Emerson died in 1709, in confident hope of "a glorias Resurection," he left land to his sons, movables to his wife, and "the sum of twenty pounds" to Hannah and her sister Abigail.[37] Elizabeth, of course, was long dead and perhaps forgotten.

When Elizabeth was born in January of 1665, Hannah was eight, Mary was five, John was almost four, and the baby Samuel not quite two. She was eleven when Hannah married, and perhaps there was special feeling between the two. Hannah named her first baby for her mother (and herself), but the second for Elizabeth. By this time Elizabeth was rapidly growing up in a house filled with siblings and marked by recurring seasons of travail and loss. She saw nine younger children born to her mother, five of whom died. None of this was unusual in New England, but something in Elizabeth's personal experience made her different. Perhaps she began in early childhood to press a little harder for her parents' attention than most, arousing first the annoyance and then the anger of her father. "I was always of an Haughty and Stubborn spirit," she later confessed.[38]

In the spring of 1676, when Elizabeth was eleven, Michael Emerson made his one and only appearance in Essex County Court as a defendant. With some reluctance perhaps, since he was then serving as juryman from Haverhill, the magistrates fined him "for cruel and excessive beating of his daughter with a flail swingle and for kicking her."[39] Note the word *excessive*. Elizabeth, unlike other children in the family, may have responded to her father's first whippings with open defiance rather than obedient submission, her resistance fueling his anger, and his anger reinforcing her resistance, until he had finally passed the line drawn in this society between godly sternness and cruelty. Six months later the court abated his fine and released him from the bond of good behavior.[40]

As she entered her teens, Elizabeth's rebellion took another form. She began to keep "bad company" and was, by her own confession, led to the "sin of uncleanness," and eventually became pregnant. Like many girls before her, she might have married hastily, faced the condemnation of church and court, and gone on to live a respectable life. But when she accused Timothy Swan of getting her with child, her reputation in Haverhill was too poor to make the charges stick. Swan's father told the justice of the peace, Nathaniel Saltonstall, that he had charged his son "not to go into that wicked house and his son had obeyed and furthermore his son could not abide the jade."[41] Wicked house—the phrase sticks in the mind, but cannot be precisely defined. Did it refer only to Elizabeth or did it extend to her father? In April, Elizabeth gave birth to a daughter, named Dorothie (perhaps defiantly) after Timothy Swan's older sister.[42]

For the next five years she continued to live at home as "Elizabeth Emerson singlewoman," perhaps keeping her little daughter in her parents' house. If she ever regained her maidenly figure after the first pregnancy, she soon lost it, putting on so much weight that by the winter of 1691, though the neighbors suspected she was with child, they could not be sure. When her mother finally queried her, she denied it, though some alert women in the neighborhood obviously kept close watch. On the morning of May 10, 1691, a Sabbath, under warrant from Major Saltonstall, two men of the town with Hannah Browne, Judeth Webster, Goodwife Hannah Swan, and widow Mary Neff came to the Emerson house while Elizabeth's parents were at public meeting. That they would come on Sunday suggests that they were alarmed. That they would come while the Emersons were away suggests that they expected opposition, though we cannot be certain.

They found Elizabeth washing dishes but looking "very ill." While the women took her into the chamber to investigate her condition, the men went to the garden. There they found two little bodies sewn up in a bag and buried in a shallow grave. The women were not sure whether the babies had been born dead or alive.

One of them had its umbilical cord twisted about its neck and one "of its hands clapt upon the same," but "wheather itt were a willful act of murder by the mother or any Else ... we do certainly believe that the children perished for want of help & caer att time of travell."[43] Curiously, one of the women who examined Elizabeth that day was the very same Mary Neff who would accompany her sister Hannah into the wilderness and return with her to Boston with ten Indian scalps.

What exactly had happened in that "wicked house" in Haverhill? The next day Elizabeth told her story to an unknown official (perhaps Nathaniel Saltonstall) as she lay on her bed in her parents' house. Her tale, recorded in the clipped responses of the formal examination, etches the desolation which awaited a young woman who could neither submit nor escape. The setting itself, a trundle bed at her parents' feet, speaks eloquently of Elizabeth's dependence and of the desperate need of the parents to control this puzzling and wayward daughter.

Q: What is yor Husband's name?
A: I have never an one.

Q: Were you ever married?
A: No: never.

Q: Have you not been a second time Delivered, & had Two Children or Twins this month?
A: Yea, I have.

Q: When were they born?
A: On Thursday night last, before day toward Friday morning. But I am not certain of the time of the night.

Q: Where were they born?
A: On the bed at my Fathers bed foot, where I now am.

Q: Did you call for help in yor travel?
A: No: There was no body to call but my Father & Mother, & I was afraid to call my Mother for fear of killing her.

Q: Did you acquaint your Father or Mother with it afterwards?
A: No, not a Word: I was afraid.

Fearful of hurting her mother and perhaps simply fearful of her father, she gave birth silently on a trundle bed at their feet, gagging her own pain with the greater fear of discovery. She insisted that neither child cried at birth.

> Q: Did you not do them to death, by violence, sitting down upon them, smothering them, or by any other meanes?
> A: No: by no meanes.
>
> Q: Where did you hide them before buried?
> A: In the chest there; by my bed.

The magistrate was incredulous. Elizabeth had simply hidden the babies and, though weak, had gone about her work as though nothing had happened.

> Q: Who helpt you sow them up in the bag they were found in?
> A: No body.
>
> Q: When did you sow them up in the cloth they were buried in?
> A: On Saturday night last.
>
> Q: Where were your Father & Mother?
> A: My Mother was gone to Milking & my Father was abroad.[44]

Though pressed by the examiner, Elizabeth's parents insisted they had not known that she was pregnant nor had they known of the birth or the burial.[45] Perhaps they simply refused to notice what at least some of their neighbors saw. Perhaps they were incapable of noticing. They were absolved in a preliminary hearing. Elizabeth was taken to Boston, where she was tried by a jury and on September 22, 1691, found guilty of murder.[46] On June 8, 1693, she was hanged, but not before sitting in Cotton Mather's church and listening to a sermon on the madness of sin. Mather begged Elizabeth to vomit all of her sins. "I Question whether ever any Prisoner in this World, enjoy's such means of Grace as you have done since your Imprisonment," he exclaimed, "and it may be there never was a Prisoner more Hard-Hearted, and more Untruthful."[47]

Still, though her repentance had been incomplete, she had left a last confession, which Mather read for the edification of the youth of the congregation. A modern reader might reject the moral of Elizabeth's story without denying the validity of her conclusion: "I believe, the chief thing that hath, brought me, into my present Condition, is my Disobedience to my Parents: I despised all their Godly Counseils and Reproffs; and I was always of an Haughty and Stubborn Spirit. So that now I am become a dreadful Instance of the Curse of God belonging to Disobedient Children."[48]

In Elizabeth's story a romanticist will certainly find the dark secret of the Emerson family and a psychologist the developmental pattern which will explain the heroism of her sister Hannah. A historian, on the other hand, can simply remind them both that early New Englanders would not have seen it that way at all.

Chapter Eleven

CAPTIVES

Between 1689 and 1730 nearly three hundred women, men, and children were taken captive from northern New England. For frontier wives, the possibility of capture must have meant a contraction of boundaries in these years, an augmented fear of going to the well after dark or of sending children to a nearby wooded fringe to gather berries. But paradoxically, perhaps, the fact of capture might have meant an expansion. For those actually taken, new worlds both of terror and of possibility were opened. The captive described in the ministerial literature was invariably an innocent Christian seized by rude savages and subjected to capricious taunts and torments mitigated only by Providential intervention. Captivity thus became a ritualistic journey of salvation, a passage through suffering and despair toward saving faith. In reality, captivity was sometimes a journey toward a new home, a new occupation, new friends and family, or at the very least toward earthly experiences little imagined in the farms and villages left behind.

Only by looking at all the known captives—those who escaped, those who returned, those who died, and those who stayed with the Indians or the French—can we understand the significance of the dramatically visible heroines of the wartime literature. Because captivity was an extraordinary experience shared by ordinary men and women, it is worth exploring for another reason as well. Although cold, hunger, fear, and forced contact with an enemy culture were experiences shared by captives of all ages and both sexes, captivity often took adults and children, females and males in different directions, illuminating role boundaries which might not be otherwise apparent.

EARLY IN THIS CENTURY Alice Baker and Emma Coleman set out to collect all known information about New England captives taken to Canada, adding to the colonial documents and local traditions many baptismal and marriage records gleaned from Canadian archives. Building upon this information, we can trace 270 captives taken from the region between 1689 and 1730.[1]

Like Hannah Duston, most prisoners were taken from their own houses in attacks involving several dwellings in their neighborhood if not an entire village. The towns of origin of the 270 captives place Mather's "Valley of Achor" unmistakably in the region of New England north of Cape Ann. Sixteen of the recorded captives came from Hannah Duston's town of Haverhill and a few others from the Essex County towns of Newbury, Salisbury, and Amesbury. Almost all of the others came from the New Hampshire and Maine settlements north of the Merrimack. It is not surprising, given the massive assaults on York in 1692 and on Oyster

Table 5. New England Captives

	Total	Escaped	Ransomed	Died	Stayed	Unknown
ALL FEMALES	128	2%	50%	3%	27%	16%
Over 21	52	6%	63%	6%	4%	21%
12–21	19	0%	36%	0%	58%	5%
Under 12	38	0%	40%	2%	42%	15%
Age not known	19	0%	52%	0%	31%	15%
ALL MALES	142	8%	50%	10%	13%	18%
Over 21	60	10%	61%	11%	3%	13%
12–21	21	19%	42%	14%	23%	0%
Under 12	41	2%	46%	10%	17%	24%
Age not known	20	0%	35%	5%	20%	40%

1. Compiled from Emma Lewis Coleman, *New England Captives Carried to Canada* (Portland, Me., 1925), individual biographies in Volume I, Chapters 6–10, 12–14; Volume II, Chapters 15–17.

River in 1694, that a fifth of the captives came from these two towns. With York, the towns along the Piscataqua River—Dover, Exeter, Oyster River, Kittery, and Salmon Falls—accounted for more than half. Twenty came from the more compact village of Wells, Maine, while the scattered plantations above Wells—Scarborough, Casco, Saco, Cape Elizabeth, Yarmouth, Pemaquid—accounted for the remaining eighty.

James Axtell has suggested that in later wars Indian captivity was primarily an experience of women and children.[2] In northern New England in these years this was not so. Although unmarried girls and boys under the age of twenty-one accounted for two-thirds of the captives, this proportion was not much different than in the general population. Among adults, fifty-two women appear on Coleman's lists and sixty men. The overall proportion of males to females was almost equal: 142 to 128.

Axtell has also described the phenomenon of the "white Indian," the captive who chose to stay, or was enticed into staying, with his or her captors. Again there is little evidence of this in northern New England, perhaps because the Abenaki Indians, who accounted for many of the raids, were less interested in adoption than in ransom. Coleman found information on only four "white Indians" from northern New England. Joanna Ordway of Newbury, who was sixteen when taken, remained in Canada and married an Abenaki. Tradition says that Martha Clark of Casco and Samuel Gill of Salisbury also stayed with the tribe which captured them. Sarah Hanson of Cocheco was adopted by Canadian Indians, but eventually married a Frenchman. There may have been more, since eighteen percent of male captives and sixteen percent of female were simply lost to the record. Among documented cases, however, "Anglo-French" are far more numerous than "white Indians."

Age was a key factor in determining the outcome of captivity. Captives over twenty were half again as likely to return as those under. Even more important than age, however, was gender. Although equal proportions of males and females were eventually ransomed, males were more likely to escape or to die, females to stay with their captors. Males resisted; females adapted. Still, escape was an uncommon feat for either sex. Only eight percent of males as compared with two percent of females managed to get away, and among all the escaped prisoners, male or female, only Hannah Duston and her companions returned with enemy scalps.

Hannah Duston's escape was unusual, but her physical condition at the time of capture was not. Fully one fifth of adult female captives from northern New England were either pregnant or newly delivered of a child. Their ability to cope with captivity is striking. Hannah Bradley of Haverhill and Tamsen Drew of Oyster River lost infants born in Indian camps, but three Maine women, Anne Batson, Sarah Cole, and Hopewell Hutchins, all in the second trimester of pregnancy when taken, delivered healthy children, baptized soon after birth by solicitous Canadian priests. Five other women, including Hannah Duston, marched northward while still experiencing post-partum symptoms.

According to Cotton Mather, Catherine Adams of Wells was dragged from her house only eight days after delivery. When told to walk, she was unable to stir, even with the help of a stick, but with prayer a new strength came into her. She trudged twenty miles the first day, was up to her neck in water six times, and at night "fell over head and ears" into a swamp. To the minister, it was miraculous that "She got not the least Cough nor Cold by all this: She is come home alive unto us."[3] Within the larger record of captivity her health seems less miraculous than commonplace. Whatever their condition, women taken from northern New England survived. Death claimed only three of fifty-two adult captives.

This is in sharp contrast to the record from another part of New England. Nine of twenty-three women taken from Deerfield in western Massachusetts in 1705 died or were killed. To John Williams, the Deerfield pastor who was himself among the captives, the death of fainting women came to be expected. Williams' own wife, who had lain in a few weeks before, nearly drowned while crossing a stream and was killed by an Indian soon after. Another captive "Who being nigh the time of travail, was wearied with her journey" was slain, as were four others also said to have been "tired."[4] Ministers were not required to explain why God gave one woman the strength to move on and another only the courage to die, but historians cannot so easily assign events to Providence. The frequent mention of physical fatigue and physical disability in Williams' account suggests that most Deerfield women were killed because they could not or would not keep up the pace required by the flight into Canada. Perhaps women from the northern frontier with its sawmills and isolated garrison houses may have been more accustomed to wilderness travel than women taken from Deerfield's village center.

In sorting out such differences, however, we must look at the captors as well as the captives. The Abenaki Indians pushed their English captives far beyond their own presumed ability: Hannah Swarton wrote of traveling "over steep and hideous Mountains one while and another while over Swamps and Thickets of Fallen Trees, lying one, two, three foot from the ground, which I have stepped on, from one to another, nigh a thousand in a day; carrying a great Burden on my Back."[5] But almost as frequently the narratives testify to Indian assistance in coping with the unaccustomed rigors of life on the trail. Elizabeth Hanson left a particularly detailed account. Her Indian master carried her newborn baby and sometimes even her blanket "tho' he had, as is said, a very heavy Burden of his own." Though Elizabeth climbed mountains so steep that she "was forc'd to creep up on my Hands and Knees," her master helped her. "When we came at very bad Places, he would lend me his Hand, or coming behind, would push me up before him: In all which he shewed some Humanity and Civility more than I could have expected."[6]

"Humanity" certainly had something to do with the treatment the captives received, but there were additional motives. Since prisoners were taken for ransom, for enslavement, or for adoption, their captors had a real stake in their survival. Here the differences between the Deerfield and northern New England captives become most apparent. The Deerfield women were all taken by Mohawk Indians in a single winter attack on their village. The northern New Englanders were taken by Abenaki Indians in much smaller groups in a series of attacks over a period of thirty years. An unusually large group of captives both increased the liability and decreased the value of any one individual. Even if they might bring a good ransom, pregnant or post-parturient women were a high-risk group. For a tribe primarily interested in adoption, as these Mohawks seem to have been, they were worth less effort than a sturdy child.[7]

For whatever reason, most wives taken captive from northern

New England survived. Returning to towns like Haverhill or Oyster River or York or Berwick, they gave their communities an image of "wilderness courage" more vivid and more immediate than any promoted by the Boston press. Their heroism was less spectacular than that of Hannah Duston, but it was noted and appreciated by their countrymen. Sylvanus Davis wrote a long letter to "be Communicated To the Inhabitants of the Province of Maine" based on intelligence collected by Esther Lee during her short period with the eastern tribes.[8] Grace Higiman, Tamsen Drew, and Ann Jenkins traveled to Boston in 1695 to testify before the governor and council regarding the activities of an Indian named Bombazeen. Higiman demonstrated a particularly sharp memory for names, numbers, dates, and geographical detail, and after three years among the Canadian Indians she felt free to offer the councilors advice on military strategy as well as specific information. "I apprehend That if the yearly supply from France to St. John's could be intercepted they would be greatly distressed and forced to draw off," she told them.[9]

In King Philip's War frontier women had been employed in diplomatic negotiations. After a year among the Abenakis, Elizabeth Hammon wrote and delivered a letter from her captors describing possible terms of settlement with the English. As the wife of a trader, she was already adept at communicating with the Indians.[10] Cotton Mather recorded two instances of similar service by women in King William's War. When ten English captives were redeemed at Sagadahock in 1691, the Indians were "very loth" to part with Mistress Hull "because being able to Write Well, they made her serve them in the Quality of a Secretary." Goody Stockford, an otherwise unidentified captive, was a more direct intermediary between the two sides. She returned to the English as a messenger, then went back to the Indians with a shallop full of "Charity" with which to redeem other prisoners.[11]

It would be interesting to know whether captivity affected the lives of these women after their return. After two or three years in foreign parts did they come back to their struggling villages with new ideas or skills? Did the ability to survive wilderness trials and to adapt to an alien culture change their self-perceptions? Did captivity increase their respect for either enemy or only fan wartime hatred and resentment? We cannot know. Few captives left written records; almost all returned to the obscurity from whence they were taken.

IF THE MAJORITY of New England captives returned to their homes, an appreciable minority did not. The behavior of these New Englanders raises the complicated problem of assimilation. Why did some choose to remain with their captors? Here again gender was a crucial factor.

Figures from Deerfield show that many more girls than boys remained among the Indians. Unfortunately, there is not enough evidence from northern New England to draw any conclusions about the importance of Indian assimilation. The record for the French, on the other hand, is clear. Statistics confirm the perceptions of the Boston ministry that if New Englanders in captivity were threatened by "savages," they were even more strenuously enticed by "papists." Twenty-nine females and fourteen males from northern New England made new lives for themselves in Canada. That twice as many females as males remained with the enemy can be attributed to three factors: the primacy of marriage, the influence of religion, and the supportive power of female networks.

Marriage was the single most important factor in determining which female captives returned and which stayed in New France. Only one married woman stayed, and, as we shall see, her situation was exceptional. The two other adults who remained in Canada had both been widowed by the war, while all the other expatriate females were single women and girls. In fact, fifty-eight percent of female captives between the ages of twelve and twenty-one found new lives in the land of their enemy. This is, of course, precisely the age group which in New England would have been putting lamb bones under pillows or counting daisies or otherwise thinking about what the future might bring. If these captives did not prove as resolute as New England ministers might have hoped, it was because they had always known that their future life would depend more than anything else on the choice of a mate. Every girl knew that she would eventually leave her father and mother and perhaps even her community to marry. To leave the country, the language, and the culture of one's childhood was *not* expected, of course, but in courtship proximity is more important than any other factor. Maine and New Hampshire were far away and French (and sometimes Indian) suitors insistent. Furthermore, there was no parent's guiding hand to restrain a youthful infatuation.

In New France the captives had found a country in which marriage may have been even easier than in New England. The first English captives arrived in Canada after the colonization policies of Jean-Baptiste Colbert, Louis XIV's minister of internal affairs, had already proved successful. Observers in the late 1660s reported a line of settlement along the St. Lawrence; farms were replacing forests, crafts and trades were appearing. It is clear from contemporary documents that industrious settlers of both sexes were welcome in the French settlements, though, as in all pioneer societies, women may have been especially welcome.[12] Furthermore, it would have been easier for females to assimilate simply because a wife usually assumes the status of her husband. The wife of an Indian or a Frenchman could become Indian or French by virtue of marriage.

The importance of the marriage choice becomes even more apparent if we look at the three adult captives who remained. Abigail Turbet's story is somewhat obscure; she died not long after making the decision to stay, so it is difficult to know if she would have returned eventually, yet she probably had little reason to do so. Her husband had died during her captivity and she had no children.[13] There is no question about Abigail Willey's motivation, however. For her, a forced journey to Canada brought freedom from bondage of a different sort. She had no desire to return to her husband, whom she had previously accused in court of insane jealousy and repeated cruelty. He was perhaps just as ready to forget her, for when he went to sea in 1696, he made out a deed of gift which ignored the existence of a wife in Canada. French and Indians effected a separation which New Hampshire courts had denied. For more than a decade Abigail lived as a single woman in New France, part of the time in the service of Messire Hector de Callières, governor of the Island of Montreal. In 1710, now listed as a widow, she married Edouard de Flecheur.[14]

Grizel Otis was also a widow. Her husband had been killed in the attack upon Dover. Within six months in New France she had married Philippe Robitaille, a Montreal cooper. But for Grizel there was an additional factor—religion. Although her husband had been a Quaker, her mother had been Irish and probably Catholic as well. Soon after her arrival she was baptized by a Canadian priest, as were her three-month-old baby, Christine, her two-year-old daughter, and four stepchildren and grandchildren. All of these children and grandchildren grew up in Canada, married there, and, with the notable exception of Christine, remained for the rest of their lives.[15] Captivity brought Grizel a new opportunity for marriage, but, perhaps even more important, it returned her to the faith of her mother.

The story of Grizel Otis Robitaille also illustrates the significance of the network of female captives which developed in Montreal. Grizel's easy assimilation into French faith and society may have been a bridge for Abigail Willey, who was related to her by marriage.[16] Although she seems to have had no prior connection with Abigail Turbet, in 1705 she witnessed Turbet's deathbed abjuration of the Protestant faith and her acceptance of Catholicism.[17] For some New England women, Canada offered an opportunity for a new life, but in New France opportunity was often linked to religious institutions fully as zealous as any in New England and to a system of support provided by godly women.

Unlike the Protestant communities of New England, New France offered women not one but two life choices, each exemplified in the biographies of two Maine girls: Esther Sayward, who in 1712 became Madame Pierre de Lestage, and her sister Mary, who a few years earlier had taken vows and become Soeur Marie-des-Anges.[18] Both girls had been captured as children and educated by the Sisters of the Congrégation de Notre-Dame in Montreal.

Women stand side by side with men in the legendary accounts of the founding of Montreal, the one city in North America unequivocally established through religion.[19] As a sister of the Congrégation de Notre-Dame, Mary Sayward belonged to one of two important Montreal institutions founded and continued by women. As nuns of L'Hôtel-Dieu (hospital), Mary Silver, Mary Ann Davis, and Ruth Littlefield were associated with the other.[20]

Mary Silver of Haverhill was sixteen when she was captured in 1708. Two years later her mother petitioned the General Court, begging help in securing her release. She was worried about her daughter's soul, as well she might have been, for two months earlier Mary had been baptized in Montreal with the High and Mighty Seigneur Messire Philippe de Rigaud, Marquis de Vaudreuil, Chevalier of the military Order of Saint-Louis, and Governor General of New France, standing as godfather. A year later Vaudreuil wrote Governor Dudley of Massachusetts that Mary was as free as any of the English captives to return, but that he wouldn't force someone to go back who wanted to stay. Mary had already entered the order of St. Joseph as a Soeur L'Hôtel-Dieu, as had another Haverhill girl, Mary Ann Davis, who had been captured fourteen years before. Seven-year-old Ruth Littlefield of Wells, who would eventually join them as a hospitalière, was probably among the children being educated at the nearby convent school.[21]

The religious influence of the New England converts spread outward from Montreal. When a mission and school were established at Sault-au-Récollet in 1701, Mary Sayward went there as superior. There she taught Indian girls and young English captives brought from her homeland. She may have been the "papist Englishwoman" who tried to comfort Joseph Bartlett of Newbury when he was brought to the mission in 1708. In 1712 she heard Hannah Hurst, a Deerfield captive, declare her wish to live among the Indians and marry there, and although there is only circumstantial evidence of this, she may also have met her cousin Esther Wheelwright of Wells, who was taken from the Abenakis in 1709 and who afterward became the fifth and most famous of the New England nuns.[22] Esther, who took final vows in 1714, was twice superior of the Ursuline convent of Quebec. Though she eventually re-established contact with her family in Maine, she never renounced her new religion. "God himself assures us," she wrote her mother in 1747, that "he who leaves for his sake, Father, Mother, Brothers and Sisters, shall have an hundred fold in this life, and Life eternal in the next."[23]

Since the New England captives who stayed in Canada included daughters of prominent families, it is little wonder that officials at home worried over the threat of French Catholicism. John Williams, the minister of Deerfield, devoted most of his captivity narrative to the spiritual threat of "papacy." In a wartime tract directed to the inhabitants of the frontier, Cotton Mather urged New England captives to fortify themselves through knowledge of the scriptures, strict observance of the Sabbath, and mutual supports through meetings and prayer.[24] A tract printed in Boston was an ineffective shield against the French assault. English girls who arrived in Montreal, Quebec, or the outlying missions encountered a world which was highly religious, oriented toward conversion, and at the same time almost exclusively feminine.

French proselytizing touched adult women as well as their daughters. Although Elizabeth Hanson, Hannah Swarton, and Margaret Stilson resisted Catholic influence and eventually returned to tell of their triumph, almost a third of adult female captives made at least some capitulation to the French. Only Grizel Otis, Abigail Willey, and Abigail Turbet fully converted, but Anne Batson of Scarborough, Tamsen Drew of Oyster River, Mary Plaisted of York, Sarah Cole of Saco, and Mehitable Goodwin, Elizabeth Tozier, and Martha Grant of Salmon Falls all accepted Catholic baptism, though they eventually returned to live in New England. Among adult males, only one—Tamsen Drew's husband, Thomas—accepted baptism. There is no indication of coercion here. Though the priests might take an infant from its mother's arms to sprinkle it against the fires of Hell, they did not forcibly baptize adults. The "susceptibility" of these women to Catholicism is best explained in social terms. In New France the religious institutions which were most intimately involved with captives were dominated by women.

The most frequent name on baptismal records of New England captives of all ages, both those who returned and those who stayed, is that of M. Henri-Etoine de Mériel, who was not only priest of the parish of Notre-Dame but also chaplain of the Hôtel-Dieu and confessor of the pupils and sisters of the Congrégation de Notre-Dame.[25] Though Father Mériel was himself interested in the captives, the fact that twice as many females as males succumbed to French influence points beyond the zealous father to the sisters who nursed and taught them after their purchase from the Indians. Nearly all of the girls who married and stayed in New France were first nurtured by nuns and baptized under their care. Local tradition says that after a year with the sisters, eight-year-old Sarah Gerrish of Dover went home in tears, hiding a little crucifix under her armpit.[26] The ministry to the captives became even more effective with the addition of the English sisters, including Mary Silver, who eventually succeeded Father Mériel as catechist. The network of female captives in New France—from Grizel Otis Robitaille, who established her family in Montreal in 1689, to the last of the captives in the wars of the eighteenth century—deserves further study, but its existence seems certain.[27]

By putting one foot in front of the other, New England women and their daughters survived the trek to Canada. Once there, they responded in different ways. Some interpreted their captivity, much as the ministers did, as a spiritual quest for courage and faith. Others accepted it as both an opportunity and a trial. Little girls responded to the nurture they were given, sometimes embracing a faith foreign to New England. Older girls, especially those in their teens or early twenties, frequently chose to marry rather than to wait months and years for ransom. Most adult women kept their eyes on home and eventually returned, though not without accepting French friendship and eventually French religion. If female New Englanders resisted captivity less strenuously than males, their adaptation was never merely passive. They proved themselves "movables," like the pots, pans, and cows which formed the chief female inheritance in either country.

ONE OF THE MOST VISIBLE—and movable—of New England captives was Christine Otis of Dover, New Hampshire. The details of her life portray the often dramatic contrast between literary heroism and life. Christine was taken to Canada as an infant with her mother, Grizel Otis Robitaille. She grew up in New France, was educated by the sisters of the Congrégation, and in 1707 at the age of eighteen married Louis Le Beau. In 1713 he died, leaving her with two daughters. A year later she married Captain Thomas Baker, a Deerfield captive who had escaped in 1705 and who now returned to Montreal as an interpreter with a party of English negotiators. Christine followed her new husband back to Massachusetts, though French officials denied her permission to take her children by Le Beau. In 1722, with support from the Massachusetts government, she briefly returned to Montreal to assist in retrieving some English captives, and again she petitioned—unsuccessfully—for custody of her daughters.[28]

In 1729 she received an earnest letter from her mother's confessor, François Seguenot, who addressed her as "my dear Christina, poor stray sheep," urging her to return to New France. Christine's own response to this letter is unknown, but her husband was concerned enough about it to give it "to a Gentleman well vers'd in that Language to transcribe, in order to employ some person to answer it." Both the translated letter and the answer appeared that year as *A Letter from a Romish Priest in Canada*. A personal appeal which had perhaps originated with Christine's mother thus became a ministerial polemic, as the anonymous Protestant tangled with the Jesuit point by point in a debate over scriptural interpretation and ecclesiastical history. Christine's own soul was obviously of less interest to either side than the argument it made possible.

In a telling passage the Protestant apologized for the level of the discourse. "I perceive Madam," he wrote, "that I am quoting Authors that are unknown to you; but you may lay the blame of it upon Mr. Seguenot, who amuses you with Stories, into the truth of which you can never examine." The condescension of Seguenot was almost as pronounced. He urged Christine to read his letter again and again, since her eternal happiness or misery was at stake, but he also asked her to show it to her ministers and requested that they reply to him in Latin or Greek if they did not know French![29] The two clergymen were conducting a professional argument using a specialized vocabulary reserved for insiders. Fine distinctions between "the Spouse of Christ" and the "invisible Church" or between "priestly sacrifice" and "the Lord's supper" probably meant little to Christine Otis Le Beau Baker, who had experienced the conflict between English Protestantism and French Catholicism on a far more personal level.

When Thomas Baker died in 1735, she decided to begin life again for a third time. Having lived the first twenty years of her life in Canada and the second twenty in Massachusetts, she took the proceeds of a land grant from the General Court and set herself up for the remaining forty as a tavernkeeper in Dover, New Hampshire, the town where her story began. Uprooted by war and transplanted by marriage, she returned to the home of her birth. There she died in 1773, a curious relic of the age of female heroism in New England.

Chapter Twelve

DAUGHTERS OF ZION

WHEN CHRISTINE OTIS BAKER returned to the Piscataqua in 1735 and joined the congregational church at Dover, she entered a world strikingly more "religious" in the formal sense than the one she had left behind as an infant captive. In 1689 there had been five congregational churches in Maine and New Hampshire; in 1735 in the very same area there were twenty-one.[1] In neighborhoods where there had once been only preaching (and that sporadically), there were now fully organized congregations with deacons and sacraments. It was ironic that Christine, whose father had once been fined for Quaker sympathies, should return from French Catholicism to the respectability of the congregational faith, for Quakers were now tolerated in Dover as elsewhere in northern New England.[2]

As a Quaker, Christine would have participated in a "Women's Meeting" which had its own leadership, its own area of jurisdiction, and its own voice in the government of monthly and quarterly meetings.[3] Having chosen equality, however, she would also have chosen a way of life at the periphery of New England society. Religion in northern New England was dominated by the congregational way.

More important to the long-range history of New England women than the fighting viragoes who resisted the enemy or the stalwart captives who surmounted the wilderness were the ordinary and invisible women who filled these churches in the first decades of the eighteenth century. Most congregations were predominantly female, though women were denied full participation in the establishment or the governance of religion. At Hampton

Falls in 1712, for example, seventy percent of the original communicants were women, yet only men signed the church covenant; women simply assented.[4] As members of churches ostensibly organized by the laity, congregational women achieved an equivocal status; they could acquiesce, but not lead.

Still, church membership was one of the few public distinctions available to women. Men could be fence-viewers, deacons, constables, captains, hog reeves, selectmen, clerks, magistrates, tithingmen, or sealers of leather. Women could be members of a gathered church. In a society in which church membership had to be earned, this was no small distinction. Furthermore, church membership was not contingent upon any other social role. A woman could be admitted to the Table of the Lord regardless of the status, economic position, or religious proclivities of her husband. As his deputy, she could reckon with a neighbor. With or without his blessing, she could settle accounts with God. Females not only achieved church membership more frequently than males, but they did so at a younger age. In two Andover churches in the years between 1711 and 1729 women on the average became church members a full decade before men of comparable age, suggesting that godly wives may indeed have led their husbands to Christ, as so many ministers hoped.[5] With or without their spouses, women in New England accepted Christ. In the church at Berwick only 39 of 155 women admitted between 1708 and 1752 were joined by their husbands.[6]

Just as church membership gave women independent status, religious teaching often ratified traditional female values, supporting old wives in their guardianship of sexual mores, elevating charity over commerce and neighborliness over trade, but, above all, transforming weakness into gentleness, obscurity into humility, changing worldly handicaps into spiritual strengths. Women may not have interpreted religion in exactly the same way as ministers, but they cared about the churches. To understand the importance of religion in northern New England, we must consider first the social and then the personal roles fulfilled by religious women in the years between 1650 and 1750.

CHURCHES WERE tax-supported public institutions. As a consequence, controversies over the settlement and maintenance of ministers, the placement of meetinghouses, or the subdivision of congregations often had economic and political ramifications. Most historians have read these events as exclusively public issues, understandably—but mistakenly—ignoring the roles of women. By piecing together scattered evidence from a number of communities, we can discern three significant roles for women in these community battles. Relying upon private power within their own families, women promoted the establishment of religion in outlying areas of older towns; using their influence within the village network as well as with their husbands, women served as guardians of ministerial reputation; and, finally, drawing upon the authority of their own powerlessness, certain women became vessels of the supernatural.

Men signed petitions, wrote the appeals, and cast the votes, but women frequently supplied the energy which established new congregations and parishes in the outlying areas of older towns. The same pattern was repeated over and over again in New England. One segment of a township, pleading distance and inconvenience, asked to be separated from the original. The old, jealous of its power of taxation, refused. The controversies which resulted fill the pages of seventeenth- and eighteenth-century records and figure prominently in community studies by twentieth-century historians. Yet, without recognizing the quite different practical problems of men and women, it is impossible to fully understand the motivations of the "outlivers." Why, for example, should aspiring freeholders in remote sections of town want to increase their own tax burden? As Richard Bushman has observed, they sometimes "wanted to support a church even before they were financially capable of doing so."[7] They may have been seeking ratification of their own separateness, but they may also have been responding to very real pressures at home. The petitions themselves suggest this. Whether written in seventeenth-century Massachusetts or eighteenth-century New Hampshire, the same argument appears again and again. Aged or feeble persons and especially mothers with young children could not walk three or four miles to meeting every Sunday, especially in winter.

Ann Jenkins and Tamsen Drew had trekked six hundred miles into Canada, but their husbands still signed the petition from Durham Point in 1718 pleading the inconvenience of coming two miles to meeting.[8] For women, the problem was not inability to walk, to manipulate a canoe, or to ride a horse. Most women were held at home by breast-feeding, by the care of infants and young children, and by concern over the reliability of servants. The same problems existed in Scotch-Irish settlements in New Hampshire in the 1700s as in Puritan settlements in Connecticut in the 1600s. They were in the nature of female life. In old age Catherine Smith recalled her first years in the new settlement of Bedford in the 1740s. "We could seldom hear a single sermon without going to Londonderry. But we did na' always stay at home. Annie Orr, and I, carried my Robert in our arms when he was ten months old, travelling on foot, to Mr. McGregor's meeting; Ben [her husband] went with us, but he did us little good, for he was not worth a fig to carry a bairn."[9]

Other fathers may have been more willing to carry their children, but they did not have to care for them during the meeting or feed them between sermons. Entreating her uncle, John Winthrop, Jr., to support the establishment of a church at Mistick, Connecticut, Hannah Gallop wrote of the problems facing mothers who came long distances to meeting and then stayed in the town all day "without any substance" so that those "that have young children sucking, manie times are brought exeding faint, & mutch weakened, & divers are not able to goe al winter."[10]

When the inhabitants of Chebacco petitioned the town of Ipswich in 1677 for liberty to call a minister, they complained of the three-to-five-mile journey to the meetinghouse. In winter the days were short and the way hazardous and long. "Though som of us, with som difficulty, doe sometimes assemble with your selves yet the greatest part are constrained to tarry at home." Children could not attend meeting, and if left at home without supervision or with unreliable servants, they were likely to "prophane that holy day." The town predictably insisted that these outlivers were not "able to bear the weight of theire owne undertakings." The taxes simply would not stretch to accommodate another minister. In Ipswich the position of the outlying inhabitants was especially sensitive because the town had been conceived as a nucleated village with farmers living in the center and traveling to the periphery to cultivate their crops. The town implied that the residents of Chebacco had brought their problem upon themselves. They might consider "that what burthen lyes upon them the first day of the week the same or greatter lyes upon theire friends in the towne the other six."[11] But, of course, it was not the *men* of Chebacco who had been inconvenienced. It was their wives and children. The price men were paying for the comfort of living on their own farms was intense pressure from their women for the right to go to church on Sunday.

That the pressure was indeed coming from the female side of the church is apparent in the next episode in the chronicle of Chebacco. While the men fought it out in town meeting and court, the women privately schemed—and then acted on their own. As the parish clerk so quietly put it in a church history written sometime afterward:

> while we were in this great conflict that all things seemed to act against us som women without the knowledge of theire husbands and with the advice of some few men went to other towns and got help and raised the house that we intended for a meeting house if we could git liberty.[12]

The wives of William Goodhue, Thomas Varney, and Abraham Martin ended up in county court, where they were fined for contempt of authority.[13] Their behavior is a classic example of the kind of demonstrative disobedience described in Chapter Ten, but it is also evidence of the concern of at least some New England women for the establishment of their church. Their impetuousness was expensive but effective. Within a few months Chebacco got permission to call a minister. When the church was gathered, it had a building to meet in.

The behavior of the wives of Chebacco is more visible than most female activity in northern New England, but their objective was probably characteristic. Women had a vested interest in the establishment of churches. The relationship between women and the ministry was not always a comfortable one, however. In illness and death or in cases of marital disruption or sexual misbehavior, the authority of the clergy might encounter the equally powerful influence of the old wives of the community. When the interests and perceptions of the two were in harmony, the combination was powerful, but when they were at odds, a clash was possible. The most obvious conflict involved folk magic. Ministers were outraged when they found parishioners draping their doorways with bay leaves or baking witch cakes at the suggestion of a neighbor, but the most serious opposition came not from cunning women, whose activities were easily dismissed as "superstitious," but from matrons who shared the minister's basic values.[14] In these cases, circumspect church members measured ministerial behavior against ministerial profession and sometimes dropped a telling remark or two into the pot of village gossip. Simmering there, it might boil over in public conflict months or even years later. Women could not control salaries, but they could control reputation, and of course they could use the same weapons in attacking ministers as they used in promoting churches—their influence with their husbands.

Conflict between ministers and influential matrons is at least one ingredient in prolonged and acrimonious church controversies in Rowley in the 1670s, in Salem Village in the 1680s, and in Durham in the 1720s. In October of 1672 Jeremiah Shepard was invited to preach at Rowley for a year. The town already had one minister, Samuel Phillips, who continued as teacher after the death of the old pastor, Ezekiel Rogers. Shepard, though younger than Phillips, was a candidate for Rogers' position. Obviously, there was the potential for jealousy, but Phillips apparently supported his young colleague during the first year. After sixteen months, though there was some dissension, Shepard's invitation was renewed, but by spring, when he asked for membership in the church as a prelude to a coming bid for ordination, a vigorous controversy emerged. The church rejected him, not being "satisfied as to his piety, nor spirit."[15]

What had the young minister done to offend the sober Christians of Rowley? The evidence is scanty but intriguing. At the end of a tumultuous meeting in which the church voted to cut Shepard off even before his time was up, Samuel Phillips wrote that Shepard had a "loose tongue," that the church did not like the company he kept, and that they suspected he neglected his studies and his family. Then he added:

> In the time of my wife's long and dangerous sickness he came below to look upon her and there took offense that she did not show him respect though my wife affirms that

she bowed her head as well as she could being then entering into her ague fit, but he never would come to see her though I wished him to do it.[16]

The coughing spell in Mistress Phillips' parlor was probably the culminating event in a long and perhaps unconscious struggle.

Mistress Phillips was not the only woman to tangle with this self-important young minister. When one of the deacons informed Shepard of the church's decision, he immediately blamed "Goody Elithorp," whose comments (to Phillips?) had apparently helped to fuel the opposition. The woman hated him so much, he said, that "if she had an opportunity he doubted not but she would cut his throat, yea, so far as a man can know a woman's heart by her words she would actually do it."[17] Shepard's dismay at the inscrutable territory of a "woman's heart" suggests one source of his difficulty. He simply did not know how to deal with an important part of his constituency.

Contempt for—or, perhaps more accurately, fear of—female power is a crucial element not only in Shepard's story but also in those of George Burroughs and Hugh Adams. Burroughs, like Jeremiah Shepard, encountered trouble as a new minister in a rural community. He arrived in Salem Village in 1681 and abruptly left in 1683 after his salary had been withheld. For a time he and his wife lived with Captain John Putnam, who later had him arrested for debt as he stood in the meetinghouse pleading for his back salary. Beyond that, little is known of his brief tenure except that his wife died during his stay in Salem. Nine years later he was brought back from Maine and tried as a wizard.[18]

Paul Boyer and Stephen Nissenbaum have been unable to fit Burroughs' story into the larger Porter-Putnam controversy which they believe dominated Salem Village politics in the years before the witchcraft outbreak of 1692.[19] This may be because personality rather than politics was the cause of the minister's troubles. During his witchcraft trial John and Rebecca Putnam told a story in public which had probably been told often in private in Salem Village, perhaps in the hearing of the afflicted girls whose supposed demonic possession brought Burroughs and the other accused witches to trial. (We will return to the religious role of those girls, but for the moment our concern is with Burroughs.) According to the Putnams, during the time that Burroughs lived in their house he had a serious argument with his wife, so serious that he asked them to come into the room and hear it out. Burroughs wanted his wife to "give him a written covenant under her hand and Seall that shee would never reveall his secrits." The Putnams were astonished. Wasn't the covenant of marriage covenant enough? All the time that Burroughs was at their house, they added, "he was a very sharp man to his wife, notwithstanding to our observations shee was a very good and dutifull wife to him."[20]

By some mysterious process the two main details in this story—the signing of a covenant and the man's anger with his wife—emerged in the spectral evidence which convicted Burroughs. To the afflicted girls, he was not only a witch but the ringleader of witches, the man who forced women to sign the Devil's black book. Furthermore, his two dead wives had appeared in their winding sheets and testified that their husband had killed them. Reports from neighbors reinforced evidence from the invisible world. It did not help Burroughs' case when two matrons from his new congregation in Maine appeared in Salem to tell of his unkindness to his second wife, describing her appeals to neighbors for help and his almost paranoid anxieties about her conversations with other women.[21] Burroughs' secrets were known in the community of women, both in Salem Village and in Maine. When public officials listened to those secrets, the result was devastating.

Hugh Adams was explicit about the source of his trouble: Elizabeth Davis. Mistress Davis' first contact with the church at Durham after its establishment in 1718 was to ask for baptism for herself and two sons. Like many other adults in this community, she was not yet formally a Christian. Her husband, Lieutenant Colonel James Davis, town moderator, assemblyman, and justice of the court of common pleas, remained outside the fold.[22] Elizabeth's squabble with Adams emerged into the public record in 1723 when she and James both applied for admission to the church at Dover four miles away which both of them had ignored for most of their lives. Adams was furious. He did not mind losing Mistress Davis as a communicant, but he did not want the embarrassment of her acceptance by a neighboring congregation.

He quickly dispatched an "ecclesiastical document" to the

"Reverend Honorable and beloved" Mr. Cushing at Dover, detailing the scandalous behavior of Davis and his wife. The Colonel had taken a false oath, Adams said; he had been instrumental in withholding the minister's salary, had coveted the parsonage land for his son, and had used his position as judge "against his own legal minister for so innocently playing at nine pins at a house no ways license for a Tavern." But his real crime was in harkening to his wife more than to the Lord of Heaven (or his pastor?). Mistress Davis had publicly railed against Adams by saying that he had spread a lie about Sobriety Thomas, had resisted his efforts to call her son to account for his involvement with said Sobriety, had mocked Christ's ordinances by saying that a disciplinary meeting was "going to be another cabal," but especially had been "a busy body at every one of her husbands Courts to be his advisor or intermedler in his passing Judgement in any case."[23] An imperious minister had met an imperious matron! Elizabeth Davis openly defied Adams and she used her influence with her husband to harass him. On November 23, 1723, she and James were admitted to the Dover Church, where they remained until continuing conflict in Durham finally resulted in Adams' expulsion from the pulpit in 1739. Not surprisingly, Colonel Davis was prominently involved in the settlement of the new minister, Nicholas Gilman.

The ministers in these three stories, though different in other ways, shared two common traits: an acute sensitivity to patriarchal authority and a failure to measure up in some way to the standards they professed. Shepard neglected his studies; Burroughs was unkind to his wife; Adams played at ninepins in a tavern. But their real flaw was more damning: they mistrusted a "woman's heart." This is not to say that every case of ministerial disruption in early New England was caused by gender conflict. It is simply to assert that personal as well as economic and social conflicts shaped religious establishment, that the ability to win the confidence of the female members of a congregation was one ingredient in ministerial stability, and that women without formal power might still wield influence.

The third way in which women influenced religion in northern New England was through ecstatic or hysteric utterance as intermediaries between the visible and invisible worlds. Two of the most dramatic examples of this occurred at Salem Village in

1692 and at Oyster River in 1742, in the very churches which had earlier ousted George Burroughs and Hugh Adams. Our objective in citing these cases is not to explain the psychological mechanism which first propelled women and girls into public view, nor to untangle the social and theological complexities which permitted them to stay there, but to delineate a religious role available to New England women.

When Deodat Lawson, a former preacher at Salem Village, heard of the apparent outbreak of demons there, he hastened to investigate. Arriving on Saturday, March 19, 1692, he observed two of the afflicted girls at the local inn and at the home of the Reverend Mr. Parris, in whose family the first demonic possessions had occurred. The next day, having accepted an invitation to preach in the meetinghouse, he encountered even more remarkable evidence of the power of Satan. Seven of the afflicted were there—Mistress Pope, a respectable matron of the town; Goody Bibber, a desperately poor and frequently contentious pariah; four maidservants, Abigail Williams, Mary Walcott, Mercy Lewis, and Elizabeth Hubbard; and one child, Anne Putnam. When Lawson opened the morning worship, the entire group fell into fits, causing him to interrupt his prayer. After the psalm was sung, one of the maidservants looked straight at the minister and said, "Now stand up, and Name your Text." When he had read it, she sniffed, "It is a long Text." The sermon had hardly begun when the formerly circumspect Mrs. Pope spoke out, "Now there is enough of that." The child, Anne Putnam, would also have testified out loud if the women around her had not prevented it. Little Anne was certain she had seen a yellow bird sitting on the minister's hat as it hung on a peg by the pulpit.[24] Because their affliction placed them outside society, the possessed could command their minister, speak in the church, and comment on the sermon as no other child, servant, or female adult could have done. Like the disorderly women of Marblehead, they were able to do things that rational persons and especially responsible male officials could not.

In Durham, New Hampshire, in 1742, children, maidservants, and several young men as well saw visions and fell into trances, but Nicholas Gilman, the new pastor in that village, saw this as evidence of God's rather than Satan's power. In the afternoon service on March 3, "Mary Reed declared in Publick the close of Her last Vision," after which Gilman "added a word of Exhortation to the People." There was no disruption here, because the minister accepted the role of the young woman as seer. When Stephen Busse saw a white dove come down into the meetinghouse on another occasion, Gilman interpreted it as a sign of God's blessing.[25]

A detailed comparison of the role of seer in the witchcraft accusations and in the Great Awakening might yield important insights into changes in female roles in northern New England.[26] One obvious difference is worth noting here. In Salem Village, visionary girls began by attacking older women. Although men, and even some very prominent men, were eventually included among the accused, in its initial stages it seems to have been an intragender conflict. Young women in tune with the supernatural accused old women of being in tune with the supernatural. The Great Awakening, in contrast, tended to break down both gender and social barriers in a common quest for a witness of the divine. Nicholas Gilman is a striking example of this. Hungering for evidence of the workings of the Holy Spirit, he fine-tuned his spirit to the responses of his listeners, leaning on them as fervently as seeking Christians leaned upon their pastors. This reversal of roles is most apparent in Gilman's relationship with Mary Reed, an obscure young woman whose very existence in Durham would be unknown except for her amazing influence upon her minister.

On March 26 she came to Gilman's house in the evening and told him "She had been exceeding full of Joy all day that it Seemd to her she was not here, and it had run in her Mind all day—this Night shall thy Soul be required." She instructed Gilman to send for her clothes and dispose of them to the poorest persons in town, then she went to bed, and after "many deep Sighs as tho' Her soul was departing" fell into an "almost breathless sleep." Since his wife was then away in Exeter, Gilman worried about how his "character and conduct . . . would be represented abroad," but when Mary awakened, she assured him that he should not "mind what men said" but should "Mind what the Spirit of Christ Says." Mary Reed stayed at the Gilman home from Saturday evening until Tuesday morning, sleeping, instructing her minister, praying, and "Singing praises to God in Extempore Verse."[27] Gilman neither counseled nor tried to "cure" Mary Reed. He marveled at her receptivity to the spirit, and when she spoke, he listened. All boundaries—of sex, of wealth, or of education—dissolved in a common rapture. Like the young women of Salem fifty years before, she had become a vessel of the supernatural.[28]

WOMEN HELPED TO SHAPE religion in northern New England, but it is important to recognize that their effectiveness was dependent upon the approval of the men who voted the taxes, called the ministers, and interpreted the visions. The more successful and dramatic witnesses of female power were also the most short-lived. The women of Chebacco meekly recanted their disobedience. Elizabeth Davis left the Durham church long before the minister she attacked. The visionary young women of Salem and Durham faded into obscurity, while the ministers who supported them soon lost favor with their congregations. The most important story of religion is to be found not on the institutional but on the personal level and especially on the level of belief. For some women, affiliation with a church may have had more social than religious significance, but for others, religion provided a way of ordering the most basic experiences of human life. To approach this inner dimension of religion, we must turn once again to the wartime literature of northern New England, to the crisis of captivity, and to the discovery of heroism which it made possible. Rare self-portraits of two women, Mary Rowlandson and Elizabeth Hanson, show strikingly different responses to pain and death, suffering and sorrow, anger and fear, but especially to the experience of subjection. For these women, Indian captivity heightened trials which all women shared. Their narratives make accessible patterns of female response which might not have been visible otherwise, and they help us to relate the development of religion to the problem of assertiveness raised in the myth of Jael.

One narrative was published in 1680, the other half a century later in 1729. One woman was a Puritan, the other a Quaker. One woman spent her captivity among a community of local Indians who had long associated with the English. The other was seized by a small band of Canadian Indians who eventually sold her to the French. One woman wrote her own story, the other simply told it to a visiting preacher, who took it down, as he said, "from her own Mouth." Obviously, differences in belief and in circumstances determined contrasts between these two stories. But for the moment let us ignore the stories' particular historical settings, and consider them as different human responses to a similar situation. Both women were deeply religious Christian Protestants. Both were captured in frightening attacks which resulted in the death of loved ones. Both carried children with them into the wilderness. Both attributed their deliverance to the mercy of God and published their stories in order to promote piety and to return thanks to Him. By examining the survival strategies which the two women used, but especially by looking at their perceptions of their captors and of themselves, we can more fully grasp the interior religious experience available to colonial women.

The primary social category in Mary Rowlandson's tale is race, in Elizabeth Hanson's gender. For Mary Rowlandson, the principal determinant of worth was religious status; for Elizabeth Hanson, religious temperament. In practical terms, Mary Rowlandson survived because she knew how to use English huswifery in the service of her captors; Elizabeth Hanson, because she was able to form a bond with Indian women who taught her what she needed to know. In religious terms, Mary Rowlandson was saved because God chose her, though she was utterly helpless and worthless outside His sustaining care. Elizabeth Hanson was saved because patience, long-suffering, and kindness were more powerful than cruelty. To understand the full significance of their contrasting personalities, we must look at each story in some detail.

Mary Rowlandson's narrative is a powerful and deeply moving piece of writing as long as the reader can suspend twentieth-century judgment and enter a world in which Indians were by definition "atheistical, proud, wild, cruel, barbarous, bruitish . . . diabolicall creatures . . . the worst of the heathen."[29] Like much heroic literature in the western world, it sketches a cosmic battle between foul heathens and fair Christians. Within the limitations of such a setting, Mary Rowlandson emerges as a courageous and ruddy heroine, resourceful, feisty, more housewife than saint, a minister's wife who gave up her pipe-smoking in captivity but not her vivid speech.

Mary Rowlandson suffered the loss of her home and the death of her wounded child, yet she clung to her knitting needles, kept a sure sense of time, and returned to Boston knowing exactly what she had eaten, where she had gotten it, and in whose pot she had cooked it. Her chief work among the Indians was knitting and sewing. Although she served as a slave in Quinnapin's family, she was resourceful in trading her services with other Indians for extra food, exchanging stockings for a quart of peas or a shirt for a bit of bear meat. Into her pocket went everything she begged or bartered—meal, meat, a parched-wheat pancake fried in bear's grease, and even a piece of stale cake handed to her by another Lancaster housewife as they were separated. The cake was perhaps a symbolic tie to the orderly world she had left behind: "there it lay, till it was so mouldy (for want of good baking) that one could not tell what it was made of; it fell all to crumbs, and grew so dry and hard, that it was like little flints; and this refreshed me many times, when I was ready to faint."[30] Characteristically, Mary could not resist commenting upon the quality of the baking even in describing the depths of her hunger.

She was prepared to survive captivity not only by her housewifely skills but also by her understanding of the nature of servility. Even though she hated and feared her captors, she knew how to please them. Growing up in a hierarchal society, she had learned what it meant to be an inferior. Among her many losses was a role shift from mistress to maid, a reversal of what she had experienced in the process of maturing and marrying. Metacom understood this humiliation; just before her redemption he told her kindly that she would soon be a mistress again.[31] Significantly, Mary's portrait of Metacom, the man who began the war, is rather benign. She was equally positive in her portrayal of her own master, Quinnapin, who comes across in the narrative as a dignified and rather distant male authority figure. The real focal point of her hatred was Wetamoo, the mistress who had immediate control of her day-to-day life in captivity.

As she was sitting in Wetamoo's wigwam, Metacom's maid came in with a child in her arms and asked Mary to give her a piece of her apron to make a diaper for it. Mary told her she would not. Even when Wetamoo commanded her to give up the apron, she refused. When the maid threatened to tear it off herself, Mary angrily retorted that if she did, she would tear the maid's petticoat. Wetamoo raised a stick "big enough to have killed me," but Mary dodged it so that it stuck into the mat of the wigwam instead.

While Wetamoo struggled to pull it out, she "ran to the Maid and gave her all my Apron."[32] Had Mary Rowlandson been in her own village instead of an Indian camp and had she been able to find a stick (or a shovel or a pot ladle), a similar trespass upon her property or her dignity might have turned into the sort of squabble so frequently reported in county court records. An inability to resist rather than any lack of assertiveness determined Mary Rowlandson's behavior.

Although she could identify to a certain extent with Metacom and with her master, she was seemingly unaware of the suffering in the Indian camp. Her hunger and cold and pain obliterated the desperation of the Indians, who were literally fleeing for their lives. When a "savage" extended human sympathy, she could only attribute it to Providence. When Wetamoo's baby died, she observed that now there would be more room in the wigwam.[33] Mary Rowlandson's narrative is deeply and pervasively racist, yet, as many scholars have shown, it is not always difference which arouses fear of an alien person or culture so much as a perceived yet repellent sameness. This is amply illustrated in Mary's story. She speaks of the Indians as "Salvage Bears" and "roaring lions," yet the most striking and pervasive animal imagery in the narrative is that which she applies to herself. In captivity she had "only a little Swill for the body, and then like a Swine, must ly down on the ground."[34]

Food is a dominant motif in her portrait of herself. She expended most of her energy begging, contriving, or working for food, and yet her hunger was never satisfied. She relished food she had always refused before, things that even dogs or pigs wouldn't touch—"nuts, acorns, hartychoaks, Lilly roots, Ground-beans, Horse guts and ears, wild birds, Bear, vennison, Beaver, Tortois, Frogs, Squirrels, Dogs, Skunks, Rattlesnakes; yea, the very Bark of Trees."[35] Eating this wild food, she became wild herself. She marveled at her own "Wolvish appetite." When given something to eat, she would burn her mouth rather than wait for it to cool. Seeing an Indian with a basket of horse liver, she begged a piece, then ate it half-cooked "with the blood about my mouth."[36] Another time she saw an English child "sucking, gnawing, chewing and slabbering" a chunk of boiled horse's foot. She took it and ate it, "and savoury it was to my taste."[37] There was no false delicacy in this Puritan wife! In fact, there are several incidents which suggest that her Indian captors were more fastidious than she and may even have found her ways somewhat repulsive. When she met Metacom for the second time, he gave her a looking glass and told her to wash herself.[38]

Mary Rowlandson's description of her own animal nature in captivity—her groveling, her begging, her unkempt state—are consistent with her theology and with her Calvinist perceptions of the depravity of humankind. In this view, all men and women are savage outside of God's covenant. But her own debasement served another purpose as well. The one quality she most consistently attributed to her Indian captors was pride—the worldly pride that would inevitably lead to a fall. She was subjected, they were haughty. The oldest of her master's three wives was "a severe and proud Dame . . . bestowing every day in dressing her self neat as much time as any of the Gentry of the land: powdering her hair, and painting her face, going with Neck-laces, with Jewels in her ears, and Bracelets upon her hands." The gentility of the Indian wife was expressed not just in her concern for clothing but in the work which she did, which was "to make Girdles of Wampon and Beads."[39] Beside her artifice Mary Rowlandson's knitting was servile, as she must have known. She was both repelled and fascinated by the pretentious and colorful clothing of her mistress.

In the experience of captivity Mary Rowlandson found a pattern of her own salvation. In the account which she left, students of religion can discern a familiar psychological type.[40] An acute consciousness of rank and order is coupled in her portrait with a deep sense of sinfulness and of the fragility of human effort. Long habit as well as immediate need put needles in her hands and peas in her pocket, but though her own skills could sustain her, they could not save her. Knowing the superiority of spiritual things, she found herself relishing the basest of material food, both resisting and embracing her own subjection. Rejecting pride, she projected it upon her captors, finding personal redemption but no charity for her enemy in the humiliation of captivity.

In comparison with Mary Rowlandson, Elizabeth Hanson is a bland and almost passive heroine, perhaps because her narrative is shorter and less colorful, but also because she embodied qualities so often associated with an insipid and confining femininity. She too willingly turned the other cheek. At the end of one long day's journey her master commanded her to fetch water, but, having sat awhile on the cold ground, she found she could not stand. So she crawled on her hands and knees along the ground until a young woman from another family took pity on her and went to get the water.[41] This incident was characteristic of her behavior throughout—never any effort to resist a command, simply a mute appeal to justice in an unquestioning and abject obedience. Yet her gentleness was no mere extension of her weakness but a consciously willed religious response. Elizabeth Hanson simply refused to meet violence with violence. According to one New Hampshire minister, the Hansons may have been captured only because Elizabeth's husband, a "stiff quaker, full of enthusiasm, and ridiculing the military power, would on no account be influenced to come into garrison."[42]

Elizabeth Hanson, like Mary Rowlandson, struggled with hunger and cold. She found it distasteful to eat the entrails of wild animals without cleaning them and marveled that what had once seemed foul could now taste sweet, yet the central focus of her narrative was not on the helplessness and vulnerability of humanity but on the power of "God's kindness" to surmount "man's cruelty." Kindness could be found in the wilderness as well as among Christians—"these People being very kind and helpful to one another, which is very commendable."[43]

After a twenty-six days' march into New France, Elizabeth found herself in an encampment of Canadian Indians, where she quickly established friendships with the women of her master's family, despite a barrier of language. Because her fourteen-day-old infant had been spared in the attack, her most persistent anxiety during the trek was a waning supply of milk. Her breasts almost dry, she warmed icy brook water in her mouth, letting it trickle out onto the nipple as the child sucked. This, with an occasional broth made from beaver guts, kept the baby from dehydrating, though by the twenty-sixth day all the joints of its backbone were visible. Finally a friendly squaw taught Elizabeth how to make pap from fine cornmeal cooked with walnut kernels which had been cleaned and ground until the mixture "looked like milk." The shared recipe saved the baby and strengthened a growing bond between the women, who were united in a common fear of the Indian master.[44]

Elizabeth Hanson's portrayal of this man is striking. Although he had beaten her, hit her little son, and threatened to kill her baby, he was never merely a "savage" in her eyes but always a struggling human being. She was terrified of his tantrums, yet she observed that "when-ever he was in such a Temper, he wanted Food, and was pinched with Hunger." Dutiful service (and perhaps her refusal to hate) were her witness against him. After a time the Lord himself "did seasonably interpose" by causing a great sickness to fall upon the man. His wife told Elizabeth that her husband considered his illness a punishment for his mistreatment of the captives. (He had already convinced himself that the baby was a "devil" because it had survived so long on the trail without food.) After his recovery he was not so passionate or so abusive. "This I took as the Lord's Doing, and it was marvellous in my Eyes."[45]

Elizabeth Hanson's hot-tempered master was never as threatening as Mary Rowlandson's "salvages." By humanizing him, she reduced him from cosmic to domestic scale. Facing the abuse of a weak and violent man, she triumphed through her own submissiveness. Like Richardson's Pamela, she knew the moral power in weakness. The underlying message of her story is clear: God will avenge the weak and powerless, but only so long as they remain weak and powerless. Aggressiveness and virtue are incompatible. In a Quaker narrative of 1729 submissiveness is a Christian rather than a peculiarly feminine quality, though the alignment of the poor captive and the equally downtrodden Indian women against the single abusive male is striking.

Mary Rowlandson's narrative had epic dimensions because her personal struggle paralleled a national struggle. Religious, political, and personal themes coalesced, as they had in the tale of Hannah Duston. Elizabeth Hanson, on the other hand, stood outside the religious establishment of northern New England. She could sympathize with the Indians because, as a Quaker, she did not fully identify with the war. The two narratives describe a religion of outsiders and of insiders. As a minister's wife and a covenanted church member, Mary Rowlandson belonged to the elect. For her, salvation came through identification with the powerful—with the saints and with God. For Elizabeth Hanson, salvation did not come through affiliation but through the incorporation or the discovery of Godlike qualities in herself or others.

Now, if we extend the analysis of their captivity beyond the specific imprisonment to the larger world of northern New England, considering the day-to-day and perhaps hardly realized subjection imposed by the hierarchal and patriarchal nature of the society in which they lived, the strikingly different responses of the two women suggest two religious modes available to women. (We are talking here about personal religious responses, not about specific "Puritan" or "Quaker" qualities.) A woman like Mary Rowlandson, struggling to maintain order against the wilderness within, would identify strongly with the role of housekeeper. She would be a supportive wife and a friendly neighbor to women like herself, but extremely suspicious of outsiders and perhaps even aggressive when she felt that her authority or her property had been challenged. Because her sense of worth came through affiliation rather than through merit, she would ally strongly with a minister and a church. A woman like Elizabeth Hanson might identify more closely with the nurturing roles. She would be more trusting of her neighbors, more likely to cross barriers of gender and race in a religious context, but, ironically, even more submissive and obedient, even less likely to resist perceived injustice or oppression, even more reluctant to assume male qualities, and, as a consequence, more fully "feminine" in the nineteenth-century sense. Although she would have substituted the word *Christian* for the word *woman*, Elizabeth Hanson would have understood the meaning of Hawthorne's comment that "woman must strike through her own heart to reach a human life, whatever were the motive that impelled her."[46]

There is something disturbingly familiar about the heroism of Elizabeth Hanson. As Ann Douglas has described it, popular literature in nineteenth-century America was permeated with just such innocent victims—pacific civilians, for example, "massacred or mutilated in a war for which" they had "no responsibility," or guiltless wives of the temperance literature, or long-suffering and ever-patient mothers.[47] Such imagery was not invented in the nineteenth century, of course, as Hanson's story reminds us. It is inherent in Christianity. Nor was it passed on to nineteenth-century America by Quakers, though it was, as Douglas demonstrates, promoted by religious "outsiders"—that is, by members of churches which were tolerated (as Dover's Quakers were) but on the periphery of social and political life.[48]

Hanson's heroism foreshadows later literature, but not because it was new. Hers was one variant among a number of possible religious responses. In northern New England, through most of the colonial period, religion was never far from politics, despite the predominance of women in the churches. Avenging Jaels existed side by side with passive victims because the nationalized religion of the Old Testament coexisted with the personalized religion of the New.

WHEN HANNAH DUSTON sat in Cotton Mather's church on that morning in 1697, she heard herself simultaneously praised as a deliverer of Zion and admonished as a religious laggard. "You are not now the Slaves of Indians, as you were a few Dayes ago," Mather told the captives, "but if you continue Unhumbled, in your Sins, You will be the Slaves of Devils."[49] In his private discussion with her, Mather must have discovered that she, like many other men and women of her generation, had neglected the church. Though baptized as children, they had failed either to "own the covenant" or to present the evidence of conversion necessary for full membership.

Cotton Mather was determined to set New England's heroic Jael squarely upon the road to salvation. Perhaps his sermon had some effect, but, if so, the timing was curious. Hannah Duston owned the covenant in Haverhill First Church in June of 1719, just twenty-two years after her deliverance from the Indians. She was admitted to the Lord's table five years later, in March of 1724, at the age of sixty-seven. In her profession taken down by Haverhill's minister, she spoke of her captivity as "the Comfortablest time that ever I had; In my Affliction God made his Word Comfortable to me."[50]

Hannah Duston's long journey to the house of the Lord was not unusual. Few folks in Haverhill were owning the covenant in the last years of the seventeenth century. Perhaps their pastor was too involved with the immediate crises of war to worry about membership statistics. For Hannah, there were other distractions. Soon after her captivity she became pregnant again (for the thirteenth time in her twenty years of marriage). There were meals to be cooked and cows to be milked and a new house to build. Hannah's eventual conversion followed a rejuvenation of the church under an aggressive new minister, John Brown, and came after a period of relative stability for the town and for the Duston family.[51]

What we can't know, of course, is the state of Hannah's soul during that long period of growing and waiting. Did Mather's words return to her in the night as she stood over a sickbed or watched her parents die? "Let me tell you, A Slavery to Devils, to be in Their Hands, is worse than to be in the Hands of Indians." Pondering these words, did she ever think of her sister Elizabeth? If so, she did not say so. She said she had found comfort in the scriptures, and that she had wanted to offer herself "from time to time ever since the Settlement of the present Minister," but "Delays and fears" had prevailed upon her. Now, at the "Eleventh hour," she asked to be admitted among the saints.[52] Quietly, like hundreds of other women before her, this fierce virago submitted to the law of Christ.

Hannah Duston's heroism belongs to a particular historical moment. Her violence was possible because she had been raised in a world where women slaughtered pigs and fought their neighbors; it was permissible because it was directed in wartime at a hated enemy; and it was publishable because the established religion in New England had not yet become the refuge of the meek.

Afterword

IN A SMALL BURYING GROUND in Keene, New Hampshire, there is a stone commemorating the virtues of Madam Ruth Whitney, who died in November of 1788. She had married and survived two Massachusetts ministers, had lived through community conflicts and a revolution, had seen her oldest son exiled as a loyalist, and had finally come to live in a picturesque New Hampshire town centered on a village church, where her son-in-law was growing rich as a trustee of loyalist estates and a "crisp foreclosure of mortgages." None of this turmoil was reflected in her epitaph, which, like hundreds of others, recognized the economy in familiar phrases. "As this stone cannot tell all her virtues," it said, "suffice it to say, that as a wife she was prudent and faithful, as a mother discreet and tender, as a neighbor friendly and charitable, as a Christian intelligent and exemplary."[1] The memorialist neglected to add a reference to servants. An oversight rather than any commitment to egalitarian housekeeping probably accounts for that; Madam Whitney had undoubtedly been a kind and "awful" mistress in her time.

Ideals have a staying power seldom reflected in life. Madam Whitney's world was not Dorothy Dudley's world. Yet the lives of both women were defined, if not described, in the roles paraded in their epitaphs. As this study has attempted to show, those roles were neither simple nor inconsequential.

As *housewives*, early American women spun wool and churned butter, as legend has always insisted, but they did much more. From the earliest years, housekeeping involved a variety of responsibilities, including trade. Furthermore, housekeeping was a social as well as an economic role. Even the mythical spinning wheel was tied as firmly to mothering as to manufacturing. Among the gentry, in the course of the eighteenth century, the ceremonial significance of housekeeping increased, perhaps because the roles of deputy husband and of neighbor had begun to fade, but for all classes the Rule of Industry prevailed.

As *deputy husbands*, wives crossed gender boundaries without challenging the patriarchal order of society. Settling accounts, commanding field hands, negotiating with Indians, or filling orders for planks and staves, New England women demonstrated their ability to perform male work, but in doing so they also proclaimed their loyalty to their husbands. Deputy husbands acted within rather than against traditional definitions of female responsibility, proving that in the premodern world position was always more important than task.

As *mistresses* (lower case), married women assumed their rightful place at the top of a hierarchy of age, as Mistresses (upper case), they surmounted a hierarchy of class. In either position they were continually threatened by the relatively widespread economic opportunity in the colonies and by cultural norms which made mistresses of servants and housewives of pretty gentlewomen. In New England only a perch among the coastal elite—or a houseful of healthy daughters—assured freedom from worry over the unreliability of help.

As *consorts*, women balanced the often contradictory demands of chastity and affability, modesty and desirability, spirituality and sexuality. In the ideal realm the role of consort veered from a vision of Eve as a meet help for Adam to an image of a luscious lady in a satin gown. In the world of the village the real tension was between generations and between the sexes, though by 1750 there was as yet only a glimpse of changes which would come later in the century as young folks challenged old folks and unmarried women struggled to assume responsibility for their own sexual property.

As *mothers*, women were praised for their piety and sometimes mistrusted for their tenderness, but they were not ignored. In names passed on to their children, as well as in literature, New Englanders acknowledged families of sentiment which were not always coextensive with the families of property reflected in wills and deeds. The custom of calling any old woman—even a witch—"Mother" testified not only to the extensive nature of the maternal role but to its close association with biological mysteries of birth and death. Motherhood in the larger sense was perceived as a kind of travail, an unavoidable though potentially rewarding labor ordained by God.

As *neighbors*, women watched and warded the female community, enforcing the rules of industry, of modesty, and of charity, through gossip and sometimes through direct intervention. The power of neighbors was conservative—a slothful wife or a wayward widow would get little mercy—but it was also supportive. Cemented by networks of trade and especially by the communal rituals of birth, neighbors helped to counterbalance the vertical authority of men over women and rich over poor.

As *Christians,* women enlarged the meaning of their own lives without really changing its dimensions. Scriptures and sermons elevated the industry of housewives, the kindness of mistresses, the tenderness of mothers, the charity of neighbors. As promulgated in New England, Christianity idealized marital love and encouraged intellectual activities usually left to males—but it also nurtured submissiveness, softened rebellion, and ratified a social order in which men preached and women listened.

Women who became *heroines* were separated from ordinary women by circumstances as much as by character. In wartime, deputy husbands could become viragoes and Christians could become saints. Taken together, these two forms of heroism juxtaposed female violence with female piety in a way impossible a century later as Christian virtues and womanly virtues merged in a sentimental religion of outsiders which gradually replaced the state religion of New England's heroic age. Heroism offered women praise, yet had a darker side forged in the racism of the Indian wars and the brutality of village life.

In the study of early New England, gender is as important a category as race, wealth, age, geography, or religion. If women had indeed lived in a fixed and enchanted circle, sealed off from the disparate, squabbling, and struggling world of neighborhoods and towns, their story would still be important to an understanding of the colonial past. But, as we have seen, the circle of female life spun outward into the web of community and religious life. In homes and in neighborhoods women protected and promoted their own interests, using their influence as consorts and mothers, their authority as housewives and deputy husbands, their power as friendly neighbors, and their stature as experienced Christians. The story of women is important not simply because it *affected* what we have come to know as the history of early New England but because it was an integral and essential part of that history. It is hardly possible to write about "community" in such a setting while ignoring the distinct interests of women, or to write about "family" while focusing entirely upon fathers and sons—as in fact a number of important works in colonial history have done. To borrow a metaphor from midwifery, women have for too long been seen as bearers of a history to which men have contributed the "spiritous part."

Historians cannot be blamed, of course, for failing to see what society as a whole had long ignored. The recovery of women's history is part of a larger movement to reassess and redefine the position of women in the contemporary world. *Good Wives* is addressed not just to colonial history but to the larger history of American women. In recent years that history has been moving from an early preoccupation with mid-nineteenth-century reform and has persuasively demonstrated the significance of the ordinary and the domestic. Yet even the best of recent work sees the colonial period (whether defined as pre-nineteenth-century or pre-revolutionary) as a static backdrop to later changes. This study has suggested that many key features of those changes, including the magnification of motherhood, the idealization of conjugal love, and the elevation of female religiosity, were clearly visible in northern New England before 1750. Other themes of the early nineteenth century, such as the organization of charitable or moral reform societies, had antecedents in the informal but crucial interaction of women in colonial neighborhoods.

This is not to deny significant differences between seventeenth- and nineteenth-century women, but it is to argue that a search for a "turning point" in women's history may be misplaced. The story of female experience in America is not to be found in a linear progression from darkness into light, from constricted to expanding opportunities, from negative to positive valuation (or vice versa), but in a convoluted and sometimes tangled embroidery of loss and gain, accommodation and resistance. There can be no simple explanation of female status because that status is in itself so complex. To enlarge the role of deputy husband might mean to contract the often highly cherished roles of housekeeper and mother. To enhance the domestic might mean to neglect the communal, to control reproduction to lose one's sexual nature, to abjure violence to abandon the right to resist.

Such changes were neither willfully imposed nor consciously chosen. They were part of much larger changes in the history of the western world, yet they are best understood in the close exploration of the lives of ordinary women and men living in particular places and times.

> *(Sarah Sevey) is my Name,*
> *England is my Nation,*
> *(Portsmouth) is my dwelling place,*
> *And Christ is my salvation.*

From Portsmouth in 1733 to Jay, Maine, in 1810, New England girls worked similar sentiments onto the linen ground of their samplers.[2] Their lives were defined not only by gender but by a political structure, a geographic and demographic setting, and a matrix of cultural and religious values. If a fuller understanding of colonial history requires women's history, then the reverse is also true.

To borrow a metaphor from Puritan sermon literature, good social history, like marriage, requires "mutual supports."

Abbreviations

AB *Works*	*The Works of Anne Bradstreet*, ed. John Howard Ellis (Gloucester, Mass.: Peter Smith, 1962)
AQ	*American Quarterly*
CHS	Connecticut Historical Society
CSM	Colonial Society of Massachusetts
ECR	*Records and Files of the Quarterly Courts of Essex County, Massachusetts*, I–IX (Salem: Essex Institute, 1911–1975)
EI	The Essex Institute, Salem, Mass.
EIHC	*The Essex Institute Historical Collections*
EPR	*The Probate Records of Essex County*, I–III (Salem, Mass.: Essex Institute, 1916–1920)
Essex Probate	Manuscript Probate records, Essex County Probate Court, Salem, Mass.
Holyoke Diaries	*The Holyoke Diaries*, ed. George Francis Dow (Salem, Mass.: Essex Institute, 1911)
MHS	Massachusetts Historical Society, Boston, Mass.
MeHS	Maine Historical Society, Portland, Me.
MPCR	*Province and Court Records of Maine*, I–VI (Portland: Maine Historical Society, 1928–1975)
NEHGR	*New England Historical and Genealogical Register*
NEHGS	New England Historic Genealogical Society
NEQ	*New England Quarterly*
NH Court	Manuscript Court Records, New Hampshire State Archives, Concord, N.H.
NHHS	New Hampshire Historical Society
NHSA	New Hampshire State Archives
NHSP	*New Hampshire Provincial and State Papers*, I–XL (Nashua, Concord, and Manchester, N.H.: 1867–1940)
NLD	Sybil Noyes, Charles Thornton Libby, and Walter Goodwin Davis, *A Genealogical Dictionary of Maine and New Hampshire* (Portland, Me.: Southworth-Anthoensen Press, 1928)
Saltonstall Papers	*The Saltonstall Papers, 1607–1814*, I–II, ed. Robert

	E. Moody (Boston: Massachusetts Historical Society, 1972)
Witchcraft Papers	*The Salem Witchcraft Papers*, I–III, ed. Paul Boyer and Stephen Nissenbaum (New York: Da Capo Press, 1977)
WMQ	*William & Mary Quarterly*
York Probate	Manuscript Probate Records, York County Probate Court, Alfred, Me.

Notes

Introduction

1. Thomas Dudley to Mrs. Mercy Woodbridge, Dec. 28, 1643, CHS *Collections* (Hartford, 1924), XXI, 25. The editor incorrectly identified the "mother" referred to in the letter as Dudley's second wife.
2. AB *Works*, p. 220.
3. Thomas Dudley to Mrs. Mercy Woodbridge, p. 26.
4. Rev. Timothy Woodbridge to Rev. John Woodbridge, July 27, 1691, CHS *Collections* (1924), XXI, 339–340.
5. Hannah Moody gravestone, Old Burying Ground, York Village, Me. Died Jan. 29, 1727/8.
6. Seaborn Cotton Commonplace Book, NEHGS, pp. 177–188.
7. F. Ivan Nye and Viktor Gecas, "The Role Concept: Review and Delineation," in F. Ivan Nye, ed., *Role Structure and Analysis of the Family* (Beverly Hills and London: Sage Publications, 1976), pp. 3–14.
8. Robert V. Wells, "Quaker Marriage Patterns in a Colonial Perspective," *WMQ*, 3d Ser., XXIX (1972), 428, 438.
9. Philip J. Greven, Jr., *Four Generations: Population, Land, and Family in Colonial Andover, Massachusetts* (Ithaca, N.Y., and London: Cornell U. Press, 1970), pp. 31–37, 117–122, 206–210; Daniel Scott Smith, "The Demographic History of Colonial New England," *Journal of Economic History*, XXXII (1972), 165–183.
10. Thomas Dudley to Mrs. Mercy Woodbridge, p. 26.
11. Sir William Blackstone, *Commentaries on the Laws of England* (Oxford: Clarendon Press, 1765–1769), I, 442, quoted and discussed in Marylynn Salmon, "Equality or Submersion?" in Carol Ruth Berkin and Mary Beth Norton, *Women of America* (Boston: Houghton Mifflin, 1979), pp. 93–98.
12. Karen Andrésen, "Marah Revisited: Widowhood in Colonial New Hampshire," paper presented at the Berkshire Conference on Women's History, Vassar College, June 1981; Richard Morris, *Studies in the History of American Law* (New York: Columbia U. Press, 1930), pp. 155–156; Alexander Keyssar, "Widowhood in Eighteenth-Century Massachusetts," *Perspectives in American History*, VIII (1974), 101–103.
13. Samuel Willard, *A Complete Body of Divinity* (Boston, 1726), pp.

609–612; for more detailed discussion of this point, see Laurel Thatcher Ulrich, "Vertuous Women Found: New England Ministerial Literature, 1668–1735," *AQ*, XXVIII (1976), 28–30.

14. William Secker, *A Wedding Ring* (Boston, 1690), n.p.
15. Thomas Dudley to Mrs. Mercy Woodbridge, p. 26.

Chapter One

THE WAYS OF HER HOUSEHOLD

1. E.g., John Dod and William Hinde, *Bathshebaes Instructions to Her Son Lemuel* (London, 1614) and Cotton Mather, *Ornaments for the Daughters of Zion, or the Character and Happiness of a Virtuous Woman* (Cambridge, Mass., 1692). For later use, see Lonna Malmsheimer, "Daughters of Zion: New England Roots of American Feminism," *NEQ*, Sept. 1977, p. 492.

2. William H. Chafe, *Women and Equality: Changing Patterns in American Culture* (New York: Oxford U. Press, 1977), p. 17; Mary P. Ryan, *Womanhood in America from Colonial Times to the Present* (New York: New Viewpoints, 1975), p. 30; Ann Douglas, *The Feminization of American Culture* (New York: Alfred A. Knopf, 1977), pp. 53–54; and Nancy F. Cott, *The Bonds of Womanhood* (New Haven and London: Yale U. Press, 1977), p. 21.

3. Unless otherwise noted, the information which follows comes from the Francis Plummer will and inventory, *EPR*, II, 319–322.

4. Joshua Coffin, *A Sketch of the History of Newbury, Newburyport, and West Newbury* (Boston, 1845; Hampton, N.H.: Peter E. Randall, 1977), p. 315.

5. Abbott Lowell Cummings, *The Framed Houses of Massachusetts Bay, 1625–1725* (Cambridge, Mass., and London: Harvard U. Press, 1979), pp. 31–32.

6. Cummings, *Framed Houses*, pp. 29–31.

7. Darrett B. Rutman, *Husbandmen of Plymouth* (Boston: Beacon Press, 1967), pp. 10–11. Other Newbury families did use corn, including the local miller, who ate "samp"; *ECR*, III, 50, and Coffin, *Newbury*, p. 43. On oats, see MHS *Collections*, 5th Ser., I, 97, and Jay Allen Anderson, "A Solid Sufficiency: An Ethnography of Yeoman Foodways in Stuart England" (Ph.D. Dissertation, U. of Pennsylvania, 1971), pp. 171, 203–204, 265, 267, 268.

8. Cf. menus in Anderson, "Solid Sufficiency," pp. 263–270, and in an anonymous reminiscence of life in mid-18th-century New Hampshire in NHHS *Collections*, V (1837), 225–226.

9. Quoted in Anderson, "Solid Sufficiency," p. 232.

10. Cummings, *Framed Houses*, pp. 4, 120–122; Anderson, "Solid Sufficiency," p. 157; Jane Carson, *Colonial Virginia Cookery* (Charlottesville: U. Press of Virginia, 1968), p. 104; Frances Phipps, *Colonial Kitchens: Their Furnishings and Their Gardens* (New York: Hawthorn Books, 1972), p. 94 ff.

11. Anderson, "Solid Sufficiency," pp. 171–172; Carson, *Colonial Virginia Cookery*, p. 106.

12. Carson, *Colonial Virginia Cookery*, pp. 104–105.

13. Anderson, "Solid Sufficiency," pp. 63, 65, 118; Howard S. Russell, *A Long, Deep Furrow: Three Centuries of Farming in New England* (Hanover, N.H.: U. Press of New England, 1976), p.160; NHHS *Collections*, V (1837), 225.

14. Anderson, "Solid Sufficiency," pp. 120–132.

15. Anderson, "Solid Sufficiency," pp. 99–108.

16. Sanborn C. Brown, *Wines and Beers of Old New England* (Hanover, N.H.: U. Press of New England, 1978), pp. 87–97.

17. Brown, *Wines and Beers*, pp. 50–63, 70–77; Anderson, "Solid Sufficiency," pp. 89–98.

18. *ECR*, IV, 194–195, 297–298.

19. Essex Probate, CCCVII, 58–59.

20. "Part of Salem in 1700," pocket map in James Duncan Phillips, *Salem in the Seventeenth Century* (Boston: Houghton Mifflin, 1933), H-6.

21. Sidney Perley, *The History of Salem, Massachusetts* (Salem, 1924), I, 435, 441.

22. Phillips, *Salem in the Seventeenth Century*, pp. 328, 314, 318, 317, and James Duncan Phillips, *Salem in the Eighteenth Century* (Boston: Houghton Mifflin, 1937), pp. 20–21.

23. The nature of petty trade in colonial America is largely unstudied. I have relied on Karen Friedman, "Victualling Colonial Boston," *Agricultural History*, XLVII (July 1973), 189–205, and suggestive glimpses in Benjamin Coleman, *Some Reasons and Arguments Offered to the Good People of Boston and Adjacent Places, for the Setting Up Markets in Boston* (Boston, 1719), pp. 5–9.

24. Phillips, *Salem in the Eighteenth Century*, p. 25, quoting Edward Ward, 1699.

25. One of the accusations against Mary Bradbury was that she sold maggoty cheese. *Witchcraft Papers*, I, 117–129.

26. Cummings, *Framed Houses*, pp. 29–31.

27. "Washing and diet" are often grouped in charges for boarders; e.g., *MPCR*, IV, 205–206. A maid in one New Hampshire house testified to having made a pair of linen sleeves in April which were stolen from the

washline in May; NH Court, IV, 237. For infant's clothing, see Claire Elizabeth Fox, "Pregnancy, Childbirth and Early Infancy in Anglo-American Culture: 1675–1830" (Ph.D. Dissertation, U. of Pennsylvania, 1966), pp. 240–245, and Essex Probate, CCCXXI, 96, which lists infant's linen: 57 clouts, 27 caps, 2 headbands, 1 swather, 50 belly bands and bibs, and 6 shirts.

28. Susan Burrows Swan, *Plain and Fancy: American Women and Their Needlework, 1700–1850* (New York: Holt, Rinehart and Winston, 1977), p. 38.

29. Swan, *Plain and Fancy*, pp. 18–19, 34–35.

30. Alice Clark, *Working Life of Women in the Seventeenth Century* (London: G. Routledge & Sons; New York: E. P. Dutton; 1919), p. 95.

31. "Letter-Book of Samuel Sewall," MHS *Collections*, 6th Ser., I, 19. Spinning wheels were staple equipment in traditional dame schools, as a number of engravings show. Lucy Larcom, *A New England Girlhood* (repr. Gloucester: Peter Smith, 1973), p. 43, recalls "Aunt Hannah" spinning at her flax wheel and singing hymns for the children.

32. York Probate, II, 26.

33. *NLD*, p. 727.

34. Charles Clark, *The Eastern Frontier* (New York: Alfred A. Knopf, 1970), pp. 67–72.

35. *MPCR*, IV, 91–92, 175, 176, 206, 263, 307, 310.

36. *NLD*, p. 726.

37. MeHS *Collections*, IX, 58–59, 457, 466; MHS *Collections*, 6th Ser., I, 126–165, 182–184, 186–189; *Journals of the Rev. Thomas Smith...*, ed. William Willis (Portland, Me.: 1849), pp. 85–86, 87, 88, 96.

38. Cotton Mather, *Decennium Luctuosum* (Boston, 1699), repr. Charles H. Lincoln, ed., *Narratives of the Indian Wars* (New York: Charles Scribner's Sons, 1913), pp. 266–267.

39. Richard M. Candee, "Wooden Buildings in Early Maine and New Hampshire: A Technological and Cultural History 1600–1720" (Ph.D. Dissertation, U. of Pennsylvania, 1976), pp. 255ff.

40. Candee, "Wooden Buildings," pp. 18, 42–48. Secondary accounts have not discussed the sharing of shelter with animals, but there are some tantalizing hints in John Josselyn, *An Account of Two Voyages Made During the Years 1638, 1663* (Boston, 1865), p. 193, on chickens fed under the table in rainy weather; *ECR*, IV, 159, on "goeing into the other roome to give my piggs corne"; and *Saltonstall Papers*, I, 219, on being "billeted" with "ould Jersey" during Indian troubles.

41. The Rev. John Pike noted that "The Indians killed Henry Barns, Edward Hammonds & his wife, as they were at work in a field at Spruce-Creek" in Kittery. MHS *Proceedings* (1876), p. 129. Also see *ECR*, II,

372–373, 22, 442; *The Diary of Matthew Patten* (Concord, N.H., 1903), pp. 6, 11, 19, 68, 84, 129, 141; and G. E. and K. R. Fussell, *The English Countrywoman* (New York: Benjamin Blom, 1971), pp. 95–96.

42. Sarah Orne Jewett, *The Old Town of Berwick* (Berwick, Me.: Old Berwick Historical Society, 1967), n.p., quoting a local story about Margery Sullivan, whose son John became governor of New Hampshire and whose son James became governor of Massachusetts.

43. *NLD*, pp. 726, 729.

Chapter Two
DEPUTY HUSBANDS

1. Page Smith, *Daughters of the Promised Land* (Boston and Toronto: Little, Brown, 1970), p. 54; Elizabeth A. Dexter, *Colonial Women of Affairs* (Boston and New York: Houghton Mifflin, 1924), p. 37; Linda Grant Depauw and Conover Hunt, *"Remember the Ladies": Women in America 1750–1815* (New York: Viking Press, 1976), p. 62; Richard B. Morris, *Studies in the History of American Law* (New York: Columbia U. Press, 1930), pp. 128–129.

2. Mary Beth Norton, "Eighteenth-Century American Women in Peace and War: The Case of the Loyalists," *WMQ*, 3d Ser., XXXIII (1976), 386–409.

3. Alexander Keyssar, "Widowhood in Eighteenth-Century Massachusetts: A Problem in the History of the Family," *Perspectives in American History*, VIII (1974), pp. 99–111. Also see Karen E. Andrésen, "Marah Revisited: The Widow in Early New Hampshire," paper delivered at Berkshire Conference on Women's History, Vassar College, June 1981.

4. *ECR*, V, 57.

5. Thomas Fuller, *The Holy and the Profane State* (1642), quoted in G. E. and K. R. Fussell, *The English Countrywoman* (New York: Benjamin Blom, 1971), p. 47. Also see Cotton Mather, *Ornaments for the Daughters of Zion* (Cambridge, 1692), p. 101.

6. Even widows with grown sons were frequently given joint administration. From 75 to 80% of widows in my sample of New Hampshire wills, 1650–1730, were named executors (N=93). *NHSP*, XXXI, 20–42, 115–167, 459–513; XXXII, 374–434.

7. *ECR*, II, 295–297.

8. *ECR*, VIII, 278, 411; NH Court, I, 1, 35.

9. *ECR*, VI, 412.

10. NH Court, II, 325.

11. *NLD*, pp. 88, 190, 738, 737.

12. *ECR*, II, 291, 407–409.

13. J. Hector St. John de Crèvecoeur, *Letters from an American Farmer* (New York: E. P. Dutton, 1912), p. 146.

14. Barton Papers, I, 7, EI.

15. Barton Papers, I, 30, EI.

16. Barton Papers, I, 25, EI.

17. NH Court, I, 2, 543.

18. NH Court, II, 471; *NLD*, pp. 57, 628–629.

19. Coffin Papers, I, 89–131, EI.

20. Kenneth A. Lockridge, *Literacy in Colonial New England* (New York: W. W. Norton, 1974), pp. 38–42. I would emphasize that the discrepancy is in *writing*, not necessarily in reading.

21. John Gould Account Book, 1697–1723, EI.

22. Anonymous Portsmouth Account Book, NEHGS, p. 203 and passim.

23. *ECR*, VIII, 279–283.

24. E.g., Abraham How Account Book, Ipswich Historical Society, Ipswich, Mass.; John Burnham Account Book, EI; Nicholas Perryman Ledger, NHHS. The Perryman Ledger has accounts from both Marblehead and Exeter.

25. Thomas Bartlett Account Book, p. 41, EI.

26. Bartlett Account, p. 93.

27. Account Book of Thomas Chute, MeHS, pp. 6, 194. For other references to occasional activities by Mrs. Chute, see pp. 99, 148, 152, 168, 171, 172, 177, 195.

28. *ECR*, VIII, 10.

29. NH Court, III, 223, 228, 235; I, 2, 427, 429; *NHSP*, XXXX, 255, 263, 323–324.

30. NH Court, III, 228.

31. "Testimony Regarding Testimentary Deed," Thomas Bartlett Papers, EI.

32. Mary Russell to Mr. Curwen, Feb. 1757, Corwin Papers, III, EI.

33. Mary Beth Norton, *Liberty's Daughters: The Revolutionary Experience of American Women, 1750–1800* (Boston-Toronto: Little, Brown, 1980), p. 225.

Chapter Three

A FRIENDLY NEIGHBOR

1. NH Court, V, 309.

2. *ECR*, III, 194.

3. *ECR*, III, 140.

4. *ECR*, III, 275.
5. James Duncan Phillips, *Salem in the Eighteenth Century* (Boston and New York: Houghton Mifflin, 1937), p. 175.
6. David H. Flaherty, *Privacy in Colonial New England* (Charlottesville: U. Press of Virginia, 1972), p. 99.
7. Flaherty, *Privacy*, pp. 111–112.
8. *ECR*, VIII, 286–287; NH Court, V, 135.
9. Thomas Franklin Waters, *Ipswich in the Massachusetts Bay Colony*, I (Ipswich, Mass.: Ipswich Historical Society, 1905), 512–513.
10. Edward S. Perzel, "Landholding in Ipswich," *EIHC*, CIV (1968), 303, 322–324.
11. Part II of the first volume of Waters, *Ipswich*, pp. 317–489, traces ownership of town lots.
12. Waters, *Ipswich*, I, 113; *ECR*, IV, 240; V, 306. Robert J. Dinkin, "Seating the Meeting House in Early Massachusetts," *NEQ*, XLIII (1970), 450–464.
13. Waters, *Ipswich*, I, 108, 113, 424–427; John D. Cushing, "Town Commons of New England, 1640–1840," *Old Time New England*, LI (1961), 90–92.
14. *ECR*, V, 31–33.
15. *ECR*, V, 38, 157.
16. *ECR*, V, 138, 141, 143, 147, 155, 186, 189, 218, 219, 220, 227, 283, 284, 292, 303, 306, 318, 413, 414.
17. *ECR*, V, 315, 155.
18. *ECR*, V, 414–417. Also see pp. 141, 143, 146, 218, 319.
19. *ECR*, V, 143–146. *Ipswich Vital Records*, I, 402; II, 467; James Savage, *A Genealogical Dictionary of the First Settlers of New England*, IV (Boston: Little, Brown, 1862), 643; Waters, *Ipswich*, I, 477, 443, 454.
20. Waters, *Ipswich*, I, 442; *NEHGR*, VIII, 23; *EPR*, I, 222–225, 167; III, 388; John Langdon Sibley, *Bibliographical Sketches of Graduates of Harvard University*, I (Cambridge, Mass.: Charles William Sever, 1873), 166–167, 170.
21. *Witchcraft Papers*, I, 117–129.
22. *ECR*, IV, 141, 181; V, 31–33.
23. *ECR*, III, 140–141.
24. *ECR*, III, 193.
25. Waters, *Ipswich*, I, 415, 439, 345; *EPR*, III, 388–389.
26. *ECR*, III, 244–246.
27. *ECR*, III, 246.
28. *ECR*, III, 245.
29. *ECR*, IV, 239–242.
30. *ECR*, V, 155–157.

31. *ECR*, V, 414; Essex Probate, 14262, Deposition of Ezekiell Northend.

32. Waters, *Ipswich*, I, 478–480, Map 5.

33. *ECR*, V, 231.

34. *ECR*, IV, 240–243.

35. Dinkin, "Seating," p. 462; Ola Winslow, *Meetinghouse Hill* (New York: W. W. Norton, 1972, 1952), pp. 144–146.

36. *ECR*, IV, 341.

37. *ECR*, V, 306–307; IV, 240–243.

38. Waters, *Ipswich*, I, 114. Cf. *ECR*, IV, 146, and Joshua Coffin, *A Sketch of the History of Newbury, Newburyport, and West Newbury* (Boston, 1845; Hampton, N.H.: Peter E. Randall, 1977), p. 167.

Chapter Four

PRETTY GENTLEWOMEN

1. *The Letters of Benjamin Franklin and Jane Mecom*, ed. Carl van Doren (Princeton, N.J.: Princeton U. Press, 1950), p. 35.

2. Samples of this literature are quoted in G. E. & K. R. Fussell, *The English Countrywoman* (New York: Benjamin Blom, 1971), p. 107. For a modern echo of the stereotype, see Linda Grant Depauw and Conover Hunt, *"Remember the Ladies": Women in America, 1750–1815* (New York: Viking Press, 1976), p. 126.

3. James Duncan Phillips, *Salem in the Eighteenth Century* (Boston: Houghton Mifflin, 1937), pp. 252–257.

4. *The Holyoke Diaries*, ed. George Francis Dow (Salem, Mass.: Essex Institute, 1911), pp. 48–81. These entries represent about a third of those referring to housekeeping in the period between January 1761 and January 1773.

5. *Holyoke Diaries*, p. 59; [Hannah Wooley], *The Accomplish'd Lady's Delight* (London, 1675), p. 253.

6. Inventory of Ursula Cutt, Portsmouth, Aug. 7, 1694, MS Probate Records, NHSA. (Karen Andrésen shared this document with me.) Cotton Mather, *Decennium Luctuosum* (Boston, 1699), p. 253; MHS *Proceedings*, 1875–1876, p. 128.

7. *Saltonstall Papers*, I, 176.

8. *Saltonstall Papers*, I, 189–190.

9. *Saltonstall Papers*, I, 218–221, 224, 235.

10. *Saltonstall Papers*, I, 242.

11. *Saltonstall Papers*, I, 228. On Nathaniel's conviviality and apparent fondness for drink, *Diary of Samuel Sewall*, ed. M. Halsey Thomas (New York: Farrar, Straus and Giroux, 1973), I, 374; *Saltonstall Papers*, I, 211–212.

12. Susan Burrows Swan, *Plain and Fancy: American Women and Their Needlework, 1700–1850* (New York: Holt, Rinehart and Winston, 1977), pp. 47–57; and *A Winterthur Guide to American Needlework* (New York: Crown Publishers, 1976), pp. 26–40. For poetic treatment of the same themes, see Jane Colman Turrell's "Invitation into the Country" in Benjamin Colman, *Reliquiae Turellae* (Boston, 1735), p. 84. For more detail on gentility and on the "servant question," see my "Good Wives: A Study in Role Definition in Northern New England, 1650–1750" (Ph.D. Dissertation, U. of New Hampshire, 1980), pp. 155–164, 170–172.

13. MHS *Collections*, 6th Ser., IV, 228–229. The editor of the Belknap Papers thinks Jeremy wrote the poem himself, though he attributed the poem to "Ruthy" in a letter to a friend.

14. Laurie Crumpacker, " 'My Time Is Not My Own But God's': Religion and Daily Work in the Journal of Esther Burr, 1754–1758," paper delivered at Old Sturbridge Village, March 1977, pp. 5, 8–11.

15. Philip J. Greven, Jr., *The Protestant Temperament* (New York: Alfred A. Knopf, 1977).

16. Holyoke Papers, Box I, Folder 2, EI.

17. *A Family History in Letters and Documents, 1667–1837*, ed. Mrs. Charles P. Noyes (St. Paul, Minn., 1919), pp. 55–60.

18. *Family History*, pp. 66, 65.

19. *Family History*, p. 54; Constance Le Neve Gilman Ames, *The Story of the Gilmans* (Yakima, Wash., 1950), p. 73.

20. Holyoke Diaries, e.g., pp. 3, 15, 21–22; "The Diary of Nicholas Gilman," ed. William Kidder (M.A. Thesis, U. of New Hampshire, 1967), e.g., pp. 153, 203, 134.

21. Book of the Church of Newbury, Mass., 1635–1828, MS, Old Newbury Historical Society, Newbury, Mass., May 1752.

22. *The Simple Cobler of Aggawam in America* (London, 1647), pp. 25–31.

23. Ray Wilbur shared this reference from the manuscript diary of Joseph Moody, which he is editing.

24. *Hoop-Petticoats Arraigned* (Boston, 1722), p. 7.

25. Rolla Milton Tryon, *Household Manufacturers in the United States* (New York: Augustus M. Kelley, 1917), pp. 124ff.; Mary Crawford, *Social Life in Old New England* (Boston: Little, Brown, 1914), pp. 266–268.

26. Cotton Mather, *Ornaments for the Daughters of Zion* (Cambridge, Mass., 1692), pp. 2, 73–74, 81–83, 100–101, 5, 7–8.

27. Laurel Thatcher Ulrich, "Vertuous Women Found: New England Ministerial Literature, 1668–1735," *AQ*, XXVII, 25–26, 32–35.

28. AB *Works*, pp. 4, iii–xiv.

29. AB *Works*, pp. iii–iv.

30. Thomas Prince, *Christ Abolishing Death* (Boston, 1736), p. 39.

31. NH Court, I, 1, 157.

32. Joseph W. P. Frost, *Sir William Pepperrell* (New York: Newcomen Society, 1951), p. 30.

33. MHS *Collections*, 6th Ser., VI, 168–171.

34. Belcher Manuscript Letter Book, MHS, II, Oct. 25, 1731 (on turnips); II, Nov. 22, 1731 (on feminine piety); II, June 20, 1732, and VI, Feb. 15, 1739/40 (on conflict over marriage).

Chapter Five

THE SERPENT BEGUILED ME

1. The Greenland-Rolfe case described below was reconstructed from depositions in *ECR*, III, 47–55, 65–67, 70, 75, 88–91. All dialogue is in the original. Greenland eventually removed to Kittery, where he was continually in trouble and where his wife was accused of witchcraft. *NLD*, 288; NH Court, I, 1, 267.

2. Lawrence Stone, *The Family, Sex, and Marriage in England 1500–1800* (London: Harper & Row, 1977), p. 523; Keith Thomas, "The Double Standard," *Journal of the History of Ideas*, XX (1959), 203.

3. *ECR*, III, 66.

4. Edmund S. Morgan, "The Puritans and Sex," *NEQ*, XV (1942), 591–607.

5. Michael Zuckerman, "Pilgrims in the Wilderness: Community, Modernity, and the Maypole at Merry Mount," *NEQ*, L (1977), 265–267.

6. Philip J. Greven, Jr., *The Protestant Temperament* (New York: Alfred A. Knopf, 1977), pp. 24–140.

7. Thomas, "Double Standard," p. 213 and passim.

8. *ECR*, III, 88, 48.

9. *The Laws and Liberties of Massachusetts, 1648* (Cambridge, Mass.: Harvard U. Press, 1929), pp. 6, 23; George Lee Haskins, *Law and Authority in Early Massachusetts* (New York: Macmillan, 1960), pp. 149–150.

10. Haskins, *Law and Authority*, p. 149; Morgan, "Puritans and Sex," p. 602.

11. William H. Whitmore, ed., *The Colonial Laws of Massachusetts . . . 1660* (Boston, 1880), p. 257. Stone, *Family, Sex, and Marriage*, p. 623, believes New England courts gave up trying to punish a sin. The continuing conviction of married fornicators argues against this. Between 1653 and 1727 the York courts tried 274 cases of fornication, 61% involving couples who had already married, eliminating the economic mo-

tive for prosecution. The midwives' testimony was crucial in cases of single women; e.g., *MPCR*, VI, 121–126.

12. In describing the effort of colonial New Englanders to achieve sexual privacy, David Flaherty clearly demonstrates its lack. *Privacy in Colonial New England* (Charlottesville: U. Press of Virginia, 1972), pp. 76–84.

13. NH Court, VII, 225, 227.
14. *ECR*, V, 351–354; *MPCR*, I, 85.
15. *ECR*, II, 35.
16. *ECR*, II, 420.
17. *ECR*, V, 351–354.
18. *ECR*, V, 228–229; G. E. and K. R. Fussell, *The English Countrywoman* (New York: Benjamin Blom, 1971), p. 27; Stone, *Family, Sex, and Marriage*, p. 520.
19. E.g., Nicholas Noyes, "A Consolatory Poem," in Cotton Mather, *Meat Out of the Eater* (Boston, 1703), p. 186; Cotton Mather, *Virtue in Its Verdure* (Boston, 1725), p. 23, and *Life Swiftly Passing* (Boston, 1716), p. 3; Benjamin Colman, *A Devout Contemplation* (Boston, 1714), p. i.
20. *MPCR*, I, 176.
21. *ECR*, III, 90.
22. *ECR*, VIII, 99, 259–263, 288–289, 296, 308, 433.
23. Morgan, "Puritans and Sex," p. 594 and passim; Eli Faber, "Puritan Criminals: The Economic, Social, and Intellectual Background to Crime in Seventeenth-Century Massachusetts," *Perspectives in American History*, XI (1977–1978), 85.
24. Sherry Ortner, "Is Female to Male as Nature Is to Culture?" in *Woman, Culture, and Society*, ed. Michelle Zimbalist Rosaldo and Louise Lamphere (Stanford, Calif.: Stanford U. Press, 1974), pp. 67–87.
25. E.g., Cotton Mather, *Ornaments for the Daughters of Zion* (Boston, 1692), p. 50. I have never found a reference to original sin as "Eve's Sin." As in the primer, "In *Adam*'s fall we die all."
26. Natalie Davis, *Society and Culture in Early Modern France* (Stanford, Calif.: Stanford U. Press, 1975), pp. 124–125.
27. William Hubbard, *A Narrative of the Troubles with the Indians* (Boston, 1677), pp. 61, 77; [Elizabeth Hanson], *God's Mercy Surmounting Man's Cruelty* (Philadelphia, 1728), pp. 35–36; Cotton Mather, *Good Fetch'd Out of Evil* (Boston, 1700), pp. 33–34.
28. *The Works of Aristotle* (Philadelphia, 1798), pp. 16–19; Stone, *Family, Sex, and Marriage*, p. 281; Nancy F. Cott, "Eighteenth-Century Family and Social Life Revealed in Massachusetts Divorce Records," *Journal of Social History*, X (1976), 33–35; Charles Carlton, "The

Widow's Tale: Male Myths and Female Reality in Sixteenth and Seventeenth Century England," *Albion*, X (1978), 118–129.

29. E.g., *MPCR*, II, 43, 92; IV, 48–50; VI, 98.

30. *ECR*, V, 21–22.

31. *ECR*, III, 194. It is hardly surprising that in *formal* court actions, male witnesses would predominate (Cott, pp. 26–27), especially in 18th-century divorce cases, which went to the Council rather than to county courts.

32. *MPCR*, I, 140–143.

33. *ECR*, V, 52–55.

34. *MPCR*, III, 378–380.

35. *MPCR*, I, 142–143.

36. *ECR*, V, 54–55.

37. *MPCR*, III, 379.

38. Daniel Scott Smith and Michael S. Hindus, "Premarital Pregnancy in America 1640–1971," *Journal of Interdisciplinary History*, V (Spring 1975), 537–570.

39. Laurie Crumpacker and Carol Karlsen, paper delivered at the Fourth Berkshire Conference on the History of Women, Mt. Holyoke, August 1978. For additional evidence that *Pamela* was read in New England, see *Gentleman's Progress: The Itinerarium of Dr. Alexander Hamilton, 1744*, ed. Carl Bridenbaugh (Chapel Hill, N.C.: U. of North Carolina Press for Institute of Early American History and Culture, 1948), p. 112; and Clifford K. Shipton, *New England Life in the Eighteenth Century* (Cambridge, Mass.: Harvard U. Press, 1963), p. 185.

40. Thomas, "Double Standard," pp. 214–215.

41. Robert A. Erickson, "Mother Jewkes, Pamela, and the Midwives," *ELH*, XLIII (1976), 500–516.

Chapter Six

CONSORT

1. Ian Maclean, *The Renaissance Notion of Woman* (Cambridge: Cambridge U. Press, 1980), pp. 8–27; "The Convenant Idea and the Puritan View of Marriage," *Journal of the History of Ideas*, XXXII (1971), 108–109.

2. John Cotton, *A Meet Help* (Boston, 1699), p. 15, quoted in Edmund S. Morgan, *The Puritan Family* (New York: Harper & Row, 1966), p. 29. For contrasting interpretations of Puritan notions, see William and Malleville Haller, "The Puritan Art of Love," *Huntington Library Quarterly*, V (1941–1942), 235–272, and Kathleen M. Davies, "The Sacred Condition of Equality—How Original Were Puritan Doctrines of Marriage?", *Social History*, V (May 1977), 563–580.

3. William Secker, *A Wedding Ring* (Boston, 1690), n.p.

4. John Calvin, *Commentary on the First Book of Moses*, trans. John King (Grand Rapids, Mich.: Wm. B. Eerdmans, 1963), I, 129–130.

5. John Calvin, *Commentary on the First Epistle ... to the Corinthians*, trans. John Fraser (Grand Rapids, Mich.: Wm. B. Eerdmans, 1960), pp. 130–131. Also see Mary Maples Dunn, "Saints and Sisters: Congregational and Quaker Women in the Early Colonial Period," in Janet Wilson James, ed., *Women in American Religion* (Philadelphia: U. of Pennsylvania Press, 1980), pp. 28–30.

6. *ECR*, III, 193–194.

7. Samuel Willard, *A Complete Body of Divinity* (Boston, 1726), p. 612.

8. John Allin, *The Spouse of Christ* (Cambridge, Mass., 1672), p. 9.

9. Cotton Mather, *The Mystical Marriage* (Boston, 1728), p. 6.

10. *EPR*, II, 278–279; also see Andrew Oliver, *Portraits of John and Abigail Adams* (Cambridge, Mass.: Harvard U. Press, 1967), p. 137; and Lucy Larcom, *A New England Girlhood* (Gloucester, Mass.: Peter Smith, 1973), p. 25, for persistence of the tradition.

11. Mehitable Parkman to Mr. Deliverance Parkman, Salem, 1683, Curwen Family Papers, EI.

12. Cotton Mather, *Meat Out of the Eater* (Boston, 1703), p. 209.

13. D. Kelly Weisberg, "Under Greet Temptations Heer: Women and Divorce in Puritan Massachusetts," *Feminist Studies*, II (1975), 183–194, and Nancy F. Cott, "Divorce and the Changing Status of Women in Eighteenth-Century Massachusetts," *WMQ*, 3d Ser. XXXIII (1976), 589–590, 612.

14. Elizabeth Wade White, *Anne Bradstreet: "The Tenth Muse"* (New York: Oxford U. Press, 1971), pp. 51–52, 89–90, 158, 174–177; *Suffolk Deeds*, I (Boston, 1880), 83–84; AB *Works*, pp. 394–398.

15. AB *Works*, pp. 394–395.

16. Rosamund Rosenmeier, " 'Divine Translation': A Contribution to the Study of Anne Bradstreet's Method in the Marriage Poems," *Early American Literature*, XII (Fall 1977), 121–135.

17. *Records of the First Church in Boston 1630–1868*, ed. Richard D. Pierce, CSM *Publications*, XXXIX (1961), 46; White, *Bradstreet*, p. 174.

18. *Suffolk Deeds*, I, 84.

19. *Records of the First Church*, p. 49.

20. *Records of the First Church*, p. 25.

21. White, *Bradstreet*, pp. 175–176.

22. AB *Works*, pp. 374, 380.

23. John Milton, *Paradise Lost* (London, 1667), Book VII, Lines 1100–1110.

24. *Paradise Lost*, IV, 492–497, 690–700.

25. *New England Weekly Journal*, Aug. 21, 1727. For other examples, see George F. Sensabaugh, *Milton in Early America* (Princeton, N.J.: Princeton U. Press, 1964), p. 43ff.

26. Samuel Eliot Morison, "The Letter-Book of Hugh Hall," CSM *Publications*, XXXII (1933–1937), 518.

27. Ebenezer Turell, *The Life and Character of the Reverend Mr. Colman* (Boston, 1749), p. 36.

28. *The Notebook of John Smibert*, ed. Andrew Oliver (Boston: MHS, 1969), pp. 88–94. The following discussion of portraits is based upon my unpublished paper, "Rosebuds and Bibles: Feminine Iconography in 18th Century New England Portraits," a study of 331 paintings by John Smibert, Robert Feke, John Greenwood, Joseph Blackburn, Joseph Badger, and John Singleton Copley.

29. Henry Wilder Foote, *Robert Feke: Colonial Portrait Painter* (Cambridge, Mass.: Harvard U. Press, 1930), pp. 123–124.

30. Décolletage and flowing ringlets appear in 77% of the 232 female portraits I studied. Biographical data in Jules David Prown, *John Singleton Copley in America, 1738–1774* (Cambridge, Mass.: Harvard U. Press, 1966), suggest that cultural divisions were reflected in clothing; 34% of Copley's congregational sitters, but only 15% of the Anglicans, had covered hair. The age distribution was similar.

31. James Bowdoin, *A Paraphrase on Part of the Oeconomy of Human Life* (Boston, 1759), p. 17. Portraits of Bowdoin and his wife appear in Marvin S. Sadik, *Colonial and Federal Portraits at Bowdoin College* (Brunswick, Me.: Bowdoin College Museum of Art, 1966), pp. 49–51.

32. Thomas Prince, *Precious in the Sight of the Lord* (Boston, 1735), pp. 23–24. The painting is reproduced in *Antiques*, 95 (February, 1969), p. 368.

33. Susan Burrows Swan, *Plain and Fancy: American Women and Their Needlework, 1700–1850* (New York: Holt, Rinehart and Winston, 1977), pp. 22, 57, 64, 106, 144–145, and *A Winterthur Guide to American Needlework* (New York: Crown Publishers, 1976), pp. 32–40; Lloyd E. Hawes, "Adam and Eve in the Decorative Arts," *Antiques*, 84 (September, 1963), pp. 279–281; Anita Schorsch, *Pastoral Dreams* (New York: Universe Books, 1977), p. 71; Glee Krueger, *New England Samplers to 1840* (Old Sturbridge Village, 1978), figures 21, 22, 23.

34. Old Gaol Museum, York, Maine. The provenance of the hangings is somewhat in doubt, according to the curator, Eldridge Pendleton, though the approximate date and coastal New England origin do seem correct, and the sentiment jibes with what is known of Mary Bulman. The Watts poem is "Meditation in a Grove" from *Horae Lyricae*,

1706. Ann Pollard Rowe, "Crewel Embroidered Bed Hangings in Old and New England," *Bulletin: Museum of Fine Arts, Boston,* LXXI (1973), 101–166; Edward E. Bourne, *History of Wells and Kennebunk* (Portland, Me.: B. Thuston & Co., 1875), pp. 381–383; and Benjamin and Mary Colman to William Pepperrell, MHS *Collections,* 6th Ser., X, 373.

35. Curwen Papers, I, 8–13, EI. (George signed his name "Corwin," though all the Corwins and Curwens are grouped with the Curwen papers.)

36. The letters have been reprinted in Usher Parsons, *The Life of Sir William Pepperrell* (Boston, 1856), pp. 220–222.

37. Parsons, *William Pepperrell,* pp. 222–223.

38. For some sense of the complexity of this change, see Lawrence Stone, *The Family, Sex, and Marriage in England, 1500–1800* (New York: Harper & Row, 1977), pp. 103, 181–191, and Randolph Trumbach, *The Rise of the Egalitarian Family* (New York: Academic Press, 1978), pp. 97–113.

39. Paul Boyer and Stephen Nissenbaum, *Salem Possessed: The Social Origins of Witchcraft* (Cambridge, Mass.: Harvard U. Press, 1974), pp. 1, 23.

40. *The Journals of Ashley Bowen of Marblehead,* CSM *Publications,* XLIV (1973), 47.

41. *ECR,* III, 271–272, 457ff.; IV, 424; V, 267, 312; VI, 344.

42. *ECR,* V, 188, 143–147, 228–229.

43. *ECR,* V, 186–189.

44. Secker, *Wedding Ring,* n.p.

45. *ECR,* II, 100, 217, 340.

46. Daniel Scott Smith and Michael S. Hindus, "Premarital Pregnancy in America 1640–1971: An Overview and Interpretation," *Journal of Interdisciplinary History,* V (Spring 1975), 537–570; Robert Gross, *The Minutemen and Their World* (New York: Hill and Wang, 1976), p. 235; Nancy F. Cott, "Passionlessness: An Interpretation of Victorian Sexual Ideology, 1790–1850," in Nancy F. Cott and Elizabeth H. Pleck, *A Heritage of Her Own* (New York: Simon and Schuster, 1979), p. 166.

47. Henry Reed Stiles, *Bundling: Its Origins, Progress and Decline in America* (Mt. Vernon, N.Y.: Peter Pauper Press, n.d., repr. 1871), p. 67.

48. Stiles, *Bundling,* p. 66.

49. Dana Doten, *The Art of Bundling* (New York: Countryman Press, 1938), pp. 148–152.

50. *Journals of Ashley Bowen,* pp. 47–49.

51. *Journals of Ashley Bowen,* pp. 49–50, 232, 271–273.

Chapter Seven
TRAVAIL

1. *ECR*, VI, 156; IV, 379–380; Julia Cherry Spruill, *Women's Life and Work in the Southern Colonies* (New York: W. W. Norton, 1972, 1938), pp. 50, 325; letter from Susan Swan, curator of textiles at Winterthur Museum, to the author, Aug. 2, 1979.

2. Diary of Zaccheus Collins, I, 1726–1750, n.p., EI; *The Diary of Matthew Patten of Bedford, N.H.* (Concord, N.H., 1903), pp. 206–207; *ECR*, II, 36–38.

3. *Journals of the Rev. Thomas Smith and the Rev. Samuel Deane*, ed. William Willis (Portland, Me.: Joseph S. Bailey, 1849), pp. 22–23. For the size of Falmouth, see p. 10.

4. Elizabeth Bing, *Six Practical Lessons for an Easier Childbirth* (New York: Grosset & Dunlap, 1967); Suzanne Arms, *Immaculate Deception: A New Look at Women and Childbirth in America* (Boston: Houghton Mifflin, 1975); Constance A. Bean, *Labor and Delivery: An Observer's Diary* (New York: Doubleday, 1977), ch. 6–7.

5. John Oliver, *A Present for Teeming American Women* (Boston, 1694), p. 3; *ECR*, V, 267; "The Experienced Midwife," in *The Works of Aristotle* (Philadelphia, 1798), pp. 36, 45, 62. On the origin of this work, see Otho T. Beall, Jr., "Aristotle's Master Piece in America: A Landmark in the Folklore of Medicine," *WMQ*, 3d Ser., XX (1963), 207–223. For the antiquity of some of "Aristotle's" lore, see Thomas Rogers Forbes, *The Midwife and the Witch* (New Haven and London: Yale U. Press, 1966), pp. 36–38.

6. "The Diary of Nicholas Gilman," ed. William Kidder (unpublished M.A. Thesis, U. of New Hampshire, 1967), pp. 115, 134.

7. *Diary of Cotton Mather*, MHS *Collections*, 7th Ser., VII, 444–445.

8. See Irving S. Cutter and Henry R. Viets, *A Short History of Midwifery* (Philadelphia and London: W. B. Saunders, 1964), p. 9, for the reference to Riverius, *The Practice of Physick*.

9. "Experienced Midwife," p. 61.

10. *Patten Diary*, pp. 64, 91, 120, 146; "Experienced Midwife," pp. 36, 40, 46.

11. The Lamaze method is based on this idea. For an intriguing description of labor "coaching," see Bean, *Labor and Delivery*, ch. 2.

12. Catherine M. Scholten, "On the Importance of the Obstetrick Art: Changing Customs of Childbirth in America, 1760 to 1825," *WMQ*, 3d Ser., XXXIV, 433. Other delivery positions included kneeling on a pallet and standing with the support of two other women.

13. "Experienced Midwife," p. 38.
14. "Experienced Midwife," p. 65; *The Diary of Samuel Sewall*, ed. M. Halsey Thomas (New York: Farrar, Straus and Giroux, 1973), I, 41.
15. "Experienced Midwife," pp. 43-44.
16. "Experienced Midwife," p. 51; Cotton Mather, *Elizabeth in Her Holy Retirement* (Boston, 1710), p. 2.
17. AB *Works*, p. 395; Sarah Goodhue, "A Valedictory and Monitory Writing," in Thomas F. Waters, *Ipswich in the Massachusetts Bay Colony, 1633–1700*, I (Ipswich, Mass.: Ipswich Historical Society, 1905), pp. 519-524.
18. Reverend Seaborn Cotton Commonplace Book, pp. 177-188, NEHGS.
19. Nicholson J. Eastman and Louis M. Hellman, *William's Obstetrics* (New York: Appleton-Century-Crofts, 1966), pp. 702, 724-745.
20. Seaborn Cotton, pp. 183-188.
21. "Nicholas Gilman Diary," p. 134.
22. *Patten Diary*, p. 253.
23. John 16:21-22.
24. Diary of Mary Greenland Cleaveland (1742-1762) in Cleaveland Family Papers, EI.
25. *The Notebook of the Reverend John Fiske*, 1644-1675, ed. Robert G. Pope, MHS *Collections* (Boston, 1974), pp. 49-50; Mary Maples Dunn, "Saints and Sisters: Congregational and Quaker Women in the Early Colonial Period," in Janet Wilson James, ed. *Women in American Religion* (Philadelphia: U. of Pennsylvania Press, 1980), pp. 33-34. For another such case, see MHS *Collections*, 4th Ser., VIII (1868), 361-362.
26. Hugh Adams, "A Narrative of Remarkable Instances of a Particular Faith, and Answers of Prayers," MHS, p. 36.
27. Adams, "Narrative," pp. 33, 5, 2, 3-4.
28. Adams, "Narrative," p. 38.
29. *Holyoke Diaries*. In a typical account for this period, "hard labor" appears four times between June 25 and Dec. 19, 1756. For later interest in forceps, see EAH to James Jackson, Jan. 14, 1800, James Jackson Manuscripts, MHS.
30. Judy Barrett Litoff, *American Midwives: 1860 to the Present* (Westport, Conn., and London: Greenwood Press, 1978), pp. 7-14.
31. Scholten, "Importance," pp. 444-445.
32. Claire Elizabeth Fox, "Pregnancy, Childbirth and Early Infancy in Anglo-American Culture: 1675-1830" (Unpub. Ph.D. Dissertation, U. of Pennsylvania, 1966), pp. 240-245.
33. *Holyoke Diaries*, pp. xvi, 73.
34. *Holyoke Diaries*, pp. 77, 70, 73, 81, 95, 107.

35. *Holyoke Diaries*, pp. 73, 77, 81.
36. *Holyoke Diaries*, p. 58, for a typical sequence.
37. Susan Swan, *Plain and Fancy: American Women and Their Needlework, 1700–1850* (New York: Holt, Rinehart and Winston, 1976), p. 123.
38. "Experienced Midwife," pp. 21–26.
39. *ECR*, VII, 278.
40. *ECR*, II, 36–38.
41. "Experienced Midwife," p. 21; Mather, *Elizabeth in Her Holy Retirement*, p. 21.
42. *ECR*, II, 38.
43. *ECR*, II, 38.
44. *Vital Records of Gloucester* (Topsfield, Mass.: Topsfield Historical Society, 1917), p. 395.
45. "Nicholas Gilman Diary," pp. 79–135.
46. *Diaries of Benjamin Lynde and of Benjamin Lynde, Jr.* (Boston, 1880), pp. 36, 163.
47. John Demos, *A Little Commonwealth: Family Life in Plymouth Colony* (New York: Oxford U. Press, 1971), p. 133; Philip J. Greven, Jr., *Four Generations: Population, Land, and Family in Colonial Andover, Massachusetts* (Ithaca and London: Cornell U. Press, 1970), pp. 30, 112; James Axtell, *The School Upon a Hill* (New Haven, Conn.: Yale U. Press, 1974), p. 82. The extent of wet-nursing in mid-18th-century cities is unknown, though among some urban women breast-feeding was favored as a contraceptive. Mary Beth Norton, *Liberty's Daughters* (Boston: Little, Brown, 1980), pp. 232–233.
48. E.g., *ECR*, III, 46, and MHS *Collections*, 5th Ser., I (1871), 104.
49. Samuel X. Radbill, "The Role of Animals in Infant Feeding," in Wayland D. Hand, ed., *American Folk Medicine: A Symposium* (Berkeley, Los Angeles, London: U. of California Press, 1976), pp. 21–30; "Experienced Midwife," p. 96.
50. *Vital Records of Lynn, Mass.* (Salem, Mass.: Essex Institute, 1905), I, 114, 117, 119; II, 105, 463, 461; *History of Bedford, N.H., from 1737* (Concord, N.H., 1903), pp. 694–698; "Joseph Green His Book," CSM Publications, XXXIV (1943), 197–253; *EIHC*, VII (1866), 215–224; X (1869), 73–104; and XXXVI (1900), 325–330.
51. *Patten Diary*, p. 200.
52. Zaccheus Collins, unpaged diary, EI.
53. "Joseph Green Diary," *EIHC*, X, 86.
54. *Patten Diary*, pp. 20–21.
55. *Patten Diary*, p. 28.
56. "Joseph Green Diary," *EIHC*, VIII, 222.

57. "Nicholas Gilman Diary," pp. 219–220.
58. *Holyoke Diaries*, p. 3.
59. John Demos, "Underlying Themes in the Witchcraft of Seventeenth-Century New England," in Stanley N. Katz, ed., *Essays in Politics and Social Development: Colonial America* (Boston: Little, Brown, 1971), p. 132.
60. Axtell, *School*, p. 88.
61. Samuel Moody, *The Children of the Covenant Under the Promise of Divine Teachings* (Boston, 1716), p. 34.
62. AB *Works*, p. 152.
63. Sewall, *Diary*, I, 444.

Chapter Eight
MOTHER OF ALL LIVING

1. The stones are in Old Newbury Burying Ground opposite the Coffin house, 16 High Road. The epitaphs have been printed in Joshua Coffin, *A Sketch of the History of Newbury, Newburyport, and West Newbury* (Boston, 1845; Hampton, N.H.: Peter E. Randall, 1977), p. 402.
2. Long before the current wave of "family history," Edmund S. Morgan argued that by the end of the 17th century "theology became the handmaid of genealogy" in New England. *The Puritan Family* (New York: Harper & Row, 1966, 1944), p. 186.
3. Tristram Coffin will, reprinted in James W. Spring, "The Coffin House in Newbury, Massachusetts," *Old-Time New England*, XX (1929), 10–11.
4. James Henretta, "Families and Farms: *Mentalité* in Preindustrial America," *WMQ*, 3d Ser., XXXV, 1 (January 1978), pp. 21–32.
5. Data on Coffin descendants gathered from *Old-Time New England*, XX, 1, pp. 8, 11–12; Coffin, *Newbury*, pp. 318, 298, 204, 308, 299, 293, 307; *NLD*, p. 604; and George Kuhn Clarke, *The Descendants of Nathaniel Clarke and His Wife Elizabeth Somerby of Newbury, Massachusetts* (Boston, 1902), pp. 28–29. Unless otherwise indicated, the following discussion is based on these sources.
6. The cradle is in the Tristram Coffin House, Newbury, Mass., Society for the Preservation of New England Antiquities. Linda Grant Depauw and Conover Hunt call these "senility cradles," *"Remember the Ladies": Women in America, 1750–1815* (New York: Viking Press, 1976), p. 161.
7. Philip J. Greven, Jr., *Four Generations: Population, Land, and*

Family in Colonial Andover, Massachusetts (Ithaca, N.Y., and London: Cornell U. Press, 1970), pp. 30, 11, 16; Susan L. Norton, "Population Growth in Colonial America: A Study of Ipswich, Massachusetts," *Population Studies*, XXV (1971), 440–442; Darrett B. and Anita H. Rutman, "Now-Wives and Sons-in-Law: Parental Death in a Seventeenth-Century Virginia County," in Thad W. Tate and David L. Ammerman, ed., *The Chesapeake in the Seventeenth Century* (Williamsburg, Va.: Institute of Early American History and Culture, 1979), pp. 162, 167–168; Maris Vinovskis, "Mortality Rates," *Journal of Economic History*, XXXII (1972), 198–199; Charles E. Clark, *The Eastern Frontier* (New York: Alfred A. Knopf, 1970), pp. 274–277; Coffin, *Newbury*, p. 204.

8. Coffin, *Newbury*, p. 299.

9. Charles G. Steffen, "The Sewall Children in Colonial New England," *NEHGR*, CXXXI (1977), 163–171, shows the importance of extended kin networks in one family with extensive Salem-Newbury connections.

10. Daniel Scott Smith, in an unpublished study of Hingham, has shown the importance of *lineal* naming patterns well into the 19th century, but no one has yet studied New England naming patterns using female as well as male lines. Mary Beth Norton, *Liberty's Daughters* (Boston-Toronto: Little, Brown, 1980), pp. 85–86. In reconstructing the Coffin-Greenleaf families, I used, in addition to sources listed in Note 5, the genealogies in *NEHGR*, XXIV, 149–154, 305–315, and a manuscript Coffin genealogy at the Society for the Preservation of New England Antiquities, Boston.

11. *Saltonstall Papers*, I, 185.

12. Cotton Mather, *Maternal Consolations of God* (Boston, 1714), pp. 24–25.

13. Cotton Mather, *Tabitha Rediviva, An Essay to Describe and Commend the Good Works of a Virtuous Woman* (Boston, 1713), p. 23.

14. Benjamin Colman, *Some of the Honors That Religion Does unto the Fruitful Mothers in Israel* (Boston, 1715), p. 7.

15. E.g., Samuel Moody, *The Children of the Covenant* (Boston, 1716), p. 24; John Cotton, *Spiritual Milk for Boston Babes* (Cambridge, Mass., 1656), for positive imagery; Benjamin Wadsworth, *The Well-Ordered Family* (Boston, 1712), p. 92; John Flavell, *A Discourse* (Boston, 1728), p. 5, for cautionary comments. Joseph and Anna Gerrish lamented that Joseph Green, minister at Salem Village, had died young, "his breast full of milk"; Jeffrey Papers, EI.

16. Sarah Goodhue, "A Valedictory and Monitory Writing," in Thomas Franklin Waters, *Ipswich in the Massachusetts Bay Colony*, I (Ipswich, Mass.: Ipswich Historical Society, 1905), pp. 519–524.

17. Philip J. Greven, Jr., *The Protestant Temperament* (New York: Alfred A. Knopf, 1977), Part One, passim; John Demos, *A Little Commonwealth* (New York: Oxford U. Press, 1970), pp. 131-139; Lawrence Stone, *The Family, Sex, and Marriage in England, 1500-1800* (London: Harper & Row, 1977), pp. 209-215; and David Stannard, *The Puritan Way of Death* (New York: Oxford U. Press, 1977), pp. 64-66.
18. Greven, *Protestant Temperament*, pp. 22-24.
19. *ECR*, IV, 310, 403.
20. *ECR*, II, 275-276. Also see *ECR*, II, 28, and V, 417-418.
21. *ECR*, II, 335-338; James Axtell, *School Upon a Hill* (New Haven, Conn.: Yale U. Press, 1974), pp. 156-159; Edwin Powers, *Crime and Punishment in Early Massachusetts* (Boston: Beacon Press, 1966), pp. 283-285; *Records of the Court of Assistants* (Boston, 1928), III, 138-139.
22. *Saltonstall Papers*, I, 176.
23. *NHSP*, XXXX, 127; *ECR*, III, 282; "Diary of Nicholas Gilman," ed. William Kidder (Unpublished M.A. Thesis, U. of New Hampshire, 1967), p. 192; Hannah Pickering entries for Jan. 17-23, 1712, in Burbank Diary, EI. Cf. Barbara A. Hanawalt, "Childrearing Among the Lower Classes of Late Medieval England," *Journal of Interdisciplinary History*, VIII (1977), 1-22.
24. Moody, *Children of the Covenant*, p. 42.
25. Lucy Larcom, *A New England Girlhood* (Boston, 1889, repr. Gloucester, Mass.: Peter Smith, 1973), pp. 39-45; *The Journals of Ashley Bowen*, ed. Philip Chadwick Foster Smith, CSM *Publications*, XLIV (1973), 184; *Holyoke Diaries*, ed. George Francis Down (Salem, Mass.: Essex Institute, 1911), p. 63; *ECR*, VI, 156, 353.
26. E.g., Jonathan Belcher Letterbook, II, Nov. 12, 1731; Nov. 22, 1731; Feb. 7, 1731/2; III, April 2, 1733; Nov. 5, 1733; IV, Nov. 25, 1734, MHS.
27. Chadwick Hansen, *Witchcraft at Salem* (New York: George Braziller, 1969), pp. 2-3; Alan Macfarlane, *Witchcraft in Tudor and Stuart England* (New York and Evanston: Harper & Row, 1970), pp. 82-85, 154 (Plate 7), 214; *Witchcraft Papers*, I, 83, 94-95, 97-99, 104, 105, 107, 111-112, 191, 217, 244; II, 634.
28. *MPCR*, VI, 208-216; Neal W. Wallen, Jr., "A Maine Witch," *Old Time New England*, LXI (Winter 1971), 75-81.
29. Bruno Bettelheim, *The Uses of Enchantment* (New York: Vintage Books, 1977), pp. 66-70; Paul Boyer and Stephen Nissenbaum make use of the "wicked stepmother" image in *Salem Possessed* (Cambridge, Mass., and London: Harvard U. Press, 1974), though they confine it to projected anger against a real stepmother.

30. Margaret Thatcher letter, Oct. 28, 1686, Curwen Family Papers, III, EI.

31. Stephen Jaques Journal, EI. Also quoted in Coffin, *Newbury*, p. 204.

32. *NEHGR*, XXVIII, 36–39. There is some evidence that among the gentry the preservation of genealogical information was a female role: "Samuel Sewall Letter Book," MHS *Collections*, 6th Ser., I (1886), 265; *The Diary of Samuel Sewall*, ed. M. Halsey Thomas (New York: Farrar, Straus and Giroux, 1973), I, 292; *Diaries of Benjamin Lynde and of Benjamin Lynde, Jr.* (Boston, 1880), p. 128; Charles W. Brewster, *Rambles About Portsmouth* (Portsmouth, N.H., 1869; repr. Portsmouth: New Hampshire Publishing Co., 1972), pp. 51–52.

33. Coffin, *Newbury*, pp. 310, 401; Allan I. Ludwig, *Graven Images: New England Stonecarving and Its Symbols, 1650–1815* (Middletown, Conn.: Wesleyan U. Press, 1966), pp. 236–237.

34. Old Burying Ground, Main Street, York Village, Maine. Ray Wilbur directed me to this stone and explained its significance.

35. AB *Works*, pp. 400–403.

Chapter Nine

BLESSED ABOVE WOMEN

1. *Humiliations Follow'd with Deliverances* (Boston, 1697) and *Decennium Luctuosum* (Boston, 1699).

2. "Journal of the Rev. John Pike," NHHS *Collections*, III (Concord, 1832), 48.

3. Cotton Mather, *Magnalia Christi Americana* (Boston, 1702, repr. New Haven, 1820), Book VII; *The Diary of Samuel Sewall*, ed. M. Halsey Thomas (New York: Farrar, Straus and Giroux, 1973), I, 372; George Wingate Chase, *The History of Haverhill, Massachusetts, from Its First Settlement, in 1640, to the Year 1860* (Haverhill, 1861), p. 191.

4. Mather, *Magnalia*, p. 551.

5. Mather, *Magnalia*, pp. 550–551.

6. Mather, *Humiliations*, p. 47.

7. David D. Hall, *The Faithful Shepherd* (New York: W. W. Norton, 1974), pp. 260–264, and Laurel Thatcher Ulrich, "Vertuous Women Found: New England Ministerial Literature, 1668–1735," *AQ*, XXVIII (1976), 20–40.

8. Nathaniel Hawthorne, *The Marble Faun: or, The Romance of Monte Deni* (New York and Toronto: Signet Books, 1961), p. 39.

9. Hawthorne, *Marble Faun*, p. 40.

10. Timothy Dwight, *Travels in New England and New York*, ed.

Barbara Miller Solomon (Cambridge, Mass.: Belknap Press of Harvard U. Press, 1969), pp. 297-298.

11. From *American Magazine of Useful and Entertaining Knowledge*, II (May 1836), 397, quoted in Kathryn Whitford, "Hannah Duston: The Judgement of History," *EIHC*, CVIII (1972), 318. Whitford's article has a useful survey of 19th-century treatments of Duston, including those by Whittier and Thoreau.

12. Douglas E. Leach, *Flintlock and Tomahawk: New England in King Philip's War* (New York: W. W. Norton, 1966) is a general account of this war. See also Alden T. Vaughan, *New England Frontier: Puritans and Indians 1620-1675* (Boston: Little, Brown, 1965), pp. 319-320; and for a concise summary, Gary B. Nash, *Red, White, and Black: The Peoples of Early America* (Englewood Cliffs, N.J.: Prentice-Hall, 1974), pp. 123-127.

13. Vaughan, *Frontier*, pp. 309-310; Neal Salisbury, "Red Puritans: The 'Praying Indians' of Massachusetts Bay and John Eliot," *WMQ*, 3rd Ser., XXXI (January, 1974), 54.

14. Increase Mather, *A Brief History of the Warr with the Indians* (Boston, 1676), p. 25.

15. William Hubbard, "A Narrative of the Troubles with the Indians in New-England, from Pascataqua to Pemmaquid," in *A Narrative of the Troubles* (Boston, 1677), p. 46.

16. "Narrative of the Captivity of Mrs. Mary Rowlandson, 1682," in Charles H. Lincoln, ed. *Narratives of the Indian Wars 1675-1699* (New York: Charles Scribner's Sons, 1913), p. 128.

17. Hubbard, *A Narrative of the Troubles*, pp. 61, 77; "Piscataqua," 15; [Elizabeth Hanson], *God's Mercy Surmounting Man's Cruelty* (Philadelphia, 1728), pp. 35-36; Cotton Mather, *Good Fetch'd Out of Evil* (Boston, 1706), pp. 33-34.

18. I. Mather, *Brief History*, p. 6.

19. "Captivity of Mrs. Mary Rowlandson," pp. 130-131; Douglas Leach, "The 'Whens' of Mary Rowlandson's Captivity," *NEQ*, XXXIV (Sept. 1960), 352-363, for a general account of geography.

20. Hubbard, "Pascataqua," pp. 32-33.

21. Hubbard, "Pascataqua," pp. 20-21.

22. Douglas Edward Leach, "Mary White Rowlandson," in *Notable American Women 1607-1950*, ed. Edward T. James, Janet Wilson James, and Paul S. Boyer (Cambridge, Mass.: Belknap Press of Harvard U. Press, 1971), III, 200; "Captivity of Mrs. Mary Rowlandson," p. 137.

23. William Willis, *The History of Portland* (1865, repr. Somersworth, N.H.: New Hampshire Publishing Company and Maine Historical Society, 1972), pp. 45, 50, 101.

24. "Captivity of Mrs. Mary Rowlandson," p. 119.

25. Letter from Thaddeus Clark to Mrs. Elizabeth Harvy, Aug. 14. 1676, in Emma Lewis Coleman, *New England Captives Carried to Canada* (Portland, Me.: Southworth Press, 1925), I, 210.

26. Douglas Leach, *Arms for Empire* (New York: Macmillan, 1973), pp. 80–115 passim.

27. Ulrich, "Vertuous Women," passim; and William Andrews, "The Printed Funeral Sermons of Cotton Mather," *Early American Literature*, V (Fall 1970), 24–44.

28. C. Mather, *Decennium*, p. 237.

29. Jeremy Belknap, *The History of New-Hampshire* (Philadelphia, 1784), I, 338–339. Belknap says Oyster River stories were collected from aged persons by John Smith, Esq., a descendant of one of the suffering families.

30. Belknap, *New-Hampshire*, I, 357.

31. Nicholas Perryman Ledger, Exeter, N.H., 1723–1754, MS, NHHS, p. 7.

32. Samuel Penhallow, *The History of the Wars of New-England with the Eastern Indians* (Boston, 1726; repr. NHHS *Collections*, 1824, 1871), I, 107.

33. Penhallow, *Wars*, p. 28; and Cotton Mather, *Good Fetch'd Out of Evil*, p. 38.

34. See, for example, the letter from Pendleton Fletcher, dated Sept. 8, 1721, MeHS *Collections*, IX, 466.

35. (Philadelphia, 1728).

36. C. Mather, *Frontiers Well-Defended* (Boston, 1707), pp. 4–5.

37. Cotton Mather, *Duodecennium Luctuosum* (Boston, 1714), p. 8.

38. This statement is based on a count of captives listed in Coleman, *New England Captives*, ch. 11.

39. "A Narrative of Hannah Swarton," in C. Mather, *Humiliations*, p. 55.

40. John Gyles, *Memoirs of Odd Adventures* (Boston, 1736), p. 4.

41. Gyles, *Memoirs*, p. 4.

42. Gyles, *Memoirs*, p. 4.

43. Gyles, *Memoirs*, p. 34.

44. Cotton Mather, *Decennium*, pp. 198–199. Mather said he received his information from John Pike, the minister at Dover. Pike *did* flee to safety, living in Portsmouth during much of the war.

45. "Letter-Book of Samuel Sewall," MHS *Collections*, 6th Ser. (Boston, 1886), I, 394.

46. Cotton Mather, *El Shaddai* (Boston, 1725), p. 21.

Chapter Ten
VIRAGOES

1. Cotton Mather, *Humiliations Follow'd with Deliverances* (Boston, 1697), pp. 42-48.

2. Charles Henry Pope in *The Haverhill Emersons* (Boston: Murray and Emery, 1913), p. 21, hoped that the "mantle of charity" would cover Elizabeth's name.

3. Eleanor Emmons Maccoby and Carol Nagy Jacklin, *The Psychology of Sex Differences* (Stanford, Calif.: Stanford U. Press, 1974), pp. 243-247.

4. This statement is based upon a count of all court cases involving any form of physical assault in three volumes of the Essex County Court Records, Volume II (41 cases), Volume V (37 cases), and Volume VIII (30 cases). Females were assailants in 21 of 108 cases, victims in 34. Women in a working-class section of London in the late 19th century committed 18 violent crimes for every 100 committed by men. Nancy Tomes, "A 'Torrent of Abuse': Crimes of Violence Between Working-Class Men and Women in London, 1840-1875," *Journal of Social History*, XI (Spring 1978), 330.

5. Emanuel Marx, *The Social Context of Violent Behavior: A Social Anthropological Study in an Israeli Immigrant Town* (London, Henley, and Boston: Routledge & Kegan Paul, 1976), pp. 96-99.

6. Anne Bradstreet, "Meditations," in *The Works of Anne Bradstreet*, ed. John Harvard Ellis (Gloucester, Mass.: Peter Smith, 1962), p. 65.

7. All of the Quarterly Courts punished wife beaters, but they seldom allowed women to leave an abusive husband and, especially if there was any evidence of provocation, they were lenient. E.g., *MPCR*, II, 403, 460; *ECR*, V, 377; *NHSP*, XXX, 20, 83, 166. See also Nancy Cott, "Divorce and the Changing Status of Women in Eighteenth-Century Massachusetts," *WMQ*, 3d Ser., XXXIII (October 1976), 608-609.

8. *ECR*, III, 224-225.

9. *MPCR*, I, 262.

10. *ECR*, VIII, 222-224.

11. *ECR*, VIII, 272-273. Elderly mothers were sometimes victims of family violence and also accused and recanted their accusations. E.g., *ECR*, II, 443-446. For a similar case, see *MPCR*, VI, 9-11, 20. Again the son-in-law is admonished and eventually cleared.

12. *ECR*, V, 312.

13. *MPCR*, IV, 278, 281, 284, 285-287.

14. "Deposition and complaint of Thomas Maule against Elizabeth Darby," EI.

15. *ECR*, V, 59–60.

16. *ECR*, VI, 9. There are numerous examples of this sort of neighborly brawling. E.g., *ECR*, II, 50, 249; III, 32–34, 57–58, 274, 414; VIII, 97, 296; *MPCR*, IV, 91, 111, 270–271; VI, 64–66; NH Court, I, part 1, 13–27; IX, 121.

17. George Lyman Kittredge, *Witchcraft in Old and New England* (New York: Russell & Russell, 1929), pp. 48–49, 102–103.

18. *ECR*, VIII, 226–227.

19. ECR, VIII, 46, 65.

20. *ECR*, VIII, 181–183, a fight at a barn-raising; *ECR*, VIII, 193–194, grievances accumulated during a fishing voyage; *ECR*, V, 31–33, trouble after training.

21. NH Court, I, part 1, 81, 91, 93. For identity of women, *NLD*, pp. 57–58, 132, 219, 387.

22. In the 108 cases described in note 4, men attacked other men in 66 of the 92 cases in which they were assailants. Women attacked other women in 10 cases, men in 10 cases, and both in 1. (The total number of assailants exceeds 108 because men and women acted together in several.)

23. *ECR*, VIII, 293.

24. NH Court, III, 37.

25. NH Court, III, 29, 31, 33, 35, 37, 141, 153, 155, 157, 161, 265, 267, 271, 273, 275, 279, 281.

26. NH Court, III, 37, 149.

27. *ECR*, VIII, 212–213.

28. E.g., *ECR*, VII, 41; VIII, 18–22.

29. "The Vengeful Women of Marblehead: Robert Roules Deposition of 1677," ed. James Axtell, *WMQ*, 3rd Ser., XXXI (Oct. 1974), 650–652.

30. Natalie Davis, "Women on Top," in *Society and Culture in Early Modern France* (Stanford, Calif.: Stanford U. Press, 1975), pp. 146–149.

31. NH Court, File 17285, New Hampshire State Archives.

32. Edwin Powers, *Crime and Punishment in Early Massachusetts, 1620–1692* (Boston: Beacon Press, 1966), pp. 287–290.

33. Lawrence Stone, *The Family, Sex, and Marriage in England 1500–1800* (New York: Harper & Row, 1977), pp. 473–474.

34. Powers, *Crime and Punishment*, p. 307.

35. Cotton Mather, *Warnings from the Dead* (Boston, 1693); *A Sorrowful Spectacle* (Boston, 1715); Samuel Willard, *Impenitent Sinners* (Boston, 1698); John Rogers, *Death the Certain Wages of Sin* (Boston, 1709).

36. *A Faithful Narrative of... Patience Boston* (Boston, 1738), p. 8.
37. Nicall Emerson Will, 8925, Essex Probate; Pope, *Haverhill Emersons*, pp. 14-15.
38. Pope, *Haverhill Emersons*, pp. 13-21; Mather, *Warnings from the Dead*, pp. 71-72.
39. *ECR*, VI, 139, 141; George Wingate Chase, *The History of Haverhill, Massachusetts, from Its First Settlement, in 1640, to the Year 1860* (Haverhill, 1861), p. 122.
40. *ECR*, VI, 212, 213.
41. *ECR*, IX, 603; Mather, *Warnings from the Dead*, pp. 71-72.
42. *Vital Records of Haverhill, Massachusetts*, I, 113, 290-291.
43. Suffolk County Court Records, Early Files, 2636, Suffolk County Court House, pp. 92-96.
44. Examination of Elizabeth Emerson, May 11, 1691, Suffolk Court, Early Files, 2636.
45. Examination of Michael Emerson, May 11, 1691; Examination of Hannah, the wife of Michael Emerson, May 11, 1691; Suffolk Court, Early Files, 2636.
46. Verdict of the Jury Sitting in Boston, Suffolk Court, Early Files, 2636, p. 92; *Saltonstall Papers*, I, 203.
47. Mather, *Warnings from the Dead*, p. 72.
48. Mather, *Warnings from the Dead*, p. 71.

Chapter Eleven

CAPTIVES

1. Emma Coleman, *New England Captives Carried to Canada* (Portland, Me.: Southworth Press, 1925). All statistics in this chapter are compiled from information given on individual captives in Volume I, chapters 6, 7, 8, 9, 10, 12, 13, 14, and Volume II, 15, 16, and 17. I have excluded a few names which Coleman mentioned but did not document.
2. James Axtell, "The White Indians of Colonial America," *WMQ*, 3d Ser., XXXII (Jan. 1975), 58-59.
3. Cotton Mather, *Good Fetch'd Out of Evil* (Boston, 1706).
4. John Williams, *The Redeemed Captive*, ed. Edward W. Clark (Amherst, Mass.: U. of Massachusetts Press, 1976), pp. 48-59, 51, 52.
5. "A Narrative of Hannah Swarton, Containing Wonderful Passages, Relating to Her Captivity, and Her Deliverance," in Cotton Mather, *Humiliations Follow'd with Deliverances* (Boston, 1697), p. 59.
6. [Elizabeth Hanson], *God's Mercy Surmounting Man's Cruelty* (Philadelphia, 1728), p. 9.
7. Coleman, *Captives*, II, 40-41, and individual biographies of captives.

8. *MeHS*, IX, 60.

9. "Statements of Grace Higiman and Others in Relation to Being Taken Captive by the Indians," *NEHGR*, XVIII (1864), 161–163.

10. Coleman, *Captives*, I, 69–70.

11. Cotton Mather, *Decennium Luctuosum* (Boston, 1699), pp. 227, 220.

12. W. J. Eccles, *The Canadian Frontier, 1534–1760* (New York: Holt, Rinehart and Winston, 1969), p. 71 and ch. 4, passim.

13. Coleman, *Captives*, II, 8–9; *NLD*, 131, 699.

14. Coleman, *Captives*, I, 255–259; NHHS *Collections*, VIII, 147; NH Court, VII, 225, 227.

15. Coleman, *Captives*, I, 75, 123–126, 143, 147, 149, 150–151 162–163, 321; II, 9, 21, 412; *NLD*, 520–521, 721.

16. *NLD*, 558, 754, 520–521.

17. Coleman, *Captives*, II, 8–9.

18. Coleman, *Captives*, I, 239–240; *NLD*, 367, 588, 744.

19. Eccles, *Canadian Frontier*, p. 40.

20. James Douglas, *New England and New France* (New York and London: G. P. Putnam's Sons, 1913), pp. 360–366.

21. Coleman, *Captives*, I, 357; II, 268–271, 398, 407, 409.

22. Coleman, *Captives*, I, 359; II, 96.

23. Coleman, *Captives*, I, 429.

24. Mather, *Good Fetch'd*, p. 21.

25. Coleman, *Captives*, I, 40, 358.

26. Coleman, *Captives*, I, 144–146.

27. To develop this topic fully would require a more detailed picture of the operation of both the school and the hospital than are available in Coleman's sketches, but the interlocking of names is clear even from the information she includes on godmothers and godfathers of baptized captives. Grizel Otis Robitaille is highly visible throughout.

28. Coleman, *Captives*, I, 146–154.

29. François Seguenot, *A Letter from a Romish Priest* (Boston, 1729), pp. 5, 20, 11, and preface.

Chapter Twelve

DAUGHTERS OF ZION

1. Jeremy Belknap, *The History of New-Hampshire*, II (Dover, N.H., 1812), 226–234; Everett S. Stackpole, *Old Kittery and Her Families* (Lewiston, Me.: 1903), pp. 184–199; Charles E. Clark, *Maine: A Bicentennial History* (New York: W. W. Norton, 1977), p. 45, and *The Eastern Frontier* (New York: Alfred A. Knopf, 1970), pp. 82–89.

2. Robert F. Lawrence, *The New Hampshire Churches* (Claremont, N.H., 1856), p. 320; *NLD*, pp. 520–521.

3. Lawrence, *New Hampshire Churches*, p. 320; Minutes of Dover Monthly Meeting, 1701–1784, Dover Public Library, microfilm, reel 3.

4. The Church Record of Hampton Falls, N.H., copied from the original by Emily Wilder Leavitt, MS, NEHGS, pp. 6–9.

5. Philip J. Greven, Jr., "Youth, Maturity, and Religious Conversion: A Note on the Ages of Converts in Andover, Massachusetts, 1711–1749," *EIHC*, CVIII (1972), 126–134.

6. The Records of the Church of Christ at Barwick, Dec. 21, 1701, to Oct. 14, 1829, MS, First Parish Federated Church, South Berwick, Maine.

7. Richard L. Bushman, *From Puritan to Yankee: Character and the Social Order in Connecticut, 1690–1765* (New York: W. W. Norton, 1970), p. 62. Bushman says that this was a phenomenon of "outlivers" rather than of new towns in Connecticut, which were notoriously slow to establish churches. If, as I believe, women were especially interested in convenient access to the meetinghouse, the existence of a distant church (which husbands might attend more frequently than wives) may have been a greater motive than the entire absence of church.

8. Everett S. Stackpole and Lucien Thompson, *History of the Town of Durham, New Hampshire* (Concord, N.H., n.d.) I, 169–184, has the long succession of petitions and counterpetitions from the Oyster River parish regarding the location of the meetinghouse.

9. *History of Bedford, New Hampshire, Being Statistics Compiled on the Occasion of the One Hundredth Anniversary* (Boston, 1851), p. 136. The anonymous author said the story came from Ann Orr, "who had it from the lips of old Mrs. Smith."

10. *The Winthrop Papers, Part III*, MHS *Collections*, 5th Ser., I (Boston, 1871), 104–105.

11. Records of Chebacco Parish, 1676–1726, MS, EI, pp. 7–17.

12. Records of Chebacco, p. 18.

13. *ECR*, VII, 245. In their own town they became heroines. See *Celebration of the Two Hundredth Anniversary of the Organization of the Congregational Church & Parish in Essex, Mass.* (Salem, Mass., 1884), p. 45.

14. Increase Mather, *An Essay for the Recording of Illustrious Providences* (Boston, 1684) gives examples both of folk magic and of ministerial opposition. E.g., when Mary Hortado of Salmon Falls was tormented by demons, she hung the door with bays; Mather did not doubt that the remedy worked, but deplored it. Pp. 167, 248–249. Two species of folk magic specifically prohibited by Mather in the long chapter on supersti-

tion (pp. 248–288) were employed in the parsonage at Salem Village—divining with egg white and detecting witchcraft with urine. Chadwick Hansen, *Witchcraft at Salem* (New York: George Braziller, 1969), pp. 30–32.

15. Patricia Trainor O'Malley, "Rowley, Massachusetts, 1639–1730: Dissent, Division and Delimitation in a Colonial Town" (Unpub. Ph.D. Dissertation, Boston College, 1975), pp. 61–65.

16. O'Malley, "Rowley," pp. 67–68, quoting from church book kept by Phillips.

17. O'Malley, "Rowley," p. 69.

18. Paul Boyer and Stephen Nissenbaum, *Salem Possessed* (Cambridge, Mass. and London: Harvard U. Press, 1974), pp. 54–56.

19. Boyer and Nissenbaum put the Putnams at the head of an anti-town, pro-church, pro-autonomy movement in the village. The facts don't add up very well in Burroughs' case. Captain Putnam promoted the church, but obviously disliked Burroughs. Even though he had welcomed him into his home in 1681, he publicly humiliated him in 1683. The controversy here seems personal rather than economic or political.

20. *Witchcraft Papers*, I, 176.

21. *Witchcraft Papers*, I, 172–174.

22. "Church Records of the Rev. Hugh Adams," *NEHGR*, XXX (1876), 59; NLD, p. 184.

23. *NHSP*, IX, 235–236.

24. Deodat Lawson, "A Brief and True Narrative of Witchcraft at Salem Village," in George Lincoln Burr, ed., *Narratives of the Witchcraft Cases* (New York: Barnes and Noble, 1946), pp. 152–154.

25. "The Diary of Nicholas Gilman," ed. William Kidder (Unpub. M.A. Thesis, U. of New Hampshire, 1967), pp. 253, 243.

26. Boyer and Nissenbaum, *Salem Possessed*, pp. 24–30, compare the "fits" of the Salem girls with some of the more bizarre manifestations in the Great Awakening at Northampton. I am making a slightly different point here. Mary Reed's behavior does not seem to have been tortured at all, but rather passive and quiet, but, like the girls in Salem, she conveyed information to the larger community which she received in visions.

27. "Nicholas Gilman Diary," pp. 256–263.

28. When a second visionary young woman tried to stay with Gilman, an uproar in the neighborhood drove her away.

29. "Narrative of the Captivity of Mrs. Mary Rowlandson, 1682," in Charles H. Lincoln, *Narratives of the Indian Wars 1675–1699* (New York: Charles Scribner's Sons, 1913), p. 116. The quote, from the introduction, is amply reflected in the narrative itself.

30. "Captivity of Mrs. Mary Rowlandson, pp. 130, 131, 132, 133, 135, 144, 146.
31. "Captivity of Mrs. Mary Rowlandson," p. 154.
32. "Captivity of Mrs. Mary Rowlandson," p. 142.
33. "Captivity of Mrs. Mary Rowlandson," p. 144.
34. "Captivity of Mrs. Mary Rowlandson," p. 145, 161.
35. "Captivity of Mrs. Mary Rowlandson," p. 159.
36. "Captivity of Mrs. Mary Rowlandson," p. 132–133.
37. "Captivity of Mrs. Mary Rowlandson," p. 149.
38. "Captivity of Mrs. Mary Rowlandson," p. 150.
39. "Captivity of Mrs. Mary Rowlandson," p. 150–154.
40. E.g., Murray G. Murphey, "The Psychodynamics of Puritan Conversion," *American Quarterly*, XXXI (Summer 1979), 140–147, for the relation between religion and personality.
41. [Elizabeth Hanson], "God's Mercy Surmounting Man's Cruelty," in *The Garland Library of Narrative of North American Indian Captivities*, ed. Wilcomb E. Washburn (New York: Garland Publishing, 1977), p. 31.
42. Samuel Penhallow, *The History of the Wars of New-England with the Eastern Indians* (Boston, 1726), reprinted in NHHS *Collections* (1824, 1871), I, 109.
43. [Hanson], "God's Mercy," p. 16.
44. [Hanson], "God's Mercy", p. 24–25.
45. [Hanson], "God's Mercy," p. 23–30.
46. See note 9, chapter 9.
47. Ann Douglas, *The Feminization of American Culture* (New York: Alfred A. Knopf, 1977), pp. 126–127 and ch. 4, passim.
48. Barbara Welter first advanced this argument in "The Feminization of American Religion: 1800–1860," in *Insights and Parallels*, ed. William L. O'Neill (Minneapolis, Minn.: Burgess Publishing Company, 1973), pp. 305–331.
49. Cotton Mather, *Humiliations Follow'd with Deliverances* (Boston, 1697), pp. 42–48.
50. Haverhill Church Book, Haverhill Public Library, Haverhill, Mass., n.p.; the profession of faith is now on display at Buttonwoods, the museum of the Haverhill Historical Society. It has been reprinted in "The Story of Hannah Duston" (Haverhill, Mass.: Duston-Dustin Family Association, 1959), pp. 13–14.
51. The rejuvenation of the church is quite apparent in the Church Book. In a summary, Brown wrote: "The Number above set down by Mr Gardner is 17. The Number of the persons here named below on this page is 55. & I think but 3 records have come to ye Lord's Table!" Excla-

mation points are unusual in church records. Brown was obviously proud of his record. Thomas Duston's affairs are detailed in "Story of Hannah Duston," pp. 16–24. The brick house in Haverhill is a restoration.

52. "Story of Hannah Duston," quoting the confession, pp. 13–14.

Afterword

1. Mrs. Josiah Carpenter, *Gravestone Inscriptions . . . in the State of New Hampshire* (Cambridge, Mass.: Riverside Press, 1913), p. 23. Mrs. Whitney was the widow of the Rev. David Stearns of Lunenburg, Massachusetts, and the Rev. Aaron Whitney of Petersham. Clifford K. Shipton, *Biographical Sketches of Those Who Attended Harvard College* (Cambridge, Mass.: Harvard U. Press, 1933–1975), X, 260; XII, 63; XIII, 645–646; XIV, 90–92, 377–378, for accounts of husbands and sons.

2. Caroline Cole Hollingsworth, "Embroidery in the Society's Collection," *Old Time New England*, LVI (1966), 69; Glee Krueger, *New England Samplers to 1840* (Sturbridge, Mass.: Old Sturbridge Village, 1978), figures 12 and 18; Ethel Stanwood Bolton and Eva Johnston Coe, *American Samplers* (Boston: Massachusetts Society of Colonial Dames of America, 1921), pp. 244, 316. Bolton and Coe date this verse from 1708 in America, but do not indicate where it was first used. Sometimes the "nation" is England, sometimes New England.

Bibliographic Essay

TWELVE YEARS AGO, in an essay urging the restoration of "the actual record of women's contributions" in the American past, Gerda Lerner recommended concentration on the post-revolutionary era, suggesting that "the story of colonial women can be quite fully traced through secondary literature." ("New Approaches to the Study of Women in American History," *Journal of Social History*, III:1 [Fall 1969], pp. 53–62). In retrospect, her statement seems astonishing, yet, given the dearth of research on American women in any era, it was understandable. For colonial women, there were, after all, a number of notable volumes produced in the later nineteenth or early twentieth century: Alice Morse Earle's many books, including *Colonial Dames and Good Wives* (Boston, 1895) and *Home Life in Colonial Days* (New York, 1898); Elizabeth Anthony Dexter's *Colonial Women of Affairs* (Boston, 1924); Mary Summer Benson's *Women in Eighteenth-Century America* (New York, 1935); and Julia Cherry Spruill's *Women's Life and Work in the Southern Colonies* (Chapel Hill, N.C., 1938).

These were pioneering works, important but limited, primarily anecdotal rather than analytical, heavily weighted toward the eighteenth century, and of course untuned to the sorts of economic and social distinctions which later historians would find essential. Their insights were not pursued in later works. Eugenie Leonard, Sophie Drinker, and Miriam Holden's exhaustive but uncritical bibliography, *The American Woman in Colonial and Revolutionary Times, 1565–1800* (Philadelphia, 1962), gives the illusion of fullness where none exists. Tracing their entries for the pre-revolutionary period can only confirm the superficial attention which women have received until recently in colonial histories.

As a consequence, in most surveys and in many specialized studies of nineteenth-century women the colonial period was seen as a static, dimly sketched but at the same time essential backdrop to later changes. If the emphasis was on the emergence of feminism, as in Eleanor Flexner's *Century of Struggle* (Cambridge, Mass., 1959), the colonial period was seen as an era of suppression and superstition. If the emphasis was on the development of "Victorian" womanhood, as in Page Smith's *Daughters of the Promised Land* (Boston and Toronto, 1970), early America became a world of shared work and healthy sensuality.

Although the position of Puritan women was sympathetically considered in Edmund S. Morgan's *The Puritan Family* (Boston, 1944), most excursions into family history gave little attention to wives and mothers. Byron Fairchild's *Messrs. William Pepperell* (Ithaca, N.Y., 1954) was correctly named: the various Mistresses Pepperell do not appear. Equally narrow in their concept of family were John Waters, whose *Otis Family in Provincial and Revolutionary Massachusetts* (Chapel Hill, N.C., 1968) ignored even so revolutionary an Otis as Mercy Warren, and Philip J. Greven, Jr., whose *Four Generations* (Ithaca, N.Y., 1970) might better have been titled "Fathers and Sons." Family historians less concerned with political and economic than with psychological issues have necessarily given greater attention to women. John Demos, in *A Little Commonwealth* (New York, 1970), considered the position of wives and mothers as well as husbands, fathers, children, and servants. Curiously, however, a focus on child-rearing has not always produced awareness of gender differences, perhaps because the psychological models upon which such studies are based have seen the psychology of women as the mirror image of the psychology of men. Philip Greven's *The Protestant Temperament* (New York, 1977) is almost as single-mindedly male as *Four Generations*, if only because his few female examples fit his theoretical frame so poorly. Psycho-history has yet to profit from the revisionist approaches of such psychologists as Jean Baker Miller, *Toward a New Psychology of Women* (Boston, 1976) or Nancy Chodorow, *The Reproduction of Mothering* (Los Angeles, 1978).

At the same time, a number of historians, bringing narrow questions to largely unexplored materials, have begun to question many assumptions about the position of women in the early American past. Nancy F. Cott explored marital status as seen through divorce records in two articles, "Divorce and the Changing Status of Women in Eighteenth-Century Massachusetts," *William and Mary Quarterly*, 3rd ser., XXXII (1976), 586–614, and "Eighteenth-Century Family and Social Life Revealed in Massachusetts Divorce Records," *Journal of Social History*, X (1976), 20–43. Mary Beth Norton undermined the assumptions of Elizabeth Anthony Dexter in her survey of the loyalist papers, described in "Eighteenth-Century American Women in Peace and War: The Case of the Loyalists," *William and Mary Quarterly*, 3rd ser., XXXII (1976), 386–409. She has developed this argument using other materials in *Liberty's Daughters: The Revolutionary Experience of American Women, 1750–1800* (Boston, 1980). Interpretations of female religious status based upon sermon literature appeared in Laurel Thatcher Ulrich, "Vertuous Women Found: New England Ministerial Literature, 1668–1735," *American Quarterly*, XXVIII (1976), 20–40; Margaret W. Masson, "The Typology of the Female as a Model for the Regenerate: Puritan Preaching, 1690–1730," *Signs*, II (1976), 304–315; and Lonna Malmsheimer, "Daughters of Zion: New England Roots of American Feminism," *New England Quarterly*, Sept. 1977, pp. 484–504. Mary Maples Dunn compared two religious traditions in "Saints and Sisters: Congregational and Quaker Women in the Early Colonial Period," *American Quarterly*, XXX (1978). Using probate records, Alexander Keyssar challenged earlier notions in his study of "Widowhood in Eighteenth-Century Massachusetts: A Problem in the History of the Family," *Perspectives in American History*, VIII (1974), 83–119. Daniel Scott Smith and Michael Hindus raised new issues in a study of marriage and birth records, "Premarital Pregnancy in America 1640–1971: An Overview and Interpretation," *Journal of Interdisciplinary History*, V (Spring 1975), 537–570. Such articles demonstrate the fruitfulness of close examination of specific issues. The study of colonial women, especially as seen in the larger context of early American culture, has barely begun.

In the colonial period, of course, it is seldom possible to locate and identify "female" materials. The record of women's lives is there, but it is largely uncatalogued and undefined. The footnotes to individual chapters form a more complete essay on sources than can possibly be written here. A full list of all the materials used would be more misleading than helpful, since few references yielded more than a scrap or two of information on female life. Five major classes of documents can be more fully described, however.

1. *Court Records* were the single most important source for female attitudes and especially for female speech. Fortunately, northern New England has two magnificent collections of printed court records. Harriet Tapley's transcription of seventeenth-century Essex County records includes eight volumes published in the early twentieth century and a ninth volume added more recently: *Records and Files of the Quarterly Courts of Essex County* (Salem, Mass.: Essex Institute, 1911–1975). Additional Essex court papers have been printed in *The Salem Witchcraft Papers*, ed. Paul Boyer and Stephen Nissenbaum, 3 vols. (New York, 1977). Manuscript court papers from seventeenth-century New Hampshire have been mounted in eleven volumes kept at the New Hampshire State Archives, Concord. For eighteenth-century New Hampshire and for Essex County, later court papers are filed by individual case, making it almost impossible to use them for the sort of information gathered here. *The Maine Province and Court Records*, on the other hand, continue into the eighteenth century in an ongoing project of the Maine Historical Society at Portland.

2. *Probate Records*, including inventories, have been published for

early Essex County and Maine but not for New Hampshire. (The Maine inventories are in the first volume of the *Maine Province and Court Records.* The Essex inventories are in *The Probate Records of Essex County,* 3 vols. [Salem, Mass., 1916–1920].) Published records barely hint at the abundance of manuscript probate records in state and county archives. New Hampshire probate records are in manuscript at the state archives and on microfilm at the New Hampshire Historical Society. Maine inventories are in the York County Court House, Alfred, Maine. Essex County inventories are at the Essex County Registry of Probate in Salem, where a lone historian may compete for attention with droves of twentieth-century lawyers. For a helpful introduction to the use of probate records, see Gloria L. Main, "Probate Records as a Source for Early American History," *William and Mary Quarterly,* 3rd Ser., XXXII (1975), 89–99, and in the same issue, Daniel Scott Smith, "Underregistration and Bias in Probate Records: An Analysis of Data from Eighteenth Century Hingham, Massachusetts," 100–112.

3. *Family Papers* for the period before 1750 often consist of deeds, wills, and business accounts, though a few collections offer series of letters. The richest source of family papers for northern New England is the Essex Institute. The most useful collections for this project were the Holyoke Family Collection, including thirteen boxes spanning three centuries; the Curwen Family Manuscripts, mounted in three volumes; and the Barton Family Papers, including the Marston family correspondence in volume one. The published *Saltonstall Papers, 1607–1815,* Robert E. Moody, ed. (Boston, 1972), have an almost unique set of letters from a mother to a daughter. The Massachusetts Historical Society has published both the William Pepperrell Papers and the Jonathan Belcher Papers. Both have occasional references to their wives, though no female correspondence has survived. The unpublished Belcher letters are useful and have been conveniently indexed at the end of the published volume (Massachusetts Historical Society *Collections,* VI).

4. Diaries for the region have been catalogued in William Matthews, *American Diaries: An Annotated Bibliography* (Berkeley, Calif., 1945) and in *American Diaries in Manuscript 1580–1954* (Athens, Ga., 1974). Unfortunately, there are no female diaries before 1750. The most detailed male diaries are those of Matthew Patten, Joseph Green, Zaccheus Collins, and Nicholas Gilman, described in Chapter Seven. Mary Holyoke's diary is part of a larger Holyoke collection, including almanac diaries in the Holyoke Family Collection at the Essex Institute and those family diaries published as *The Holyoke Diaries 1709–1856* (Salem, Mass., 1911). The Mary Cleaveland "Diary" at the Essex Institute is a mere fragment. Male account books, on the other hand, exist in great

abundance. They occasionally give glimpses of daily life, though they require industrious mining for every jewel uncovered. Account books are catalogued separately at the New Hampshire Historical Society and at the Essex Institute.

5. *Church Records* can be found in archives, in trunks in church basements, or in the custody of church clerks who spend the winter in Florida. For clues to whereabouts of congregational-church records, see Harold F. Worthley, *An Inventory of the Records of the Particular Churches of Massachusetts Gathered 1620–1805* (Cambridge, Mass., 1970). There is much more to be learned about the activities of women in churches from a close examination of membership patterns and of disciplinary action. For a brilliant example of what can be done with local church records, see Mary P. Ryan, "A Woman's Awakening: Evangelical Religion and the Families of Utica, New York, 1800–1840," *American Quarterly*, XXX (1978), 602–623.

Lyle Koehler's *A Search for Power: The Weaker Sex in Seventeenth Century New England* (Urbana: U. of Illinois Press, 1980) appeared after this book was complete. The research is impressive and the bibliography and source notes are an excellent guide to the kinds of materials available for other parts of New England. Unfortunately, the book itself is marred by a curiously polemical style and by what sometimes appears as deliberate distortion of evidence.

Index

A

Abbott, Sarah, fights with Alice Cate, 191
account books, 44–5
Adams, Catherine, endurance in captivity of, 205
Adams, Hugh:
  assists at childbirth, 132–3
  in Durham church controversy, 222–3
adultery, 94, 95, 112
aggression, 170–2, 183, 185, 193, 232
  see also violence
agriculture, domestic, 15, *table 16*, 21–2, 25, 32, 70, 71
  slaughtering pigs, 22–3
Allin, John, on union in marriage, 108
Appleton, Elizabeth Rogers, family history, 160–1
Axtell, James:
  on captivity, 204
  on conversion and weaning, 142

B

Baker, Alice, 203
Baker, Christine Otis Le Beau, captivity and return of, 213–14, 215
baking, 20–1
barter economy, 26–7
bastardy, 96, 198
Bathsheba, *see* Proverbs 31
Batson, Anne, captivity of, 205, 212
Bedford (N.H.), residents of: *for ac-counts of, see* Patten, Elizabeth; Smith, Catherine
beer:
  "groaning" (at childbirth), 127
  -making, 23
Belcher, Jonathan, on ideal wife, 84–6
Belcher, Mary, 83–4
Belknap, Jeremy, on Oyster River heroines, 178–9
Belknap, Ruth, "Pleasures of a Country Life . . ." (poem), 77–8, 253
Bettelheim, Bruno, 159
birth, *see* childbirth
Bishop, Mary, and charity, 61–3
Black, Faith (and Daniel), "gadding" of, 51, 61, 107
Blesdel, Debrath (and Ephraim), trades her spinning, 45–6
bodkin, 63 and *n.*, 64–5
Bond, Jane, and Robert Collins, 99–100, 101–2
bonding of women, 57, 59–60, 66, 132
  in captivity, 210–13 *passim*, 231
  see also childbirth: attendants; neighbors
bookkeeping, 44–5
Boston, Patience, infanticide, 196
Bowdoin, James, on idealized image of woman, quoted, 115–16
Bowen, Dorothy Chadwick (and Ashley), courtship of, 124–5
Boyer, Paul, 221
Boynton, Sarah, pregnancy of, 136
Brackett, Ann, captivity of, 175, 176–7
Bradley, Hannah, as heroine, 179
Bradstreet, Anne Dudley:
  and childbirth, 129

Bradstreet, Anne Dudley (*cont.*)
  on discipline of children, quoted, 187
  eulogy for mother, quoted, vii, 3
  Four Ages of Man, quoted, 144-5
  and husband, 110-11
  on (her own) motherhood, quoted, 162-3
  poetry of, 83, 111; quoted, 110-11, 113, 162-3
bread-making, 20-1
breast-feeding, *see* nursing
Browne, Judith (and Nathaniel), gossip about, 55
Bulman, Mary, crewelwork of, 116-17, 258
bundling, 122-3
Burr, Esther Edwards:
  compulsion to serve, 78
  and *Pamela* (Richardson), 104
Burroughs, George, in church controversy, 221-2
Busse, Stephen, sees vision, 225

C

Calvin, John, on Eve, 107
Cantlebury, Rebecca, premarital pregnancy of, 122
captives, 203-8, *table* 203
  age, 204
  escape of, 204-5
  gender, *table* 203, 204
  as intermediaries, 207, 213
  pregnancy/maternity of, 173-4, 205
  religious experience and influence of, 175-7, 179-80, 183, 208, 210-13 *passim*, 226-34
  remain with captors, 204, 208-13
  skills (practical) of, 175, 177, 228, 230
  survival of, 205, 206-7
  towns of origin of, 203-4
captivity narratives, 167-83, 202-14, 226-34
  Brackett, Ann, 175, 176-7
  Duston, Hannah, *see* Duston, Hannah
  Gyles, John, 181
  Hanson, Elizabeth, 179-80, 206, 212, 226-7, 230-4
  Heard, Elizabeth, 181-2, 183
  piety of, 79, 169, 174, 179-80, 202, 226-7, 230, 231, 232
  Rowlandson, Mary, 173-4, 226-30, 232-3
  Swarton, Hannah, 180, 181, 183, 206, 212
captors, 206
  assimilation with, 208-13
  attitudes toward, 228-30, 231-2
Casco Bay (Me.), residents of: *for accounts of, see* Brackett, Ann; Clark, Martha; Swarton, Hannah
Cate, Alice, fights with Sarah Abbott, 191
Catholicism:
  and captives, 210-13
  and Protestants (as threat to), 180, 181, 208
charity, 14
  Rule of (Proverbs 31), 59, 61, 62-3, 67, 83-4
chastity, 93-4, 104
  in Milton, 114
Chebacco, *see* Ipswich
cheese:
  -making, 22
  trading in, 47
childbirth, 126-35
  attendants in, 126-7, 128-9, 135
  infant deaths, 134-5, 137
  and suffering, 129-32, 145
  see also motherhood; pregnancy
children:
  care of, 14; *see also* motherhood;

Index

nursing; parenting styles; weaning
  gender identity of, 29
  hazards and dangers to, 157–8
  illegitimate, 96, 198
  mortality, 134–5, 137, 149, 152, 158, 159, 161
  violence to, 187, 188, 197
  see also childbirth
Christians, women as, 9–10, 239
  in captivity, *see* captivity narratives: piety of; religious experience of women: in captivity
  in churches, *see* churches
churches:
  controversies, 220–3
  distance to attend meetings, 217–19
  membership, 215–16
  and women, 215–26
  see also meetinghouse; ministers; Protestantism
cider-making, 23
Clark, Martha, as "white Indian," 204
Cleaveland, Mary, on birth of child, quoted, 131
clergy, *see* ministers
Clinton, Rachel (and Laurence), marriage choice of, 120
clothing:
  care of, 27–8
  of children, 29
  of gentlewoman, 71–2, 81–2
  men's, 79–81
  sewing, 29
  see also modesty
Cocheco, *see* Dover
Coffin, Judith Somerby (and Tristram):
  family names, 149–52
  maternal role, 146–9
Cole, Sarah, in captivity, 205, 212
Coleman, Emma, 203
Collins, Elizabeth (and Zaccheus), travel and pregnancy, nursing, 139–42
Collins, Robert, and Jane Bond, 99–100, 101–2
Colman, Benjamin, on Eve, quoted, 114, 153
commerce, skills in, 14, 26–7, 43
  of gentlewoman, 70
  oral basis of, 45
  simple *vs.* complex, 48–9
  see also deputy husband
consort, 9, 95, 107–25, 238
  in Milton, 114
  sexuality *vs.* spirituality, 107
  see also marriage; wife
consumer economy, 15
  for food, 26–7
contraception:
  lack of, 152, 159
  nursing as, 139
  see also fertility/fecundity
convents/nuns, Catholic, 210–13
cooking, 19–21, 26
  of gentlewoman, 71
Corwin, Sarah (and George), marriage relationship of, 118
Cotton, Anne Lake, childbirth experience of, 129–30
Cotton, Dorothy Bradstreet, 4
Cotton, Elizabeth Saltonstall Denison (and Rowland), 73, 74
Cotton, John:
  record of family births by, 129
  on women as necessary, quoted, 106
Cotton, Seaborn, 3–4
courts, and women, 54–5, 103, 156, 256
courtship, 119–21
  bundling, 121–2
  and captivity, 208–9
Creford, Edith, acts as attorney, 41
Crumpacker, Laurie, 78
Cutt, Ursula, probate inventory of (1694), 72

D

dairying, *see* agriculture, domestic
Danvers, Mass., *see* Salem Village
Davis, Elizabeth (and Lt. Col. James),
  in Durham church controversy, 222–3
Davis, Mary Ann, captivity and religious vocation of, 210, 211
Davis, Natalie, 194
Deerfield (Mass.), captives from, 205–6
  see also Hurst, Hannah; Williams, John
Demos, John, 142
Denison, Elizabeth, 73, 74
Denison, Patience Dudley:
  death of, 160
  and Rule of Charity, 58, 61–3
dependence/independence:
  and courtship, 119–20, 121–2
  economic, 36, 46–7; *see also* deputy husband
  on husband, 7–8, 36–7, 42, 48–9
  sexual, 94
  see also submission
deputy husband, 9, 36–50, 238
  as attorney, 41
  and fishing, 40–1
  Jael (Biblical heroine) as, 170
  limitations of role of, 37–8, 49–50
  and merchant shipping, 41–2
  and timber business, 39–40
Dering, Anne, as widow, 40
Devorix, Anne, as fishwife, 41
Dexter, Elizabeth A., 35
diet, 19–21
disguise, female, 194–5
disguise, male, 178–9
dissenters, religious, 112, 132
divorce, 110, 112–13
domestic role, *see* housewife
Douglas, Ann, 233
Dover (N.H.), residents of: *for accounts of, see* Belknap, Ruth; Hanson, Sarah; Heard, Elizabeth; Jones, Esther; Pike, John
Drew, Tamsen (and Thomas):
  as captive, 205, 207, 212
  and church, 217
Dudley, Dorothy, death and eulogy of, 3
Dudley, Thomas:
  and (Benjamin) Keayne, 112
  on submission to husband, quoted, 6
  at wife's death, quoted, 3, 10
Durham (Oyster River) (N.H.):
  heroines of, 178
  residents of: *for accounts of, see* Adams, Hugh; Davis, Elizabeth; Drew, Tamsen; Jenkins, Ann; Reed, Mary; Willey, Abigail
Duston, Hannah Emerson:
  aggression of, 167, 183
  captivity (1697) of, 167–70
  escape from captivity by, 167, 205
  and Jael (Biblical heroine), 168–9
  later accounts of, by Dwight, Whittier, Thoreau, Hawthorne, 171–2
  motivation of, 171
  religious conversion of, 234–5
  and sister, Elizabeth Emerson, 184–5, 197, 235
Dwight, Timothy:
  account of Hannah Duston, 171–2
  dislike for Hannah Duston, quoted, 172

E

ecstasy, religious, 223–6
education:
  power of, for men, 132, 133, 134
  of women, 43–4
Ela, Elizabeth, beaten by husband, 188
Emerson, Elizabeth, 196–201

infanticide committed by, 185, 198–201
and sister, Hannah Duston, 184–5, 197
Emerson, Hannah (and Michael), 197
epitaphs, 3
Coffin, Judith, 146, 152
Coffin, Tristram, 146
Moody, Lucy, 162
Moody, Mehetable, 161
Whitney, Ruth, 237
equality of men and women:
of Eve and Adam, 107
spiritual, 9, 107
see also submissiveness
Erickson, Robert, 105
Essex County (Mass.), household inventories:
(1670–1730), 15, *table 16*, 69 and *table*
(1700), 15, 17 and *table*
evangelical tradition, and housewife, 79, 80, 81
Eve, as model, 106–7, 117–18
in (Anne) Bradstreet's poem, 113
in courting ballad (1786), 123–4
and gentry, portraits of, 115
in Milton, 113–14
and suffering, 130, 131
Ewens, Agnes, testifies in court, 98–9
Exeter (N.H.):
incident involving female disguise (1719), 195
residents of: *for accounts of, see* Gilman, Elisabeth; Gilman, Mary

F

family, 147
governance of, 36
naming patterns, 149–52
of property, 147, 148, 152, 160, 239
of reproduction, 147, 148–9, 152
of sentiment, 147, 150, 152, 160, 238–9
Fanning, Elizabeth, violence of, 191
fertility/fecundity, 33, 146–7
and motherhood, 159–62
reproductive patterns, 139–40
and witchcraft, 158
uncontrolled, 152, 159
fires, domestic, regulation of, 20
first names, 149–52
Fiske, John, autopsy on child, 132
folk magic, 219–20, 273
see also witchcraft
food, 19–21
in captivity, 229
"groaning" cakes, 127
urban procurement of, 26–7
forenames, 149–52
fornication, 31, 94, 254
and churches, 103
Four Ages of Man, The (Bradstreet), quoted, 144–5
Furson, Joane, demonstrative protest of, 192–3

G

garrisons, 32, 67
attacked, 178
in Saltonstall home, 74–5, 79
Gatchell, Wiboroe, protects son, 156
gathering:
herbs for childbirth, 127–8
-tasks, general, 31–2
gender specialization, 37–8, 49–50
Genesis:
(2:18, 21–25), quoted, 87, 106, 107
(3:12–17, 20), quoted, 87–8, 106
gentlewoman, "pretty," 68–86
clothing of, 71–2
in coastal town, 70–1
in frontier town, 73–5
and housewife, compared to, 68–70, 71–9 *passim*, 82

gentlewoman, "pretty" (cont.)
  religious considerations, 79–86
  rural, 77–8
  work of, 70–1
Gilman, Elisabeth (and Moses), deputation of duties, 39–40
Gilman, Mary:
  pregnancy of, 128, 138, 142
  and son's clothing, 80–1
Gilman, Nicholas, 81, 157, 223
  on birth of child, 128, 138, 142; quoted, 131
  and Mary Reed, 224–6
given names, 149–52
Glitten, Mary, in childbirth, 132–3
Goodell, Elizabeth, harassed, 100, 102
Goodhue, Sarah, "Valedictory and Minitory Writing," 5, 129, 154–5
Gookin, Dorothy Cotton, 4
  and childbirth, 130
gossip and rumor, 55, 57, 66, 96, 102, 220
  see also slander
Grafton, Hannah (and Joshua), household in town, 24–30
grains, 19
grandmother, 149, 158, 159–60
gravestones, *see* epitaphs
Green, Elizabeth (and Joseph), travel and pregnancy, nursing, 139–41, 143–4
Greenland, Henry, and Mary Rolfe, 89–92, 93, 98, 254
Greven, Philip J., Jr., 79, 93, 160
"groaning" beer, cakes, at childbirth, 127
Gyles, John, captivity narrative quoted, 181

H

Hanson, Elizabeth:
  captivity narrative, 179–80, 212; quoted, 206
  as submissive heroine, 226–7, 230–4

Hanson, Sarah, as "white Indian," 204
Haverhill (Mass.), residents of: *for accounts of, see* Boynton, Sarah; Bradley, Hannah; Davis, Mary Ann; Duston, Hannah; Emerson, Elizabeth; Saltonstall, Elizabeth
Hawthorne, Nathaniel:
  aversion to Hannah Duston, 172
  Miriam (character in *Marble Faun*), 170–1
Heard, Elizabeth, as heroine, 181–2, 183
hearsay, *see* gossip and rumor
herbs, and childbirth, 127–8
heroine, 10, 239
  aggression of, 170–2, 183
  godly type of, 174, 179–80, 183
  Jael as model for, 168–9, 178–9
  and violence, 185
  virago (self-reliant) type of, 174, 175
  see also captives; captivity narratives
Hewlett, Mistress, and poultry business, 46
Higiman, Grace, captivity of, 207
Holmes, Robert, strikes wife, 188
Holyoke, Edward Augustus, 70, 79–80, 142
  and childbirth, 134
Holyoke, Mary (and Edward), 79–80
Holyoke, Mary Vial:
  daily work of, 70–1
  and Elizabeth Saltonstall, compared to, 75–7
  and infant deaths, 134–5
  travels with child, 142
house:
  rural, 32
  in town, 25–6
  in village, 18–19
housewife, 9, 13–34, 237–8
  domain of, 13–14, 38–9
  and "pretty gentlewoman," 68–70, 71–9 *passim*, 82

private or hidden nature of role, 14, 59
rural, 30-3
social context of, 33-4
in town, 24-30
in village, 18-24
see also manufacture, domestic
Hubbard, Margaret, and Sarah Row, 58
Hubbard, William, 55
Narrative of the Trouble with the Indians . . . (1677), 173-4, 175
and Sarah Row, 57, 121
Hunt, Elizabeth (and Samuel), 58
seating in meetinghouse, 65-6
theft of bodkin, 63-5
Hunt, Mary, as cheese dealer, 47
Hurst, Hannah, captivity of, 211
Hurst, Mary (Pepperrell), 82, 83-4
husband:
abusive, 187, 188, 269
-beating, 191
and childbirth, 127-8, 131
choice of, 120-2, 123, 209
role in family of, 36; see also deputy husband; family
and wife, relationship with, 8; conflict in, 109-10, 120; dependence in, 7-8, 36-7, 42, 48-9; economic, see deputy husband; legal, 6-7, 94; sexual, see consort and sexual behavior; spiritual, 108; violent, 187, 188, 269
husband, deputy, see deputy husband
Hutchinson, Anne, dissenter, 112, 132

attitudes toward, 228-30, 231-2
as captors, 204, 206
and frontier settlers, 176
and rape, 97, 174
Industry, Rule of, 59, 61, 67, 78
infanticide, *see* infant mortality: infanticide
infant mortality, 134-5, 137, 149
infanticide, 186, 195-6; of Boston, Patience, 196; of Emerson, Elizabeth, 185, 198-201
inheritance, 148
see also widow: legal status of
inventories, household:
of Cutt, Ursula (1694), 72
in Essex Co. (Mass.) (1670-1730), 15, *table* 16, 17 and *table*, 69 and *table*
in Salem (Mass.) (1700), 15, 17 and *table*
in York Co. (Me.) (1670-1730), 15, *table* 16, 69 and *table*
Ipswich (Mass.), 52-67, *map* 56
intermarriage in, 160
landholdings, 53
meetinghouse, 53-4
petitioned by Chebacco for own minister, 218-19
residents of: *for accounts of, see* Appleton, Elizabeth Rogers; Clinton, Rachel; Goodhue, Sarah; Hewlett, Mistress; Quilter, Thamar; Symonds, Samuel
social strata, 57
ironing, 28

I

illegitimacy, 96, 198
independence, *see* dependence/independence
Indian-captivity narratives, *see* captivity narratives
Indians:
assimilation with, 208-9

J

Jael (Biblical heroine):
and Duston, Hannah, compared to, 168-9
and heroines of her type, 178-9, 234
sexual overtones of, 191-2
and "Song of Deborah" (Judges 5),

Jael (Biblical heroine) (*cont.*)
    quoted, 165; summarized, 168
Jacques, Deborah, death of grandchildren, 159–60
Jenkins, Ann:
    captivity and return of, 207
    and church, 217
Jenkins, Mary (and Rowland), sexual escapade of, 100–1, 102–3
Jones, Esther, heroine at garrison, 178
journeys, *see* travel

K

Keayne, Sarah Dudley (and Benjamin),
    marriage and divorce of, 110, 111–13
Keene, Nathaniel, struck by Joanna Williams, 189
Keene, Sarah:
    suspects witchcraft, 158
    witness to Joanna Williams' violence, quoted, 189
Keyssar, Alexander, 36
King Philip's War (Metacom's Rebellion), 173
    women as negotiators during, 207
    see also captivity narratives
King William's War (1689–98), 74–5, 177–8
    women as negotiators during, 207
    see also captivity narratives
Kittery (Me.), residents of: *for accounts of, see* Jenkins, Mary; Keene, Sarah; Mendum, Goody; Weeks, Judith

L

lactation, *see* nursing
laundering, 28

Lawson, Deodat, preaches at Salem Village, 224
learning, *see* education
Littlefield, Ruth, captivity and religious vocation of, 210, 211
longevity:
    average, 149
    matriarchal, 160
    see also infant mortality

M

manufacture, domestic, 14, 15–17, *table 16*
    beer-making, 23
    cheese-making, 22
    cider-making, 23
    by gentlewoman, 70, 71
    meat-processing, 22–3
    sale/trade of, 45–7
    spinning, 29, 34, 45–6, 82
    see also needlework
marriage:
    age at, 6
    in captivity, 208–13 *passim*
    conflict in, 109–10, 120
    emotional aspects, 108, 109
    legal aspects, 6–7, 94, 119
    see also consort; courtship; deputy husband; sexual behavior; wife
Marston, Patience (and Benjamin), involvement in business of, 41–2
Marx, Emanuel, 186
maternal role, *see* motherhood
Mather, Cotton:
    and Duston, Hannah, 167–70, 184, 234
    Ornaments for the Daughters of Zion (1691), 82–3
    quoted, on: Amazonian women, 178; captives as mediators, 207; Emerson, Elizabeth, 200–1; heroic New England women, 182; man and wife, 108; (his) mother, 153;

"papist threat," 180; sufferings of
frontier, 180
warns against dangers of "papacy,"
211–12
and wife's illness, 128
Mather, Increase, *History of the War
with the Indians . . .* (1676),
173–4
meals, 19–21
meat, 19
processing, 22–3
medicines, 128, 136
meetinghouse:
controversies in, 64–6; *see also*
churches: controversies
distance of, from "outliners,"
217–19, 237
in Ipswich, 53–4
seating customs in, 54, 65, 66, 82
men, equality of women with, *see*
equality of men and women
Mendum, Goody, in slander case, 96
Mériel, Fr. Henri-Antoine de, 212,
213
Metacom, 228
Metacom's Rebellion (King Philip's
War), 173
women as negotiators during, 207
see also captivity narratives
midwife:
decline in role of, 134
and fornication cases, 98, 255
supplies, 128
military training day, 54, 64, 190
Milton, John, on Eve in *Paradise Lost*,
113–14, 115
ministers:
and church controversies, 220–3
and folk magic, 219–20, 273
and women, 219–23; affluent, 84;
in childbirth, 132–3; situations
compared, 37
see also individual ministers
Miriam (Hawthorne character),
170–1
mistress, 9, 14, 76, 238
in Ipswich, 57, 58

see also charity; gentlewoman,
"pretty"; servants
modesty, 108–9
and childbirth, 127
Rule of (Proverbs 31), 59, 64,
66–7, 83
with servants, 95
see also privacy
Moody, Samuel:
and death of daughter, 162
and Patience Boston, 196
Morgan, Edmund S., 93
motherhood, 9, 152–63, 238–9
as affectionate mode of child-rearing, 154–6
and attending church, 218–19
in captivity, 173–4, 205
extensive nature of, 157–9
and family patterns, 146–52
and fertility, 159–62
idealized, 152–3
and witchcraft, 158–9
see also childbirth; children; grandmother; nursing; pregnancy;
weaning

N

names:
and marriage, 7
patterns in families, 149–52
needlework:
as captivity skill, 228
courting pictures, 116, 120
domesticity portrayed, 116–17
fine, 77
knitting, 67, 228
samplers, sentiments of, quoted,
241
see also sewing
Neff, Mary, 167, 168, 198, 199
neighbors, 9, 239
conflicts among, 53, 189–90; *see
also* courts; gossip and rumor
patterns among, 51–67

neighbors (*cont.*)
  and sexual conduct, 101–3
  see also women: bonding of
Newbury (Mass.), residents of: *for accounts of, see* Blesdel, Debrath; Jaques, Deborah; Ordway, Joanna; Plummer, Beatrice; Rolfe, Mary; Stickney, Sarah
Nissenbaum, Stephen, 221
Norton, Mary Beth, 35, 49
nuns/convents, Catholic, 210–13
nursing, 138–9
  and assault (male), 89–90
  in captivity, 231; "sucking infant" theme, 173–4
  on church grounds, 218
  as contraception, 139
  in religious imagery, 154
  and travel, *table 140*, 141
  see also weaning

O

obedience, *see* submission
obstetrics, 134
  see also midwife
Oliver, Elizabeth (and Daniel), portrait and eulogy of, 116
Ordway, Joanna, as "white Indian," 204
Ornaments for the Daughters of Zion (Mather, 1691), 82–3
Otis, Christine, captivity and return of, 213–14, 215
Otis, Grizel (*later* Robitaille), as captive, 209–10, 212, 213
Oyster River (Dover, N.H.):
  heroines of, 178
  residents of: *for accounts of, see* Adams, Hugh; Davis, Elizabeth; Drew, Tamsen; Jenkins, Ann; Reed, Mary; Willey, Abigail

P

Pamela (Richardson), 104–5
Paradise Lost (Milton), on Eve, 113–14, 115
parenting styles, 154–6
Parkman, Mehitable, fond wife, 118–19; quoted, 109
Patten, Elizabeth (and Matthew):
  birth of child, 131
  travel and pregnancy, nursing, 139–41
Pepperrell, Andrew, and Hannah Waldo, 119
Pepperrell, Mary Hurst (and Sir William):
  fashionable clothing of, 82
  piety of, 83–4
Perkins, Elizabeth, Sr., testifies in court, 98–9
Pike, John:
  on Hannah Duston, quoted, 167
  on wife's modesty, quoted, 108
"Pleasures of a Country Life . . . , The" (Belknap), 77–8
Plummer, Beatrice (and Frances):
  and Edmund Berry, 23–4
  household of, 18–24
pocket, as symbol, 34
Porter, Joseph, slanders mother, 156
portraits of gentry, 115–16, 258
Portsmouth (N.H.), residents of: *for accounts of, see* Cutt, Ursula; Furson, Joane; Hunt, Mary
pregnancy, 135–8
  and captivity, 205
  premarital, 122, 198
  travel during, 139–41, *table 140*
  see also childbirth; motherhood
Prince, Margaret, pregnancy of, 136–7
privacy, 52, 66, 94–5
property:
  chastity as, 93–4
  family of, 147, 148, 152, 160, 239
Protestantism:
  attitudes toward women, 106, 107

and convents, monasteries, 106
and French "papism," 180, 181, 208, 210–13 passim
see also Christians, women as; churches; Puritanism; Quakers
Proverbs 31:
  and piety, 82–3
  quoted, 11–12, 14, 82–3
  Rule of Charity, 59, 61, 62–3, 67, 83–4
  Rule of Industry, 59, 61, 67, 78
  Rule of Modesty, 59, 64, 66–7, 83
  "virtuous woman" model, 14, 78, 84–5
Puritanism:
  on marriage, 109, 110
  and morality, 92, 93
Putnam, Rebecca (and Capt. John), in church controversy, 221–2, 274

Q

Quakers, 215, 232–3
Queen Anne's War (1703–1713), 177–8
Quilter, Frances (and Mark), and neighbor, 58, 60–1
Quilter, Thamar, and son Joseph, 156

R

rape:
  of Bond, Jane, 99–100, 101–2
  and Indians, 97, 174
  of Jenkins, Mary, 100–1, 102–3
  in *Pamela* (Richardson), 104–5
Reed, Mary, and Nicholas Gilman, 224, 225–6, 274

religious experience of women:
  in captivity, 175–7, 179–80, 183, 208, 210–13 *passim*, 226–34
  in churches, 215–23
  conversion of Hannah Duston, 234–5
  as dissenters, 112, 132
  ecstatic utterance, 223–6
  of gentlewomen, 79–86
remedies, medicinal, 128, 136
reproduction, *see* fertility/fecundity
Richardson, Samuel, *Pamela*, 104–5
Robitaille, Grizel Otis, captive, 209–10, 212, 213
role analysis, 5–6
Rolfe, Mary (and John), and Henry Greenland, 89–92, 93, 98
Roman Catholicism, *see* Catholicism
Roper, Sarah, thefts by, 61–5
Rosenmeier, Rosamund, 111
Row, Sarah Woodward (and William):
  choice of husband, 120–1
  jealousy of husband, 95
  and relations between social groups, 57–8
Rowlandson, Mary, 176
  captivity narrative (1682), 173–4, 226–30, 232–3
  piety of, 174, 176, 226–7, 230, 232
  practical survival skills, 177, 228, 230
  racism of, 229
  responses to patriarchal society, 233
Rowley (Mass.), church controversies in (1670s), 220–1
rumor, *see* gossip and rumor
Russell, Mary, 48–9

S

Salem (Mass.):
  domestic life in, 24–30

INDEX

Salem (Mass.) (*cont.*)
  household inventories (1700), 15, 17 and *table*
  residents of: *for accounts of, see* Cantlebury, Rebecca; Corwin, Sarah; Creford, Edith; Goodell, Elizabeth; Grafton, Hannah; Holyoke, Edward Augustus; Holyoke, Mary Vial; Marston, Patience; Parkman, Mehitable; Porter, Joseph
  witchcraft in, 120, 221–2, 225
Salem Village (Danvers, Mass.):
  church controversies in, 220–2
  demon possession incident (1692), 224
Saltonstall, Elizabeth (and Nathaniel), 73–5, 182
  death of Nathaniel's mother, 153
  and Mary Holyoke, compared, 75–7
salvation:
  and captivity, 202, 230, 232
  hope of, for dead, 161–2
Sayward, Esther (*later* Mme. Pierre de Lestage), captive, 210
Sayward, Mary (*later* Sr. Marie-des-Anges), captive, 210, 211
Secker, William, on husband and wife, quoted, 8, 107
sentiment, family of, 147, 150, 152, 160, 238–9
servants:
  in Ipswich, 57, 58
  modesty with, 95
  problems with, 74, 76; *see also* Roper, Sarah
  residence of, in household, 39
  responsibility for, 157, 158
  and tasks of mistress, 71
  violence to, 187–8
  see also mistress
Sewall, Samuel, 161, 167
  eulogy for mother, quoted, 145
  on frontier heroism, 182
sewing, 29

see also needlework
sexual behavior, 85–6, 92–9
  aggression and, 99–101, 102
  bundling, 122–3
  and courts, 103
  and dissension (religious), 112
  double standard in, 93, 94, 97
  with husband, 95–6, 108
  internal/external controls of, 96, 103
  premarital pregnancy, 122, 198
  and spirituality, 107
  see also adultery; chastity; fornication
sexual harassment, 100, 102
Shepard, Jeremiah, in church controversy, 220–1
Sherburne, Sarah, evicts second husband, 42–3
Silver, Mary, captivity of, 210–11, 213
"sitting up week," 135
skills, *see* agriculture, domestic; captives: skills (practical) of; commerce, skills in; gathering-tasks; manufacture, domestic; writing, skills in
slander:
  against parents, 156
  sexual, 96
  see also gossip and rumor
Smith, Catherine, difficulty of attending church, quoted on, 218
Smith, Page, 35
Smith, Sarah, in childbirth, 126
"Song of Deborah" (Judges 5), 165, 168
spinning, 29, 34
  moral aspects, 82
  for sale/trade, 45–6
stealing, *see* theft, cases of
Stickney, Sarah, as loose woman, 96
submissiveness:
  in captivity, 230–4 *passim*
  to God, 6
  and heroine role, 170, 172, 233–4

    to husband, 6, 24, 108
    to parents, 197–8
    and violence, 188–9
    see also dependence/independence
suffering:
    in captivity narratives, 173
    and childbirth, 129–32, 145
    of frontier settlers, 180–2
Swarton, Hannah, captivity of, 180, 181, 183, 206, 212
Symonds, Samuel, *et ux.*, and servants, 39

T

Thatcher, Margaret, on grandchildren, quoted, 159
theft, cases of:
    Hunt, Elizabeth, 63–5
    Hunt, Mary, 47
    Roper, Sarah, 61–5
Thomas, Keith, 93, 104
Thoreau, Henry David, account of Hannah Duston, 172
Topsfield (Mass.), residents of: *for accounts of, see* Black, Faith; Ewens, Agnes
towns:
    communal life in, 51–67
    domestic life in, 24–30
    houses, 25–6
    population, 52
trading, *see* commerce, skills in; deputy husband
travail of childbirth, 129–32
travel:
    and nursing, *table 140*, 141
    and pregnancy, 139–41, *table 140*
    and weaning, 141–4
Tucker, Mary, pulls hair of assailant, 190
Turbet, Abigail, captivity of, 209, 210, 212

V

violence:
    authoritarian, 186, 187–9
    defensive, 186, 189–90
    demonstrative, 186, 192–5, 219
    disorderly, 186, 190–2
    gender of assailants, 191, 269, 270
    of heroine, 185, 195
    and sex, 191–2
    typology of, 186–7
    see also aggression; children: violence to; husband-beating; infant mortality: infanticide; rape; sexual harassment; wife-beating
"virtuous woman" model, *see* Proverbs 31

W

war:
    economic consequences of, 30, 49
    and violence, 186
    see also garrisons; King Philip's War; King William's War; Queen Anne's War
Ward, Nathaniel, *Simple Cobler of Agawam*, quoted, 81–2
Watts, Isaac, "Meditation in a Grove," quoted, 117
weaning, 141–4
    see also nursing
Wear, Magdalen (and Elias), household of, 30–3
Weeks, Judith, violence to servant, 187–8
Wells (Me.), residents of: *for accounts of, see* Adams, Catherine; Littlefield, Ruth; Wheelwright, Esther
Wheelwright, Esther, captivity and religious vocation of, 211
"white Indians," 204, 208–13
Whitney, Ruth, biography and epitaph, 237

Whittier, John Greenleaf, account of
    Hannah Duston, 172
widow:
    legal status of, 7, 38, 249
    maintenance of, 148
    and sexual temptation, 97
wife:
    -beating, 101, 107, 187, 188
    roles, 9–10, 237–9
    see also consort; deputy husband;
        heroine; housewife; mistress;
        motherhood; neighbors
wife and husband, relationship of, 8
    conflict in, 109–10, 120
    dependence in, 7–8, 36–7, 42, 48–9
    economic, *see* deputy husband
    legal, 6–7, 94
    sexual, *see* consort; sexual behavior
    spiritual, 108
    violent, 187, 188, 269
    see also deputy husband; marriage
Willard, Samuel, on man and wife,
    quoted, 8, 108
Willey, Abigail (*later* Flecheur)
    captivity, second marriage of, 209,
        210, 212
    extramarital affair of, 95
Williams, Joanna, strikes neighbor,
    189
Williams, John, as captive, 205, 211
witchcraft:
    and infant death, 137
    and motherhood, 158–9
    in Salem, 120, 221–2, 225
    trial of George Burroughs, 221–2
    see also folk magic
women:
    aggression of, 170–2, 183, 185, 193,
        232; *see also* violence
    bonding of, 57, 59–60, 66, 132; in
        captivity, 210–13 *passim*, 231;
        see also childbirth: attendants;
        neighbors
    and churches, 215–26
    and courts, 54–5, 103, 156, 256
    equality with men, *see* equality of
        men and women
    violence of, *see* violence
women, disorderly, 194–5
women, older:
    and control of sexuality, 98–9, 103
    nurturing role of, 158
    see also grandmother; widow
Woodbridge, Mercy Dudley, 3, 10
Woodward, Sarah, *see* Row, Sarah
    Woodward
work:
    gender-linked, 37–8, 49–50
    gentlewoman's, 70–1
    shared, 51–2
    see also manufacture, domestic
writing, skills in, 44, 48

Y

York (Me.), residents of: *for accounts
    of, see* Boston, Patience; Bulman,
    Mary; Moody, Samuel; Wear,
    Magdalen
York County (Me.), household inven-
    tories (1670–1730), 15, *table 16*,
    69 and *table*

Z

Zuckerman, Michael, 93

About the Author

LAUREL THATCHER ULRICH was born in Sugar City, Idaho. She holds degrees from the University of New Hampshire, the University of Utah, and Simmons College. She is the 300th Anniversary University Professor at Harvard University and past president of the American Historical Association. As a MacArthur Fellow, Ulrich worked on the PBS documentary based on her book *A Midwife's Tale*. Her work is also featured on an award-winning website called dohistory.org. She is a past president of the Mormon History Association. She lives in Cambridge, Massachusetts.